Lecture Notes in Computer Science 12153

More information about this series at http://www.springer.com/series/7408

Jun Pang · Lijun Zhang (Eds.)

Dependable Software Engineering

Theories, Tools, and Applications

6th International Symposium, SETTA 2020
Guangzhou, China, November 24–27, 2020
Proceedings

 Springer

Editors
Jun Pang 🆔
University of Luxembourg
Esch-sur-Alzette, Luxembourg

Lijun Zhang 🆔
Chinese Academy of Sciences
Beijing, China

ISSN 0302-9743   ISSN 1611-3349 (electronic)
Lecture Notes in Computer Science
ISBN 978-3-030-62821-5   ISBN 978-3-030-62822-2 (eBook)
https://doi.org/10.1007/978-3-030-62822-2

LNCS Sublibrary: SL2 – Programming and Software Engineering

This Springer imprint is published by the registered company Springer Nature Switzerland AG
The registered company address is: Gewerbestrasse 11, 6330 Cham, Switzerland

Preface

This volume contains the research papers presented at the 6th Symposium on Dependable Software Engineering: Theories, Tools, and Applications (SETTA 2020) series of conferences – held during November 24–27, 2020, in Guangzhou, China. The purpose of SETTA is to bring international researchers together to exchange research results and ideas on bridging the gap between formal methods and software engineering. The interaction with the Chinese computer science and software engineering community is a central focus point. The aim is to show research interests and results from different groups so as to initiate interest-driven research collaboration. Past SETTA symposiums were successfully held in Nanjing (2015), Beijing (2016), Changsha (2017), Beijing (2018), and Shanghai (2019).

SETTA 2020 attracted 20 submissions co-authored by researchers from 10 countries. Each submission was reviewed by five Program Committee members with help from additional reviewers. The Program Committee discussed the submissions online and decided to accept 10 regular papers and 1 short paper for presentation at the conference. The program also included four invited talks given by Prof. Holger Hermanns from Saarland University, Germany, Prof. Wan Fokkink from Vrije Universiteit Amsterdam, The Netherlands, Prof. Andreas Zeller from CISPA Helmholtz Center for Information Security, Germany, and Prof. Yongwang Zhao from Zhejiang University, China. This year, together with Prof. Zhiming Liu from Southwest University, China, two special tracks were organized in addition to the research papers track: one special track on Artificial Intelligence Meets Formal Methods to provide a platform for experts of both AI and FM, from both academia and industry, to discuss important research problems across these two areas, and the other journal first papers track implemented in partnership with the *Journal of Computer Science and Technology*. The conference program also consists of the presentations selected from these two special tracks.

SETTA 2020 is sponsored by the Institute of Software, Chinese Academy of Sciences, China, and organized by the Institute of Intelligent Software, Guangzhou, China. We are grateful to the Local Organizing Committee for their hard work in making SETTA 2020 a successful event. Our warmest thanks go to the authors for submitting their papers to the conference. We thank the members of the Steering Committee for their support in organizing this event. We thank all the members of the Program Committee (PC) for completing reviews on time and being active in discussions during the review process. We also thank the additional reviewers for their effort that helped the PC to decide which submissions to accept. Special thanks go to our invited speakers for presenting their research at the conference. Finally, we thank the conference general chair, Prof. Huimin Lin, the publicity chair, Dr. Fu Song, and the local organization and Web chairs, Prof. Meng Sun and Dr. Chengchao Huang.

September 2020   Jun Pang
                                                                                                             Lijun Zhang

Organization

Program Committee

Ezio Bartocci	Vienna University of Technology, Austria
Lei Bu	Nanjing University, China
Milan Ceska	Brno University of Technology, Czech Republic
Sudipta Chattopadhyay	Singapore University of Technology and Design, Singapore
Yu-Fang Chen	Academia Sinica, Taiwan
Alessandro Cimatti	Fondazione Bruno Kessler, Italy
Yuxin Deng	East China Normal University, China
Wei Dong	National University of Defense Technology, China
Hongfei Fu	Shanghai Jiao Tong University, China
Jan Friso Groote	Eindhoven University of Technology, The Netherlands
Nan Guan	The Hong Kong Polytechnic University, Hong Kong
Dimitar Guelev	Bulgarian Academy of Sciences, Bulgaria
Xiaowei Huang	The University of Liverpool, UK
Nils Jansen	Radboud University, The Netherlands
Yu Jiang	Tsinghua University, China
Sebastian Junges	University of California, Berkeley, USA
Zhiming Liu	Southwest University, China
Stefan Mitsch	Carnegie Mellon University, USA
Jean-Francois Monin	Verimag and Université de Grenoble, France
Mohammadreza Mousavi	University of Leicester, UK
Sebastian A. Mödersheim	Technical University of Denmark, Denmark
Jun Pang	University of Luxembourg, Luxembourg
Dave Parker	University of Birmingham, UK
Mickael Randour	Université de Mons, Belgium
Zhiping Shi	Capital Normal University, China
Fu Song	ShanghaiTech University, China
Jeremy Sproston	University of Turin, Italy
Jun Sun	Singapore Management University, Singapore
Meng Sun	Peking University, China
Cong Tian	Xidian University, China
Andrea Turrini	Institute of Software, Chinese Academy of Sciences, China
Tarmo Uustalu	Reykjavik University, Iceland
Jaco van de Pol	Aarhus University, Denmark
Chenyi Zhang	Jinan University, China
Lijun Zhang	Institute of Software, Chinese Academy of Sciences, China

Additional Reviewers

Ahmadi, Mohamadreza
Becchi, Anna
Dong, Naipeng
Groß, Dennis
H. Pham, Long
Haase, Christoph
Hu, Chi
Huang, Mingzhang
Jegourel, Cyrille
Laveaux, Maurice
Li, Jiaying
Li, Ximeng
Liyun, Dai
Lu, Yuteng
Martens, Jan
Novotný, Petr

Quatmann, Tim
Sangnier, Arnaud
Shi, Hao
Suilen, Marnix
Turrini, Andrea
Wang, Rui
Willemse, Tim
Wu, Yuming
Xia, Bican
Yang, Yilong
Yang, Zhengfeng
Zhang, Liang
Zhang, Min
Zhang, Qianying
Zhang, Xiyue
Zhang, Yuanrui

Abstracts of Invited Talks

Lab Conditions for Research on Explainable Automated Decisions

Holger Hermanns[1,2]

[1] Saarland University – Computer Science, Saarland Informatics Campus,
Saarbrücken, Germany
[2] Institute of Intelligent Software, Guangzhou, China

Artificial neural networks are being proposed for automated decision making under uncertainty in many visionary contexts, including high-stake tasks such as suggesting which patient to grant a life-saving medical treatment, or navigating autonomous cars through dense traffic. Against this background, it is imperative that the decision making entities meets central societal desiderata regarding dependability, perspicuity, explainability, and robustness.

Decision making problems under uncertainty are typically captured formally as variations of Markov decision processes (MDPs). This keynote discusses a set of natural and easy to-control abstractions that altogether connect the autonomous driving challenge to the modelling world of MDPs. This is then used to study the dependability and robustness of NN-based decision entities which in turn are based on state-of-the-art NN learning techniques. We argue that this approach can be regarded as providing laboratory conditions for a systematic, structured and extensible comparative analysis of NN behaviour, of NN learning performance, as well as of NN verification and analysis techniques.

Holger Hermanns—This work receives financial support by the ERC Advanced Investigators Grant 695614 (POWVER), by the Deutsche Forschungsgemeinschaft (DFG, German Research Foundation) Grant 389792660 as part of TRR 248, see https://perspicuous-computing.science, and by the Key-Area Research and Development Program of Guangdong Province (Grant 2018B010107004).

Rely-Guarantee Reasoning About Concurrent Reactive Systems: Framework, Languages Integration and Applications

Yongwang Zhao

School of Cyber Science and Technology, College of Computer Science and Technology, Zhejiang University, Hangzhou, Zhejiang 310007, China
zhaoyongwang@gmail.com

This talk presents PiCore, a rely-guarantee reasoning framework for formal specification and verification of concurrent reactive systems (CRSs). PiCore takes the level of abstraction and reusability of the rely-guarantee method a step further by proposing an expressive event language for complex reaction structures at the system level, as well as decoupling the system and program levels. The result is a flexible rely-guarantee framework for CRSs, which is able to integrate existing rely-guarantee implementations at program level without any change of them. PiCore introduces the notion of "events" into the rely-guarantee method for system reactions and provides a *rely-guarantee interface* which is an abstraction for common rely-guarantee components for the program level. Concrete languages used to model the behaviour of events can be easily integrated with PiCore by a *rely-guarantee adapter* which implements the rely-guarantee interface. This design allows PiCore to be independent of program languages and thus to easily reuse existing rely-guarantee frameworks. To deal with complex reaction structures, we design an event specification language in PiCore supporting structural compositions of events. An event system is a structural composition of a set of events.

We have integrated two existing languages (Hoare-Parallel and CSimpl) and their rely-guarantee proof systems into the PiCore framework. As a result we create two instances of PiCore. Then, we apply the instances of the PiCore framework to two case studies, i.e. a real-world concurrent RTOS (Zephyr) and a standard of business process execution language (BPEL). We have applied PiCore to the formal specification and mechanized proof of the concurrent buddy memory allocation of Zephyr RTOS. The formal specification is fine-grained providing a high level of detail. It closely follows the Zephyr C code, covering all the data structures and imperative statements present in the implementation. We use the rely-guarantee proof system of PiCore for the formal verification of functional correctness and invariant preservation in the model, revealing three bugs in the C code. We have applied PiCore to interpret the semantics of the BPEL language by translating BPEL into PiCore. To show the correctness of this translation, we prove a strong bisimulation between the source BPEL program and the translated PiCore specification. In this way, formal verification of BPEL programs can be conducted in the PiCore framework. The strong bisimulation implies the soundness and completeness of formal verification of BPEL program in PiCore.

Contents

The Road Ahead for Supervisor Synthesis

M. A. Goorden, L. Moormann, F. F. H. Reijnen, J. J. Verbakel,
D. A. van Beek, A. T. Hofkamp, J. M. van de Mortel-Fronczak, M. A. Reniers,
W. J. Fokkink[✉], J. E. Rooda, and L. F. P. Etman

Eindhoven University of Technology, Eindhoven, The Netherlands
w.j.fokkink@vu.nl

Abstract. This paper reports on recent research advances in supervisor synthesis, as well as industrial applications and future research challenges, especially in the context of a research project funded by Rijkswaterstaat, responsible for the construction and maintenance of infrastructure in the Netherlands.

1 Introduction

Rijkswaterstaat, as part of the Dutch Ministry of Infrastructure and Water Management, is responsible for the design, construction, management, and maintenance of the main infrastructure in the Netherlands. This includes roads, bridges, tunnels, and waterway locks. In the coming decades, many such systems will be renovated or replaced, as they reach their end of life cycle or have capacity problems. In the past, they were engineered, built, and maintained on an individual project basis, resulting in a large variety of solutions to the same engineering problem. Rijkswaterstaat is seeking methods for modularization and standardization to increase quality and evolvability, decrease life-cycle costs, and enable so-called smart mobility. More and more functionality of infrastructural systems is being automated. The quality of supervisory controllers for such systems has a significant impact on their availability and reliability.

Supervisory control theory is a model-based methodology for designing supervisory controllers. Supervisor synthesis allows to automatically calculate a supervisor. From the supervisor, a supervisory controller can be derived. Taking the uncontrolled behavior of the system components as starting point, an engineer needs to formulate system requirements that rule out all undesired behavior, while allowing desired behavior. The supervisor is then synthesized automatically from the requirements together with the unrestricted system behavior. This is achieved by blocking controllable (output) events, such as starting a motor, as opposed to uncontrollable (input) events, such as sensor reports, over which the supervisor exerts no control. This automatic synthesis may at first sound as some kind of wizardry, but in essence the underlying idea is simple. Let us take the example of a bridge. The software units that drive the different components of the bridge, such as barriers, traffic lights, and the motors to lift the bridge decks, are all supposed to be operational. The supervisor is only required to

© Springer Nature Switzerland AG 2020
J. Pang and L. Zhang (Eds.): SETTA 2020, LNCS 12153, pp. 1–16, 2020.
https://doi.org/10.1007/978-3-030-62822-2_1

block illegal activities, such as opening the bridge while the barriers have not yet closed. Such illegal activities are pre-determined from the requirements and then made unreachable by blocking as few controllable events as possible.

Rijkswaterstaat, in an effort to regulate and unify the system designs of its diverse contractors, has developed a strict regime of structuring and formulating requirements, which form the starting point and basis for system implementations. Additionally, infrastructure systems under their responsibility are mostly discrete-event systems with a clear distinction between controllable and uncontrollable events. This makes supervisor synthesis a suitable engineering method for these applications, which can contribute to the aim of Rijkswaterstaat to increase the quality and evolvability of its supervisory controllers.

In the past, the applicability of supervisor synthesis in real-life systems engineering was often limited due to the heavy demand on computational power, both in time and memory. Recent research developments have helped to make this methodology applicable to large real-life infrastructural systems. This paper discusses some of these developments as well as several case studies in the context of the Rijkswaterstaat project, which all use the CIF 3 toolset. These case studies concern the development of supervisory controllers for bridges, tunnels, waterway locks, and roadside systems. We also discuss future research challenges to further strengthen the applicability of supervisor synthesis.

2   Supervisory Control Theory

The task of a supervisory controller is to control the different components and subsystems such that the entire system, called the plant, behaves as intended. A supervisory controller is part of a control stack with different layers, see Fig. 1 below. A human operator sends instructions to the supervisory controller via a graphical user interface (GUI), such as to raise a sluice gate inside a waterway lock. The GUI moreover displays sensor data from the plant, such as the height of the water inside the lock. At the plant, actuators drive the mechanical components of the plant, while sensors pick up information regarding the plant. A supervisory controller constitutes a layer between the GUI and the actuators and sensors. Signals to actuators can be blocked by the supervisory controller, i.e., are controllable, if they would lead to violation of a requirement on the plant's behavior. Signals from sensors are uncontrollable for the supervisory controller and are always allowed to occur.

Supervisory control theory, initiated by Ramadge and Wonham [26], automatically synthesizes a supervisor from formal specifications of (1) the plant components and (2) the requirements imposed on the behavior of the plant. This supervisor can then be used to derive a supervisory controller, as shown in [4,15]. Here we will focus on formal specifications expressed by so-called extended finite automata (EFAs), consisting of finite automata embellished with discrete variables. Guards and updates can be added to transitions that use such variables. EFAs have the same expressive power as finite automata [36], but tend to provide a much more concise representation of the modeled behavior.

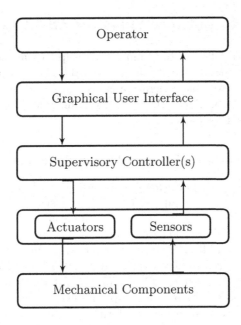

Fig. 1. Schematic view of a control system structure of an infrastructural system

The components of the plant are specified as EFAs and put in a synchronous product, meaning that a certain event, with a particular action name, can only be performed if each component that contains this event is in a state where it can perform this event. This synchronous product specifies the behavior of the entire plant. The requirements that are imposed on the plant behavior are also specified in the form of EFAs. To achieve a supervisor, the requirements are added to the synchronous product. As a result, events that can be performed by the plant may be blocked because they are not allowed by a requirement.

The requirements concern safety properties, making sure that no bad things will ever happen. To ensure liveness, meaning that eventually something good will happen, some states in the EFAs of plant components can be marked by the modeller. A marked state in the synchronous product means that all individual plant components are in a marked state, expressing that the plant is in a steady position, e.g., the bridge deck is closed, the barriers are open, and the signals are green. It must be guaranteed that the plant can always reach a marked state. Therefore, (events leading to) states that violate this property are blocked.

In summary, the synthesized supervisor is (1) *safe*, meaning that all requirements are satisfied, (2) *controllable*, meaning that it only blocks controllable events, and (3) *nonblocking*, meaning that the plant can always reach a marked state. Moreover, it is (4) *maximally permissive*, meaning that the supervisor imposes the minimum restrictions to enforce the first three properties.

A nice introduction to supervisory control theory is offered in [2].

3   Techniques to Enhance Supervisor Synthesis

This section discusses different techniques that help to scale supervisor synthesis to large-scale industrial case studies, how additional features such as fault-tolerance and counterexample generation can be included in the synthesis process, and that implementation code for a programmable logic controller (PLC) can be generated from a supervisor.

3.1   Multilevel Synthesis Through Design Structure Matrices

The number of states of a plant grows exponentially with its number of components. For example, in [29], a supervisor was synthesized for a relatively small waterway lock, called Lock III, consisting of a single chamber in the Wilhelmina canal at the city of Tilburg. The combination of 4 incoming and 4 outgoing traffic lights, 2 gate paddles, 2 culverts, 4 gates, 2 equal-water sensors, and 25 GUI buttons gives rise to an uncontrolled plant that has $6.0 \cdot 10^{32}$ states. In total systems engineers formulated 142 requirements for this plant. Its controlled state space, monitored by the maximally permissive supervisor, still consists of $5.9 \cdot 10^{24}$ states. A key challenge in performing supervisor synthesis for large real-life infrastructural systems is to cope with this inherent state space explosion problem. The experiments on Lock III reported in this section were redone especially for the current paper, to achieve consistent numbers on sizes of state spaces for the different optimizations. All models and results can be found on a Git repository[1].

In *modular* supervisor synthesis [41], for each individual requirement a different "local" supervisor is synthesized. An event is enabled by the overall supervisor if all local supervisors enable it. An important optimization with regard to modular synthesis, proposed in [25], is to consider for each requirement only those plant components that have at least one event in common with this requirement. This can lead to a drastic reduction in the sizes of the local supervisors. *Multilevel* synthesis [10] reduces the large number of local supervisors generated in modular synthesis by grouping together subsets of components and their related requirements and generating a local supervisor for each such cluster. A key underlying idea is to keep track which pairs of distinct plant components have a requirement in common, in the sense that the requirement is related to both components. This is documented in a so-called design structure matrix (DSM), with one row as well as one column for every plant component. A field in the matrix is colored gray if the components associated to its row and to its column have a requirement in common. An algorithm from [40] determines a clustering of components such that gray fields in the matrix are placed as close as possible to the diagonal. In Fig. 2, a DSM for Lock III is depicted. The clustering algorithm in this case determines clusters which can be mapped back to physical entities: gates, traffic lights, water leveling systems, and the stop and emergency stop.

---

[1] https://github.com/magoorden/SETTA2020.

Synthesis is performed for the plant components in each cluster separately, together with all related requirements for this cluster. Synthesis continues in a hierarchical fashion: next it is performed for related clusters of clusters, et cetera, until finally the overall supervisor for the entire plant is computed. Multilevel synthesis for Lock III produces local supervisors that in total require $1.8 \cdot 10^{23}$ states, as compared to the aforementioned $6.0 \cdot 10^{24}$ states for a monolithic supervisor.

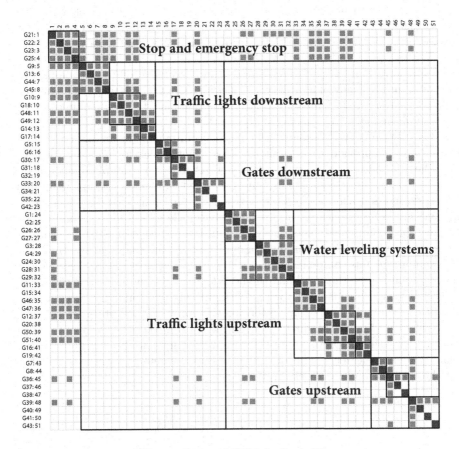

Fig. 2. Clustered DSM for Lock III

It turns out to be very important for the efficiency of multilevel synthesis to split a requirement into smaller requirements when possible [8]. The reason is that this gives rise to fewer relations between the different plant components, so that smaller clusters of components can be synthesized at the start. For example, one requirement of Lock III states that it is unsafe to open a gate when:

- the water-leveling system at the other side is not closed, or
- the gate at the other side is not closed, or

– there is no equal water over the gate.

This requirement can be divided into 13 smaller requirements: (1) split the 3 disjuncts; (2) disentangle references to multiple system states (e.g., "not closed"); and (3) disentangle references to multiple plant components (e.g., gates consist of multiple components). Overall, in [8], the 142 requirements for Lock III are split into 358 requirements. As a result, the number of states required for the local supervisors drops to $4.5 \cdot 10^{19}$ states.

Similar to splitting requirements, multilevel synthesis is also strengthened by splitting plant components into smaller components. In [9], the 35 components are split into 51 smaller components, yielding a reduction of the local supervisors to $1.5 \cdot 10^{19}$ states with respect to the original model.

Combining splitting of requirements and splitting of plant components improves the efficiency of multilevel synthesis significantly. Having 51 plant components and 358 requirements results in the number of states required for the local supervisors to drop spectacularly to $2.9 \cdot 10^{10}$ states.

Bus structures inside a plant, which have requirements in common with most of the plant components, turn out to cause a bottleneck for multilevel synthesis. The stop and emergency stop for Lock III form an example of such a bus structure. Bus components are usually considered only at the final phase of multilevel synthesis, when the overall supervisor is computed. This tends to produce a relatively large supervisor at this final phase. Therefore, in [5] it is proposed to treat bus components separately in multilevel synthesis. At each synthesis phase, concerning certain non-bus components and the requirements they have in common, the bus components that are related to at least one of these requirements are included, thus avoiding the need to treat the bus structure separately at the very end. For instance, for Lock III, treating bus components in this way produces local supervisors that in total require only $7.7 \cdot 10^8$ states.

Next to guiding the hierarchical structuring of clusters of components within multilevel synthesis, DSMs also help in capturing modeling errors of the actual plant. For example, let us consider only the stop and emergency stop of the DSM for the original model of Lock III, detailed in Fig. 3

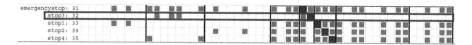

Fig. 3. Snippet of the clustered DSM for Lock III indicating a modeling error

Since the functionality of stop1, stop2, stop3, and stop4 is similar, one would expect that the rows for these four components in the DSM would be similar. However, the highlighted row for stop3 is clearly distinct from the rows for the other three components. This observation led to the detection of a small but serious copy/paste error in several requirements formulated by system engineers, where the event name stop4 should actually be stop3. Based on a series of industrial case studies, in [7] three modeling guidelines are formulated in relation to DSMs. (1) *Similar components should have similar relationships in a DSM.* (2) *A DSM should not contain an empty row or column.* (3) *A DSM should not have independent clusters.* The first two guidelines led to the detection of modeling flaws in plant components and requirements, while the third guideline led to the detection of missing requirements.

In this section Lock III was used as a running example. Another illuminating example of the strength of combining multilevel synthesis with DSMs can be found in [28], where this approach is applied to a small-scale production line, from modeling the plant and its requirements up to the automatic generation of controller code for implementation.

3.2   Additional Features for Supervisor Synthesis

We discuss several advancements and case studies in supervisor synthesis that add features needed for industrial applications and pave the way to apply supervisory control theory from formal plant models and requirements up to the generation of efficient PLC code for a controller that implements the supervisor.

Nonblockingness Check for Modular Synthesis. The Achilles' heel of modular supervisor synthesis is that a collection of nonblocking local supervisors may still induce a blocking overall supervisor, meaning that the latter supervisor contains states from which no marked state is reachable. In [18], a method is introduced to efficiently check for nonblockingness, by first performing a string of blockingness-preserving abstraction steps on the local supervisors, resulting in a simplified monolithic supervisor, which is blocking if and only if the overall supervisor induced by the local supervisors in blocking. In [11], reversals of those abstraction steps are defined, so that a blocking simplified supervisor can be used to transform the corresponding overall supervisor into a nonblocking one (which is safe, controllable, and maximally permissive).

Achieving Nonblockingness Through a Dependency Graph. In [6], properties are formulated on plant components and requirements which ensure that the resulting supervisor is nonblocking. Roughly these are: (1) plant automata are strongly connected, (2) different plant automata do not have events in common, (3) requirements express in which states some plant automata must be to perform some controllable event, and (4) the plant automata mentioned in a requirement only consist of uncontrollable events. Properties (1) and (4) ensure that plant components can always be brought in a state needed to satisfy a certain requirement, as expressed in (3). And (2) makes sure a plant component can be brought in a desired state while the other plant components remain stationary. In modular synthesis this allows to determine clusters where nonblockingness is obtained for free.

In practice, a stumbling block for this method tends to be violation of property (4). Therefore, in [12], a dependency graph is introduced, in which the nodes are plant components and there is an edge from a node P to a node Q

if a requirement expresses a condition on a controllable event that occurs in plant P, while the requirement requires plant Q to be in a certain state. Plant components that do not exhibit an infinite path in this graph, do not give rise to blocking behavior. For example, the following dependency graph in Fig. 4 is generated for the model of Lock III.

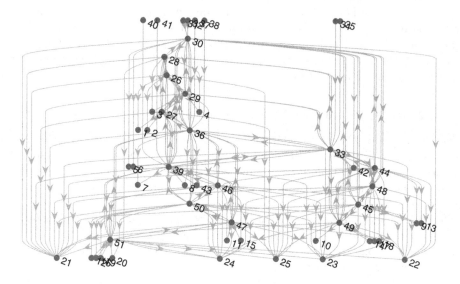

Fig. 4. The dependency graph for Lock III (Color figure online)

The strongly connected components in this graph, drawn in red, require a nonblockingness check, as well as nodes from which a path exists to a strongly connected component, drawn in purple. In total 27 plant components and related requirements of Lock III can thus be omitted from the nonblockingness check.

Symmetry Reduction. Validation of supervisory controllers is an important step to guarantee correct and safe system behavior. In [20], a method is proposed to significantly reduce the validation effort by exploiting that often different plant components are equivalent in behavior, and likewise for different requirements, modulo some renamings of events. This symmetry reduction was essential in a case study on tunnel systems. A supervisor for subsystems such as lighting, ventilation, and emergency detection in the First Heinenoordtunnel, a roadway tunnel with two traffic tubes located south of the city Rotterdam, could be validated without exploiting symmetry [21]. However, for the King Willem-Alexandertunnel at the city of Maastricht, the first two-layered roadway tunnel in the Netherlands, with two traffic tubes at each layer, the supervisor, became so large that it could only be validated after applying symmetry reduction [20]. This research line has also been combined successfully with the work on dependency graphs in [22].

Counterexample Generation. The generated supervisor may not be according to the expectations of the user, typically because it does not allow any plant behavior. In such cases it is desirable to obtain feedback on the synthesis process, for instance to detect a modeling error that causes aberrations in the generated supervisor. In [38], a collection of deduction rules are presented that allow to derive reasons for the absence of a state in a supervised system and provide feedback to the user. An adaptation of a standard synthesis algorithm is provided to automatically obtain a cause for each state that is omitted from a plant during synthesis.

Synthesis of Fault-Tolerant Supervisors. A fault-tolerant supervisor [19] enables the plant to continue its intended operations, possibly with degraded service, when some of its components fail or a fault occurs, such as a broken wire, defect sensor, or blocking actuator. In [24], after detection of a fault, an alternative supervisor is activated, designed specifically for this type of fault. An alternative approach is followed in [34], where the same supervisor controls the plant before and after the occurrence of faults. Instead, the models of the plant components and the requirements are divided into fault-free and post-fault behavior, where the latter depends on the type of fault that is diagnosed. This approach was successfully applied to synthesize a fault-tolerant supervisor for the Algera bridge over the river IJssel (see Fig. 5), which consists of two vehicle lanes, a lane for cyclists, and a lane for pedestrians. This supervisor allows the bridge to continue its operation when only one out of a pair of stop signs breaks down, and restricted operation when one of a pair of barriers remains stuck in the closed position. Furthermore, it takes appropriate action if the bridge deck opens erroneously.

Continuous-Time Simulation. A hybrid plant model is obtained by extending the discrete-event model used for synthesis with continuous behavior. This is modeled by continuous variables that change their values at the passing of time, defined by a differential equation that can depend, for example, on the current location of a plant component. Additionally, continuous variables may change their values during an event. In [30], this approach was used to simulate a supervisor for the Algera complex, consisting of the aforementioned bridge together with a waterway lock and two storm surge barriers.

Hardware-in-the-Loop Simulation. While model simulation is a powerful tool for validation, it offers only a partial analysis. Aspects related to the execution of the supervisory controller on the hardware and communication with subsystems, such as GUIs, cannot be validated with model simulation. To bridge the gap between model simulation and realization, hardware-in-the-loop simulation can be performed after model simulation and before implementation, meaning that the supervisory controller realization and its subsystems are connected to a model of the plant. In [35], an engineering method is proposed that combines supervisor synthesis with hardware-in-the-loop simulation. Models created for synthesis are refined and re-used to obtain models for model simulation and hardware-in-the-loop simulation. This method was applied successfully to

Fig. 5. The Algera complex consisting of a lock, a bascule bridge, and two storm surge barriers [https://beeldbank.rws.nl, Rijkswaterstaat/Joop van Houdt].

the Prinses Marijke complex in the Amsterdam-Rhine canal, consisting of two waterway locks and a floodgate as protection from the river Lek.

Confluence and Finite Response. While nonblockingness of a supervisor guarantees that always a marked state of the plant is reachable, it does not guarantee that a deterministic supervisory controller implemented on the basis of such a supervisor ever reaches a marked state [4]. In the transformation from a synthesized supervisor to an actual supervisory controller that drives the mechanical plant by enforcing events, it is important to know whether the supervisor exhibits *finite response* and *confluence* [3]. A state of the plane is called stable if the supervisory controller cannot enforce any event, typically because all events leaving this state are uncontrollable. Usually the marked states of a plant are stable. Finite response guarantees that each execution trace allowed by the supervisor eventually returns to a stable state, so that clearly this property is also satisfied by the supervisory controller implemented on the basis of this supervisor. This ensures that a supervisory controller cannot continuously enforce events. Confluence of a supervisor guarantees that each enforcement of events by the supervisory controller leads back to the same stable state. In [31], building on earlier work in [15], sufficient criteria are given to guarantee that a synthesized supervisor exhibits finite response, and also sufficient criteria to guarantee that it is confluent.

Generation of PLC Code. For the implementation of supervisory controllers, often a programmable logic controller is used. In [37], PLC code is generated automatically from a model of the supervisor. In recent follow-up work, the structure of generated PLC code has been improved and optimization techniques have been used to reduce its variability in execution times.

In industry, supervisory controllers need to adhere to strict safety standards. To achieve these standards, safety PLCs are used, which contain diagnostic functions to detect internal faults in the hardware and avoid unsafe situations that could be caused by such faults. For a safety PLC implementation, the supervisory controller has to be split into a regular and a safety part. In [27], a method is presented that automatically performs this split. It has been used to generate controller code for the Oisterwijksebaanbrug, a rotating bridge in the Wilhelmina canal at the city of Tilburg, which was then successfully employed for real-life operation of the bridge [32]. This application demonstrated all the necessary steps to go from a specification to an implementation of a supervisor, driving home the point that supervisory control theory is a viable engineering approach to transform a consistent and complete set of well-defined requirements into efficient PLC code for controlling industrial infrastructural systems.

Tooling. The reported case studies have all been carried out using the CIF 3 toolset [1]. It is based on networks of hybrid automata with invariants and differential algebraic equations. Automata can interact in several ways: multi-party synchronization via shared events; and shared variables (local write, global read). CIF 3 supports a rich set of data types and expressions (e.g., lists, sets, dictionaries, and tuples), functions, conditional updates, and multi-assignments. Large-scale systems can be modeled conveniently owing to parametrized process definitions and instantiations of automata, grouping of arbitrary components in sub-scopes, and an import mechanism.

The synthesis algorithm of CIF 3 (based on the algorithm of [23]) computes various predicates, such as conditions under which controllable events may take place in the controlled system, and the initialization predicate of the controlled system. These predicates are included in the supervisor that results from synthesis. Crucial for the good performance of the toolset is that internally such predicates are represented compactly in the form of binary decision diagrams. Parts of the CIF 3 tool were inspired by Supremica [16], including the use of advanced model checking techniques such as symbolic representations.

The CIF 3 simulator enables interactive visualization-based simulation of the behavior of the controlled system. It can be employed to validate models in isolation. Additionally it may be used to validate the supervisory controller when put in the context of the uncontrolled hybrid plant.

Interoperability with other languages and tools is achieved by means of model transformations, external functions, and co-simulation via the Matlab/Simulink S-function interface. PLC code generation conforming to the IEC 61131-3 standard allows for implementation of CIF 3 supervisory controllers in actual systems.

From 2020 on, development of the CIF 3 toolset continues within the Eclipse project ESCET[2] (Supervisory Control Engineering Toolset), offering an open environment in which interested academic and industrial partners can collaborate on and profit from the further development of tool support for supervisory control theory.

4   Research Challenges

We envision the following research challenges for the coming years.

- *Stronger liveness notions*: Reachability of a marked state by the plant is a rather limited notion to ensure liveness properties, which express that eventually something good will happen. It might be a good idea to integrate stronger liveness notions in the synthesis algorithms.
- *Exploit symmetry reduction*: The work on symmetry reduction in [20] may be extended from validation to optimization of synthesis algorithms. Furthermore, it could be integrated with multilevel synthesis to profit from symmetries in subclusters of components.
- *Insightful counterexample generation*: The framework in [38] can provide causes on why a certain state was trimmed by a supervisor, but often there are many such causes. Informative feedback requires a sensible selection from these causes and depicting them in an insightful manner. Moreover, counterexample generation needs to be integrated in the tooling.
- *Utilize DSMs in tools*: Structure information from a DSM regarding a plant could be exploited to optimize synthesis algorithms and tools. In particular, inside CIF 3 predicates are represented by binary decision diagrams. Their sizes are very sensitive to the ordering of systems variables against which they are constructed. In [39], it was shown that the difference between the 'right' and 'wrong' ordering for the variables in Lock III can mean a shift in computation time from a few seconds to a few hours. Initial results show that ordering variables based on a DSM can yield a significant compaction of binary decision diagrams.
- *Improve supervisory controller generation from a supervisor*: It seems possible to relax the requirements on supervisors to ensure finite response and confluence in [31]. Moreover, ideally these notions will be strengthened to ensure that a supervisory controller always eventually returns the plant to a marked state [15].
- *Integration into the engineering process*: Supervisory control synthesis needs to be made accessible for system engineers, by clear GUIs in the tools, adding features that are needed in practice, and providing proper instruction material.

---

[2] https://projects.eclipse.org/projects/technology.escet.

5   Conclusion

The 30th anniversary of the inception of supervisory control theory by Ramadge and Wonham was celebrated by a workshop on December 11, 2017, preceding the *CDC* conference in Melbourne, Australia [14]. The case studies presented in the current paper, in the context of a project with Rijkswaterstaat, show that this theory has reached a maturity level that allows it to be fully embraced by industry. The project initially focused on control systems for bridges and waterway locks, which may in the long run support smart waterways. It then extended to tunnels, taking into account important aspects such as emergency situations and escape routes. Recently it extended further to roadside systems, where managing and avoiding traffic jams is a serious point of concern.

A challenge lies ahead to support industrial partners in adapting synthesis-based engineering methods for their supervisory control systems. To strengthen the integration of supervisor synthesis within the engineering process, in [33], a graphical modeling method has been developed based on a library of standardized modules within movable bridges, inspired by work in [13,17]. Subsystems of a plant are modeled by instantiating modules from the library. The method is supported by a tool. In this way supervisors have been developed for a family of 17 real-life bridges.

Key to the success of the project has been its close connection to the actual engineering process at Rijkswaterstaat and its subcontractors. We are grateful to Rijkswaterstaat for their financial support as well as their active participation in the project. In particular we thank Maria Angenent, John van Dinther, Patrick Maessen, Bert van der Vegt, and Han Vogel.

Finally, we gratefully acknowledge the groundbreaking work by the international research community of supervisory control theory, which has served as a corner stone and inspiration for the work reported here. In particular we would like to mention Knut Åkesson, Kai Cai, José Cury, Martin Fabian, Dennis Hendriks, Stéphane Lafortune, Robi Malik, Sahar Mohajerani, Thomas Moor, Max Hering de Queiroz, Peter Ramadge, Karen Rudie, Jan van Schuppen, Rong Su, and, last but not least, W. Murray Wonham.

References

1. van Beek, D.A., et al.: CIF 3: model-based engineering of supervisory controllers. In: Ábrahám, E., Havelund, K. (eds.) TACAS 2014. LNCS, vol. 8413, pp. 575–580. Springer, Heidelberg (2014). https://doi.org/10.1007/978-3-642-54862-8_48
2. Wonham, W.M., Cai, K.: Supervisory Control of Discrete-Event Systems. CCE. Springer, Cham (2019). https://doi.org/10.1007/978-3-319-77452-7
3. Dietrich, P., Malik, R., Wonham, W., Brandin, B.: Implementation considerations in supervisory control. In: Synthesis and Control of Discrete Event Systems, pp. 185–201. Kluwer (2002)
4. Fabian, M., Hellgren, A.: PLC-based implementation of supervisory control for discrete event systems. In: 37th Conference on Decision and Control, CDC 1998, vol. 3, pp. 3305–3310. IEEE (1998)

5. Goorden, M., Dingemans, C., Reniers, M., van de Mortel-Fronczak, J., Fokkink, W., Rooda, J.: Supervisory control of multilevel discrete-event systems with a bus structure. In: 17th European Control Conference, ECC 2019, pp. 3204–3211. IEEE (2019)
6. Goorden, M., Fabian, M.: No synthesis needed, we are alright already. In: 15th Conference on Automation Science and Engineering, CASE 2019, pp. 195–202. IEEE (2019)
7. Goorden, M., van de Mortel-Fronczak, J., Etman, L., Rooda, J.: DSM-based analysis for the recognition of modeling errors in supervisory controller design. In: 21st Dependency and Structure Modeling Conference, DSM 2019, pp. 127–135 (2019)
8. Goorden, M., van de Mortel-Fronczak, J., Reniers, M., Fokkink, W., Rooda, J.: The impact of requirement splitting on the efficiency of supervisory control synthesis. In: Larsen, K.G., Willemse, T. (eds.) FMICS 2019. LNCS, vol. 11687, pp. 76–92. Springer, Cham (2019). https://doi.org/10.1007/978-3-030-27008-7_5
9. Goorden, M., van de Mortel-Fronczak, J., Reniers, M., Fokkink, W., Rooda, J.: Modeling guidelines for component-based supervisory control synthesis. In: Arbab, F., Jongmans, S.S. (eds.) FACS 2019. LNCS, vol. 12018. Springer, Cham (2020). https://doi.org/10.1007/978-3-030-40914-2_1
10. Goorden, M., van de Mortel-Fronczak, J., Reniers, M., Fokkink, W., Rooda, J.: Structuring multilevel discrete-event systems with dependency structure matrices. IEEE Trans. Autom. Control **65**(4), 1625–1639 (2019)
11. Goorden, M., Reniers, M., van de Mortel-Fronczak, J., Fokkink, W., Rooda, J.: Compositional coordinator synthesis for discrete event systems (2020). Submitted to Discrete Event Dynamic Systems
12. Goorden, M., van de Mortel-Fronczak, J., Reniers, M., Fabian, M., Fokkink, W., Rooda, J.: Model properties for efficient synthesis of nonblocking modular supervisors. arXiv preprint arXiv:2007.05795 (2020)
13. Grigorov, L., Butler, B., Cury, J., Rudie, K.: Conceptual design of discrete-event systems using templates. Discret. Event Dyn. Syst. **21**(2), 257–303 (2011)
14. Lafortune, S., Rudie, K., Tripakis, S.: Thirty years of the Ramadge-Wonham theory of supervisory control: a retrospective and future perspectives. IEEE Contr. Syst. Mag. **38**(4), 111–112 (2018)
15. Malik, P.: From Supervisory Control to Nonblocking Controllers for Discrete Event Systems. Ph.D. thesis, Universität Kaiserslautern (2003)
16. Malik, R., Åkesson, K., Flordal, H., Fabian, M.: Supremica-an efficient tool for large-scale discrete event systems. IFAC-PapersOnLine **50**(1), 5794–5799 (2017). 20th IFAC World Congress
17. Malik, R., Fabian, M., Åkesson, K.: Modelling large-scale discrete-event systems using modules, aliases, and extended finite-state automata. IFAC Proc. Vol. **44**(1), 7000–7005 (2011). 18th IFAC World Congress
18. Mohajerani, S., Malik, R., Fabian, M.: A framework for compositional nonblocking verification of extended finite-state machines. Discret. Event Dyn. Syst. **26**(1), 33–84 (2015). https://doi.org/10.1007/s10626-015-0217-y
19. Moor, T.: A discussion of fault-tolerant supervisory control in terms of formal languages. Ann. Rev. Contr. **41**, 159–169 (2016)
20. Moormann, L., Goorden, M., van de Mortel-Fronczak, J., Fokkink, W., Maessen, P., Rooda, J.: Efficient validation of supervisory controllers using symmetry reduction. In: 15th Workshop on Discrete Event Systems, WODES 2020. IFAC (2020, in press)
21. Moormann, L., Maessen, P., Goorden, M., van de Mortel-Fronczak, J., Rooda, J.: Design of a tunnel supervisory controller using synthesis-based engineering. In: ITA-AITES World Tunnel Congress, WTC 2020 (2020, in press)

22. Moormann, L., van de Mortel-Fronczak, J., Fokkink, W., Rooda, J.: Exploiting symmetry in dependency graphs for model reduction in supervisor synthesis. In: 16th Conference on Automation Science and Engineering, CASE 2020, pp. 660–667. IEEE (2020)
23. Ouedraogo, L., Kumar, R., Malik, R., Åkesson, K.: Nonblocking and safe control of discrete-event systems modeled as extended finite automata. IEEE Trans. Autom. Sci. Eng. **8**(3), 560–569 (2011)
24. Paoli, A., Sartini, M., Lafortune, S.: Active fault tolerant control of discrete event systems using online diagnostics. Automatica **47**(4), 639–649 (2011)
25. de Queiroz, M.H., Cury, J.E.R.: Modular supervisory control of large scale discrete event systems. In: Boel, R., Stremersch, G. (eds.) Discrete Event Systems. The Springer International Series in Engineering and Computer Science, vol. 569. Springer, Boston (2000). https://doi.org/10.1007/978-1-4615-4493-7_10
26. Ramadge, P., Wonham, W.: Supervisory control of a class of discrete event processes. SIAM J. Contr. Optim. **25**(1), 206–230 (1987)
27. Reijnen, F., Erens, T., van de Mortel-Fronczak, J., Rooda, J.: Supervisory control synthesis for safety PLCs. In: 15th Workshop on Discrete Event Systems, WODES 2020. IFAC (2020, in press)
28. Reijnen, F., Goorden, M., van de Mortel-Fronczak, J., Reniers, M., Rooda, J.: Application of dependency structure matrices and multilevel synthesis to a production line. In: 2nd Conference on Control Technology and Applications, CCTA 2018, pp. 458–464. IEEE (2018)
29. Reijnen, F., Goorden, M., van de Mortel-Fronczak, J., Rooda, J.: Supervisory control synthesis for a waterway lock. In: 1st Conference on Control Technology and Applications, CCTA 2017, pp. 1562–1563. IEEE (2017)
30. Reijnen, F., Goorden, M., van de Mortel-Fronczak, J., Rooda, J.: Modeling for supervisor synthesis - a lock-bridge combination case study. Discret. Event Dyn. Syst. **30**(3), 499–532 (2020)
31. Reijnen, F., Hofkamp, A., van de Mortel-Fronczak, J., Rooda, J.: Finite response and confluence of state-based supervisory controllers. In: 15th Conference on Automation Science and Engineering, CASE 2019, pp. 509–516. IEEE (2019)
32. Reijnen, F., Leliveld, E.B., van de Mortel-Fronczak, J., van Dinther, J., Rooda, J., Fokkink, W.: A synthesized fault-tolerant supervisory controller for a rotating bridge (2020, under submission)
33. Reijnen, F., van de Mortel-Fronczak, J., Reniers, M., Rooda, J.: Design of a supervisor platform for movable bridges. In: 16th Conference on Automation Science and Engineering, CASE 2020, pp. 1298–1304. IEEE (2020)
34. Reijnen, F., Reniers, M., van de Mortel-Fronczak, J., Rooda, J.: Structured synthesis of fault-tolerant supervisory controllers. IFAC-PapersOnLine **51**(24), 894–901 (2018). 10th Symposium on Fault Detection, Supervision and Safety of Technical Processes, SAFEPROCESS 2018
35. Reijnen, F., Verbakel, J., van de Mortel-Fronczak, J., Rooda, J.: Hardware-in-the-loop set-up for supervisory controllers with an application: the Prinses Marijke complex. In: 3rd Conference on Control Technology and Applications, CCTA 2019, pp. 843–850. IEEE (2019)
36. Sköldstam, M., Åkesson, K., Fabian, M.: Modeling of discrete event systems using finite automata with variables. In: 46th Conference on Decision and Control, CDC 2007, pp. 3387–3392. IEEE (2007)
37. Swartjes, L., van Beek, D., Reniers, M.: Towards the removal of synchronous behavior of events in automata. IFAC Proc. Vol. **47**(2), 188–194 (2014). 12th Workshop on Discrete Event Systems, WODES 2014

38. Swartjes, L., Reniers, M., Fokkink, W.: Deducing causes for the absence of states in supervised systems. In: 6th Conference on Control, Decision and Information Technologies, CoDIT 2019, pp. 144–149. IEEE (2019)
39. Thuijsman, S., Hendriks, D., Theunissen, R., Reniers, M., Schiffelers, R.: Computational effort of BDD-based supervisor synthesis of extended finite automata. In: 15th Conference on Automation Science and Engineering, CASE 2019, pp. 486–493. IEEE (2019)
40. Wilschut, T., Etman, L., Rooda, J., Adan, I.: Multilevel flow-based Markov clustering for design structure matrices. J. Mech. Des. **139**(12), 121402 (2017)
41. Wonham, W., Ramadge, P.: Modular supervisory control of discrete-event systems. Math. Contr. Sig. Syst. **1**(1), 13–30 (1988)

Reentrancy? Yes. Reentrancy Bug? No.

Qinxiang Cao$^{(\boxtimes)}$ and Zhongye Wang$^{(\boxtimes)}$

Shanghai Jiao Tong University, Shanghai, China
caoqinxiang@gmail.com, wangzhongye1110@sjtu.edu.cn

Abstract. In this paper, we address the reentrancy vulnerability in smart contracts using two program logics. We first propose a coarse-grained logic that extends the standard Hoare logic by a proof rule for reentry trigger commands. We prove this logic sound and complete. We propose another fine-grained logic that considers reentry triggers as entry and exit points of functions. For verifying coarse-grained specifications, these two logics have the same expressiveness, and we can derive coarse-grained judgments from fine-grained ones. In comparison, the fine-grained logic is more useful for fine-grained specifications. We use a toy language to demonstrate our results and formalize all definitions and proofs in Coq (https://github.com/BruceZoom/Reentry).

Keywords: Reentrancy · Smart contract · Hoare logic

1 Introduction

Smart contracts [26] are decentralized protocols automated by programs and deployed on blockchains, allowing trading without being supervised or intervened by any third party. Ethereum [9] is a successful implementation of this idea, where users use the Solidity [1] language to write smart contracts. However, catastrophic attacks in history unveil various vulnerabilities of Solidity contracts, including the reentrancy loophole we study, which is challenging to identify during the development of contracts and has caused the infamous DAO attack [25]. This paper targets smart contracts' functional correctness verification which takes potential reentry behavior into consideration.

Reentries and Reentrancy Bugs. Figure 1 shows a simplified version of the DAO attack. In this example, the simple bank contract maintains a state variable userBalance to store users' deposits. User contracts can reclaim their deposits by calling the withdrawBalance method, which issues the transfer at the 7th line and clears the balance at the 8th line. Solidity specifies that every transaction will trigger a fallback function in the receiver contract—this fallback function is where the receiver could respond to the transaction. However, a potential attacker could leverage this mechanism to re-enter the withdrawBalance method before the execution of the 8th line. Thus, the control flow would form an infinite

---

Parallel authorship and equal contribution. Corresponding author: Qinxiang Cao.

© Springer Nature Switzerland AG 2020
J. Pang and L. Zhang (Eds.): SETTA 2020, LNCS 12153, pp. 17–34, 2020.
https://doi.org/10.1007/978-3-030-62822-2_2

```
1   contract Bank{
2     mapping (address => uint) private userBalances;
3     function withdrawBalance() public{
4       uint amountToWithdraw = userBalances[msg.sender];
5       if(amountToWithdraw > 0){
6         // reentry point
7         msg.sender.call.value(amountToWithdraw)("");
8         userBalances[msg.sender] = 0;
9       }
10    }
11  }
12  contract Attacker{
13    Bank public bank;
14    function() payable{
15      // reentrancy attack
16      bank.withdrawBalance();
17    }
18  }
```

Fig. 1. The simplified DAO example [13]

```
1     contract Bank{
2       mapping (address => uint) private userBalances;
3       function withdraw() public {...}
4       function deposit() public payable {...}
5       function query() public returns (uint) {...}
6     }
7     contract User{
8       Bank public bank;
9       uint balance;
10      function() payable{
11        balance += msg.value;
12        // re-enter query() & deposit()
13        uint diff = balance-bank.query();
14        if(diff > 0){
15          balance -= diff;
16          bank.deposit().value(diff)();
17        }
18      }
19    }
```

Fig. 2. Potential usage of the reentrancy

recursion between these two functions. The bank will constantly send Ether[1] to the attacker until gas[2] runs out, and the attacker may eventually harvest more Ether than what it initially owns.

---

[1] Ether is the currency circulated on the Ethereum platform.

[2] Gas measures the amount of computation required for one transaction. Using up the gas undoes modifications to the state in the current call frame.

The word "reentrancy" refers to entering a function, or more generally, a contract again during its execution without an explicit invocation. It is often caused by calling functions of external contracts that have another call to functions in the host contract. Standard practices fix reentrancy bugs by forcing variable updates before possible reentry calls or by introducing a mutex lock to forbid reentry calls [12]. However, we believe a contract preserving the reentrancy feature allows more automation for users who want to make valid adjustments upon transactions. An example in Fig. 2 allows reentrancy not only to the read-only method `query`, but also the non-static method `deposit`, where the user could secure its asset by always keeping half of its balance in the bank upon transactions.

Functional Correctness and Interactive Verification. Our strategy in this paper is to develop program logics for verifying functional correctness, while potential reentry behaviors are taken into consideration. In other words, we are not going to define and find *what is wrong*, but will define *correctness* and prove contracts correct (if they are indeed correct). This strategy has been proved successful by previous works like VST [4,11] and Iris [20]. They formalize program semantics and program logics (usually a Hoare-like logic) in an interactive theorem prover (e.g. Coq) and prove them sound. Their users can use these logics to verify programs in the theorem prover.

We follow their work flow: a program semantics that describes potential reentry behaviors is first formalized; our program logics are then proved sound in Coq w.r.t. this semantics. Our program logics are extensions of Hoare logic and smart contracts' functional correctness can be described by Hoare triples.

Designing Program Logics for Reentrancies. Reasoning about reentrancies is difficult because the fallback function is invisible from the verifier. Although some existing program logics and verification tools [4] can verify functional correctness when function calls and/or function pointers appear in programs, they only reason about known functions. In other words, their users need to write very specific assumption about callee functions/function pointers in preconditions and those assumptions describes the expected functionality of those functions. For Solidity contracts, the receiver's fallback function is unknown from the sender. It can be even malicious. Due to this reason, many previous authors consider reentrancy-bug-free difficult to verify if using Hoare-like program logics [2].

Another difficulty is expressiveness. If excluding reentrancy behavior, the execution result of a smart contract would be only determined by the initial state and the contract program itself. Thus, pre/postconditions would be expressive enough to describe a program's functionality—how the initial state determines the ending states. However, due to potential reentrancy, the ending state is also determined by those receivers' fallback functions, i.e. determined by the number of reentrancies, the order of reentrancies and the arguments of reentry calls. Thus pre/postconditions are not expressive enough to describe all Solidity contracts' functionality.

For simplicity, we use a toy language to demonstrate our results. In this paper,

- We define the syntax and semantics of the toy language with reentry trigger commands in Sect. 2.
- We propose a proof rule for reentry trigger commands and develop a coarse-grained logic that can reason about reentrancy in Sect. 3. This logic is especially useful when reentry calls will not "interfere" original execution. We use this logic to prove specifications for a toy example.
- We propose another fine-grained logic to verify contracts with reentrancy in Sect. 4. We use an example to show its ability to reason about fine-grained specifications where the coarse-grained logic would fail.

We formalize two logics and all conclusions in Coq [7] (https://github.com/BruceZoom/Reentry).

Remark. The concept of the "reentrancy" is as well a term in the concurrent program context, where *"a program is reentrant if distinct executions of the program on distinct inputs cannot affect each other, whether run sequentially or concurrently"* [28]. This is a more general concept of the reentrancy in smart contracts, where we only consider reentrant programs running sequentially.

2   Preliminary

In this section, we set up a simple imperative language and its denotational semantics, which contains functions and reentry calls. They will be the focus of program logics we propose in Sect. 3 and Sect. 4.

2.1   Programming Language

Figure 3 shows the syntax of the programming language with reentry calls. We use global v and local v to denote global and local variables, where v stands for variable names. The arithmetic expressions and boolean expressions are defined as normal.

$$
\begin{aligned}
n &:= \cdots, -1, 0, 1, \cdots & \text{(number)} \\
v &:= x, y, \ldots & \text{(variable name)} \\
V &:= \text{local } v \,|\, \text{global } v & \text{(variable)} \\
E &:= n \,|\, V \,|\, E + E \,|\, E - E \,|\, E * E & \text{(expression)} \\
B &:= \text{true} \,|\, \text{false} \,|\, !B \,|\, E == E \,|\, E < E \,|\, B\&\&B & \text{(boolean expression)} \\
C &:= \text{skip} \,|\, V = E \,|\, \text{reentry} \,|\, \text{if } B \text{ then } C \text{ else } C \text{ fi} & \text{(command)} \\
&\quad |\ \text{while } B \text{ do } C \text{ od} \,|\, C; ; C \,|\, \text{Call } f\, E
\end{aligned}
$$

Fig. 3. Syntax of the language with reentry calls

In Solidity, the host contract does not explicitly issue reentry calls, and reentrancy is more like the side effect of a transfer statement. From this point of view, we may treat such transfer as two separate steps: the execution of intended operations and the execution of reentry calls. Knowing one command that might cause reentrancy, we can mark it as a reentry point and apply the effect of reentry calls to the program state at that point. In our toy language, the primitive command `reentry` defines those reentry points in programs.

Remark. Although we list the command `Call f E` in Fig. 3 for regular function invocation of f with arguments E, but for clarity, we will not consider it in the discussion throughout the paper, i.e., we only consider a language excluding the `Call` command. However, both languages share many similarities and we formalize all conclusions for both versions in Coq.

Corresponding to the distinction of local and global variables, we model the program state S as a tuple of a local state S_l and a global state S_g. The local and global states are mappings from variable names to variable values. We define evaluations of variables and updates of program states as

$$\begin{aligned}
[\![\text{local } v]\!]_S &:= [\![v]\!]_{S_l} \\
[\![\text{global } v]\!]_S &:= [\![v]\!]_{S_g} \\
S[(\text{local } v) \mapsto n] &:= (S_l[v \mapsto n], S_g) \\
S[(\text{global } v) \mapsto n] &:= (S_l, S_g[v \mapsto n])
\end{aligned}$$

On the right hand side, $[\![v]\!]_{S_-}$ is the regular evaluation of v on the global/local state S_-, and $S_-[v \mapsto n]$ is the regular update on S_- that changes the value for v to n.

Reentrancy happens in a program organized with functions, so we formalize the function model as follows.

$$\begin{aligned}
F &:= f, f_1, f_2, \cdots \\
&\Gamma : \text{list of function names} \\
&\Pi : \text{function name} \rightarrow (\text{list of variable names} \times \text{command})
\end{aligned}$$

We use a set of identifiers F to denote function names. Γ is a white-list of function names for public functions that may be invoked during reentrancy[3]. We use Π to represent function context, a mapping from function names to function arguments (lists of identifiers) and function bodies (pieces of commands), which are denoted as $\text{arg}_\Pi(f)$ and $\text{bdy}_\Pi(f)$.

Unlike Solidity, our toy language is not object-oriented. We consider the entire known function context to be one contract and use global program states to describe contract states, while local states are only for temporary variables during execution. Such practice is well-defined since we only need to see the host contract and should not make any assumption about external contracts that are unknown to developers.

---

[3] In Solidity, external contracts can only issue reentry call to public functions visible to them in the host contract, not private functions that are invisible to them.

$\text{SKIP}\ (\Pi, \Gamma, \texttt{skip}, S) \Downarrow (S)$ $\text{ASSIGN}\ (\Pi, \Gamma, x = E, S) \Downarrow (S[x \mapsto [\![E]\!]_S])$

$$\text{REENTRY}\ \frac{\Pi, \Gamma \vDash S_g \leadsto_{\text{ar}} S_g'}{(\Pi, \Gamma, \texttt{reentry}, (S_l, S_g)) \Downarrow ((S_l, S_g'))}$$

$$\text{SEQ}\ \frac{(\Pi, \Gamma, C_1, S_1) \Downarrow (S_2) \qquad (\Pi, \Gamma, C_2, S_2) \Downarrow (S_3)}{(\Pi, \Gamma, C_1; ; C_2, S_1) \Downarrow (S_3)}$$

$$\text{IF TRUE}\ \frac{[\![B]\!]_{S_1} = \mathit{true} \qquad (\Pi, \Gamma, C_1, S_1) \Downarrow (S_2)}{(\Pi, \Gamma, \texttt{if}\ B\ \texttt{then}\ C_1\ \texttt{else}\ C_2\ \texttt{fi}, S_1) \Downarrow (S_2)}$$

$$\text{IF FALSE}\ \frac{[\![B]\!]_{S_1} = \mathit{false} \qquad (\Pi, \Gamma, C_2, S_1) \Downarrow (S_2)}{(\Pi, \Gamma, \texttt{if}\ B\ \texttt{then}\ C_1\ \texttt{else}\ C_2\ \texttt{fi}, S_1) \Downarrow (S_2)}$$

$$\text{WHILE FALSE}\ \frac{[\![B]\!]_S = \mathit{false}}{(\Pi, \Gamma, \texttt{while}\ B\ \texttt{do}\ C\ \texttt{od}, S) \Downarrow (S)}$$

$$\text{WHILE TRUE}\ \frac{[\![B]\!]_{S_1} = \mathit{true} \qquad (\Pi, \Gamma, C, S_1) \Downarrow (S_2)}{(\Pi, \Gamma, \texttt{while}\ B\ \texttt{do}\ C\ \texttt{od}, S_2) \Downarrow (S_3)}{(\Pi, \Gamma, \texttt{while}\ B\ \texttt{do}\ C\ \texttt{od}, S_1) \Downarrow (S_3)}$$

$\underline{\text{EMPTY REENTRY CALL}}\ \Pi, \Gamma \vDash S_g \leadsto_{\text{ar}} S_g$

$$\underline{\text{APPEND REENTRY CALL}}\ \frac{f \in \Gamma \qquad \Pi, \Gamma \vDash S_g \leadsto_{\text{ar}} S_g'}{(\Pi, \Gamma, \texttt{bdy}_\Pi(f), (S_l', S_g')) \Downarrow ((S_l'', S_g''))}{\Pi, \Gamma \vDash S_g \leadsto_{\text{ar}} S_g''}$$

Fig. 4. Denotational semantics: we underline the new big step relation and the arbitrary evaluation relation we add

2.2 The Denotational Semantics

We present the coarse-grained denotational semantics for the toy language in Fig. 4, where $(\Pi, \Gamma, C, S_1) \Downarrow (S_2)$ means that given function context Π and white-list Γ, the execution of C can change the program state S_1 into S_2, and the arbitrary evaluation relation $\Pi, \Gamma \vDash S_g \leadsto_{\text{ar}} S_g'$ means the reentrancy can change the global state S_g into S_g'.

The evaluation relation and the arbitrary evaluation relation are mutually defined. The arbitrary evaluation relation is a binary relation of global states. We define it as the reflexive, transitive closure on the global effect of calling functions in white-list Γ. Reentry calls do not alter local program states of the caller and the arguments of the reentry call is directly instantiated into the local state of the callee. The global state after the reentry point can be any descendant of the original global state in the arbitrary evaluation relation, in accordance with the indefiniteness of the reentry call. In other words, the semantics of reentry is defined to be demonicly non-deterministic, since the receiver can be malicious. Semantics for other commands are defined as normal.

3   A Coarse-Grained Logic for Reentry Call

In this section, we extend the Hoare logic [18] by adding the REENTRY rule to reason about reentry calls. The judgement of the logic has the form of

$$\Pi, \Gamma, \Delta \vdash \{P\}C\{Q\}$$

which declares that the precondition and postcondition of command C are respectively P and Q, under the given function context Π, white-list Γ, function assumptions Δ. Function assumptions is a set of function triples with function name and the pre/post-conditions of the function:

$$\Delta := \{\{P\}f\{Q\}, \cdots\}$$

We define judgment's validity as

$$\Pi, \Gamma \vDash \{P\}C\{Q\} \overset{\text{def}}{\Leftrightarrow} \forall S_1, S_2. \, S_1 \vDash P \Rightarrow$$
$$(\Pi, \Gamma, C, S_1) \Downarrow (S_2) \Rightarrow$$
$$S_2 \vDash Q$$

where $S \vDash P$ means the program state S satisfies assertion P.

We distinguish local/global assertions with normal assertions to reason about reentry calls that only modify the global state. We define the following two predicates that restrict the scope of an assertion to either local or global, where global (local) assertions do not constrain local (global) states.

$$\text{localP}\,(P) := \forall S_l, S_{g1}, S_{g2}.(S_l, S_{g1}) \vDash P \Rightarrow (S_l, S_{g2}) \vDash P$$
$$\text{globalP}\,(P) := \forall S_{l1}, S_{l2}, S_g.(S_{l1}, S_g) \vDash P \Rightarrow (S_{l2}, S_g) \vDash P$$

3.1   Proof Rules

Figure 5 shows proof rules in this logic, where we underline the REENTRY rule that reasons about the reentrancy.

We use a global invariant I to connect several reentry calls in the REENTRY rule. To do so, every function in the white-list should have the invariant as both its precondition and postcondition in function assumptions Δ. The existence of the local assertion P ensures that the local state is untouched by reentry calls.

3.2   Soundness

We prove the soundness of the logic stated in Theorem 1.

$$\text{SKIP } \Pi, \Gamma, \Delta \vdash \{P\}\texttt{skip}\{P\}$$

$$\text{ASSIGN BACKWARD } \Pi, \Gamma, \Delta \vdash \{P[x \mapsto E]\}x = E\{P\}$$

$$\text{SEQ } \frac{\Pi, \Gamma, \Delta \vdash \{P\}C_1\{Q\} \quad \Pi, \Gamma, \Delta \vdash \{Q\}C_2\{R\}}{\Pi, \Gamma, \Delta \vdash \{P\}C_1;; C_2\{R\}}$$

$$\text{IF } \frac{\Pi, \Gamma, \Delta \vdash \{P \wedge [\![B]\!]\}C_1\{Q\} \quad \Pi, \Gamma, \Delta \vdash \{P \wedge \neg[\![B]\!]\}C_2\{Q\}}{\Pi, \Gamma, \Delta \vdash \{P\}\texttt{if } B \texttt{ then } C_1 \texttt{ else } C_2 \texttt{ fi}\{Q\}}$$

$$\text{WHILE } \frac{\Pi, \Gamma, \Delta \vdash \{I \wedge [\![B]\!]\}C\{I\}}{\Pi, \Gamma, \Delta \vdash \{I\}\texttt{while } B \texttt{ do } C \texttt{ od}\{I \wedge \neg[\![B]\!]\}}$$

$$\text{CONSEQUENCE } \frac{P \vdash P' \quad \Pi, \Gamma, \Delta \vdash \{P'\}C\{Q'\} \quad Q' \vdash Q}{\Pi, \Gamma, \Delta \vdash \{P\}C\{Q\}}$$

$$\text{REENTRY } \frac{\forall x.\mathsf{localP}(P(x)) \quad \forall x.\mathsf{globalP}(I(x)) \quad \forall f \in \Gamma, x.\{I(x)\}f\{I(x)\} \in \Delta}{\Pi, \Gamma, \Delta \vdash \{R\}\texttt{reentry}\{R\}}$$

$$\text{where } R \triangleq \exists x, P(x) \wedge I(x)$$

Fig. 5. Proof rules in the coarse-grained logic

Theorem 1 (Soundness). *Suppose that any specification in function assumptions is provable (i.e. $\forall\{P'\}f\{Q'\} \in \Delta.\Pi, \Gamma, \Delta \vdash \{P'\}bdy_\Pi(f)\{Q'\}$) and some triple $\{P\}C\{Q\}$ is provable (i.e. $\Pi, \Gamma, \Delta \vdash \{P\}C\{Q\}$), then the triple is also valid*

$$\Pi, \Gamma \vDash \{P\}C\{Q\}.$$

We follow the standard proof technique [5] by introducing the "validity from assumptions", which we denote as $\Pi, \Gamma, \Delta \vDash\!| \{P\}C\{Q\}$ and define as

$$\forall\{P'\}f'\{Q'\} \in \Delta. \Pi, \Gamma \vDash \{P'\}\texttt{bdy}_\Pi(f')\{Q'\} \Rightarrow \Pi, \Gamma \vDash \{P\}C\{Q\}$$

And our key steps are to prove the following lemmas.

Lemma 1. $\Pi, \Gamma, \Delta \vdash \{P\}C\{Q\}$ *implies* $\Pi, \Gamma, \Delta \vDash\!| \{P\}C\{Q\}$.

Proof. We can prove the lemma by induction on the structure of the proof tree, and proofs of most cases are as normal, leaving the base case for REENTRY rule. We prove the case by induction on the arbitrary evaluation relation in the semantics of **reentry** command, and the rest of the proof is trivial.

Lemma 2. *Suppose that any specification in function assumptions is provable*

$$\forall\{P\}f\{Q\} \in \Delta.\Pi, \Gamma, \Delta \vdash \{P\}bdy_\Pi(f)\{Q\}$$

Then we have these specifications are all valid

$$\forall\{P\}f\{Q\} \in \Delta.\Pi, \Gamma \vDash \{P\}bdy_\Pi(f)\{Q\}.$$

Proof. The proof for the lemma is standard [5].

The proof of Theorem 1 is obvious given these lemmas. We also prove the logic to be complete. But for the sake of space, we put the completeness proof in the long version of the paper [10].

3.3 DAO Example

Figure 6 shows the simplified implementation of the DAO example in our toy language, where (1) is vulnerable to reentrancy attack while (2) is safe with reentry calls. We use a global variable `balance` to represent the recorded deposit of the target user, and a global variable `user` to represent the Ether held by the user. The composite command `user + = balance;` l : `reentry;` (ignore the label l for now) simulates the transfer in Solidity, which transfer Ether to the user and then allow the user to perform reentry calls.

```
withdraw(){                                    withdraw(){
   if(balance > 0){                               if(balance > 0){
      user + = balance; l : reentry;                 balance = 0;
      balance = 0;                                   user + = balance; l : reentry;
}}                                              }}
```

$$(1) \hspace{6cm} (2)$$

Fig. 6. DAO in the toy language

We would like to prove the specification (3).

$$\forall m, n \in \mathbb{N}^+. \frac{\{[\![balance]\!] = n \wedge [\![user]\!] = m\}}{\text{withdraw}()\{[\![balance]\!] = 0 \wedge [\![user]\!] = m + n\}} \quad (3)$$

For the implementation in (2), we need to prove $\{I\}\text{reentry}\{I\}$ at the reentry point, where $I \triangleq [\![balance]\!] = 0 \wedge [\![user]\!] = m + n$. It is a valid invariant for the contract since $\{I\}\text{withdraw}()\{I\}$ is obviously provable, and by the REENTRY rule we can easily prove the specification.

But for (1), we would require

$$\{[\![balance]\!] = n \wedge [\![user]\!] = m + n\}\text{reentry}\{[\![balance]\!] = n \wedge [\![user]\!] = m + n\}$$

which is not provable since in the reentry call we could add more to `user` by calling `withdraw` and no invariant could be found to prove the specification.

4 A Fine-Grained Logic for Reentry Call

One problem of our coarse-grained logic is the restricted expressiveness of function specifications: we cannot express a relation between ending states and hyperparameters of reentry calls. For example, the best specification we can only prove for (1) is

$$\forall m, n \in \mathbb{N}^+. \quad \frac{\{[\![balance]\!] = n \land [\![user]\!] = m\}}{\texttt{withdraw}()\{\exists k. [\![balance]\!] = 0 \land [\![user]\!] = m + kn\}}$$

However, we would like to show that the increment of user is related to the number of reentry calls to withdraw in the specification. We can accomplish this with the fine-grained logic we propose here.

In this section, we pursue a different strategy: treating reentry as a special control flow and adding extra assertions for program states entering and leaving reentry. This idea is not totally new. Multi-postcondition are widely used for reasoning about break commands and continue commands [4]. Tan's previous work [27] also uses multi-precondition and multi-postcondition for reasoning about non-structural jumps in assembly programs. We treat a function as a multiple-entry-multiple-exit code segment, where an entry or exit is marked by a label, which we define as

$$L := \mathsf{entry} \,|\, \mathsf{exit} \,|\, l, l_1, l_2, \cdots$$

where entry and exit describe the beginning and the end of a command, and $l, l_1, l_2, \cdots$ are unique line numbers of reentry commands in a function. We define a pair of function name and label to be the index

$$\mathsf{index} := \langle f, l \rangle$$

which uniquely[4] determines a reentry point throughout the entire contract.

The key idea is to use fine-grained judgments of the form

$$\Pi \vdash \{P\}\{\boldsymbol{R_1}\}C\{\boldsymbol{R_2}\}\{Q\} \tag{4}$$

where P, Q are regular assertions that specify the regular precondition and postcondition of the program C. $\boldsymbol{R_1}, \boldsymbol{R_2}$ are mappings from indices of reentry points to assertions, which we name as reentry assertions. $\boldsymbol{R_1}$ specifies assertions that program states should satisfy when entering C through each reentry point, and $\boldsymbol{R_2}$ specifies assertions for program states to satisfy when leaving C through each reentry point. We will use $f : \{P\}\{\boldsymbol{R_1}\}\{\boldsymbol{R_2}\}\{Q\}$ as a shorthand for $\{P\}\{\boldsymbol{R_1}\}\mathsf{bdy}_\Pi f\{\boldsymbol{R_2}\}\{Q\}$ in the rest of the paper.

In short, P, Q corresponds to assertions at entry and exit, while $\boldsymbol{R_1}, \boldsymbol{R_2}$ corresponds to the preconditions and postconditions at each reentry line number. A quintuple (the fine-grained judgment) says entering through any label (except exit) with corresponding precondition satisfied, if it leaves through any label (except entry), the program state will satisfy corresponding postcondition. Comparing with our coarse-grained judgements, these fine-grained judgements allow us to connect ending states with reeentry call arguments.

Most proof rules are standard except the following one for the reentry.

$$\textsc{Reentry } \{P\}\{l : Q\}l : \texttt{reentry}\{l : P\}\{Q\}$$

The logic is sound and the proof will be very similar to the one in Tan's previous work [27]. We only focus on the validities of these judgments in this paper.

---

[4] Two functions with the same function body might share the same label.

4.1   The Fine-Grained Semantics

We propose a fine-grained auxiliary semantics in Fig. 7 to support the fine-grained logic. Due to the sake of space, we only pose some important part here. The complete definition can be found in the long version [10]. We use $(\Pi, C, L_1, S_1) \downarrow (L_2, S_2)$ to denote the fine-grained semantics of the execution trace in program C from entry L_1 to exit L_2, where the program state changes from S_1 to S_2.

For the skip command and the assignment command, the program state pairs are the same as those in the coarse-grained semantics (see Sect. 2.2). The label pairs for them are entry and exit, meaning the execution trace starts from the very beginning and terminates at the very end of the command, without triggering any reentry call.

$$\text{SKIP } (\Pi, \text{skip}, \text{entry}, S) \downarrow (\text{exit}, S)$$

$$\text{ASSIGN } (\Pi, x = E, \text{entry}, S) \downarrow (\text{exit}, S[x \mapsto [\![E]\!]s])$$

$$\text{REENTRY CALL } (\Pi, \text{reentry}, \text{entry}, S) \downarrow (l, S)$$

$$\text{REENTRY RETURN } (\Pi, \text{reentry}, l, S) \downarrow (\text{exit}, S)$$

$$\text{SEQ } \frac{(\Pi, C_1, L_1, S_1) \downarrow (\text{exit}, S_2) \quad (\Pi, C_2, \text{entry}, S_2) \downarrow (L_2, S_3)}{(\Pi, C_1; C_2, L_1, S_1) \downarrow (L_2, S_3)} \qquad \text{SEQ1 } \frac{(\Pi, C_1, L, S_1) \downarrow (l, S_2)}{(\Pi, C_1; C_2, L, S_1) \downarrow (l, S_2)}$$

$$\text{SEQ2 } \frac{(\Pi, C_2, l, S_1) \downarrow (L, S_2)}{(\Pi, C_1; C_2, l, S_1) \downarrow (L, S_2)}$$

Fig. 7. The fine-grained semantics

We treat the reentry command as an exit-entry point, where the execution trace can either leave the current function to perform arbitrary reentry calls outside the contract or return from completed reentry calls to resume execution. Therefore, we split its semantics into two parts: REENTRY CALL states that after entering the reentry command, the reentrancy-free execution trace terminates at the location pointed by the concrete label l with the program state S; REENTRY RETURN states that if the interrupted execution trace returns to the function at l, the control flow will exit the reentry point normally to resume subsequent execution. Here, the reentry trigger itself does not affect the program state, but rather the segments of reentry calls that connect entry points and exit points do the job. There are similarities among semantics for different compositional commands, and we will take the sequence command for demonstration in Fig. 8.

If the execution of program C_1 starts from some label L_1 with program state S_1 and quits from the exit with S_2, and the execution of program C_2 starts from

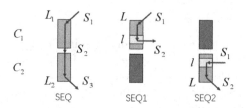

Fig. 8. Semantics for sequence command

the entry with state S_2 and terminates at some label L_2 with S_3. Then by SEQ, we may connect two execution traces and obtain the trace that starts from L_1 with state S_1 and terminates at L_2 with S_3.

If the execution of C_1 does not quit from the standard exit but instead breaks out through some reentry point l as a reentry call, then following SEQ1, the effect of C_2 is blocked because the execution trace leaves the entire program from l, before reaching the second part. Similarly, if the execution begins by returning to the reentry point at l in C_2, the execution trace will not go through C_1, which does not affect the program state according to SEQ2.

In summary, the fine-grained semantics only describes the binary relation of states on a single execution trace from one label to another. The trace should not be interrupted by any reentry call, i.e., no reentry line number is allowed as an intermediate label. The semantics is enough for supporting the definition of fine-grained validity since both only talk about preconditions and postconditions along segments of execution traces within the contract. In the long version of this paper [10], we propose another reentry semantics, which can connect those traces and bridge the fine-grained semantics to the coarse-grained semantics.

The white-list Γ does not occur in the fine-grained semantics because this semantics does not describe the real happenings during reentrancy and there is no need to know which functions are reentrant.

Based on the previous interpretation of the quintuple, we then define a quintuple having fine-grained validity ($\Pi \vDash f : \{P\}\{R_1\}\{R_2\}\{Q\}$) if and only if the following criteria hold:

- $\Pi \vDash_{PQ} f : \{P\}\{R_1\}\{R_2\}\{Q\}$ iff. for the evaluation $(\Pi, \mathsf{bdy}_\Pi(f), \mathsf{entry}, S_1) \downarrow$ (exit, S_2) from the standard entry to the standard exit of function f, if S_1 satisfies P, then S_2 satisfies Q.
- $\Pi \vDash_{PR} f : \{P\}\{R_1\}\{R_2\}\{Q\}$ iff. for the evaluation $(\Pi, \mathsf{bdy}_\Pi(f), \mathsf{entry}, S_1) \downarrow$ (l, S_2) from the standard entry to any reentry point l in function f, if S_1 satisfies P, then S_2 satisfies the reentry assertion $R_{2,\langle f,l\rangle}$ at l.
- $\Pi \vDash_{RQ} f : \{P\}\{R_1\}\{R_2\}\{Q\}$ iff. for the evaluation $(\Pi, \mathsf{bdy}_\Pi(f), l, S_1) \downarrow$ (exit, S_2) from any reentry point l to the standard exit of function f, if S_1 satisfies the reentry assertion $R_{1,\langle f,l\rangle}$ at l, then S_2 satisfies Q.
- $\Pi \vDash_{RR} f : \{P\}\{R_1\}\{R_2\}\{Q\}$ iff. for the evaluation $(\Pi, \mathsf{bdy}_\Pi(f), l_1, S_1) \downarrow$ (l_2, S_2) from any reentry point l_1 to any reentry point l_2 in f, if S_1 satisfies the reentry assertion $R_{1,\langle f,l_1\rangle}$ at l_1, then S_2 satisfies the reentry assertion $R_{2,\langle f,l_2\rangle}$ at l_2.

4.2   DAO Example Cont

We revisit the simplified DAO example (1) and use the quintuple specification below to express a more precise property about it.

$$
\begin{aligned}
\texttt{withdraw} : & \{ [\![balance]\!] = n \wedge [\![user]\!] = m \} \\
& \{ l : [\![balance]\!] = n \wedge [\![user]\!] = m' \} \\
& \{ l : [\![balance]\!] = n \wedge [\![user]\!] = m + n \} \\
& \{ [\![balance]\!] = 0 \wedge [\![user]\!] = m' \}
\end{aligned}
\tag{5}
$$

When exiting the function withdraw from the reentry point l, the variable user will increase its value by n. However, we never know what value it will be after the reentrancy finishes and returns to the function through l. But we are sure that if it enters the function through l with user set to some m', when the function terminates, it will still be m' and the balance will be 0.

This quintuple specifies that each regular/reentry call of the function would result in an increase of user with value n. Therefore, we can prove such a fact: if the user calls withdraw once and calls it k times during the reentrancy, then it will receive kn unit of Ether. The coarse-grained logic cannot achieve this.

The DAO example already show how to use our toy language to simulate real Solidity contracts and prove their specifications. We use more examples in the long version [10] to demonstrate our coarse-grained and fine-grained logic, including a more general case with multiple function reentrancy.

5   Discussion: Relationship Between Two Logics

In Sect. 3, we give a coarse-grained logic that can prove coarse-grained specifications, and in Sect. 4, we give a fine-grained logic that can prove fine-grained specifications but with more complex judgment. In comparison, coarse-grained specifications can only describe connections between a function's initial states and its ending states, while fine-grained specifications can also describe connections between reentrancy's hyper-parameters and ending states.

In reality, many Solidity contracts do not permit real reentrancy. Here are some common design pattern:

- A boolean variable is defined to indicate whether it is currently in a reentry call; and every smart contract function will check it at the beginning. Leave the function immediately if it is indeed a reentry.
- Only read-only functions are allowed in reentry.
- Only virtual read-only functions are allowed in reentry. Virtual read-only functions may be not read-only, e.g. a red-black-tree look up.

In these cases, the invariant-based proof rule is useful in verification and coarse-grained specifications have enough expressiveness. In comparison, there are still applications which exploits Solidity's fallback setting. In those cases, fine-grained specifications are needed to describe functional correctness and our fine-grained logic is needed in verification.

If a smart contract will be used in both of these scenario, do verifiers need to verify it twice using both logics? The answer is no. Given that users have proved some fine-grained properties in the fine-grained logic, they may directly derive valid coarse-grained specifications using those results. There is no need to go through another proof in the coarse-grained logic. For the sake of space, we leave technique details and proofs in the long version [10].

6 Related Work

There have been surveys looking into the loopholes similar to the reentrancy bug of Ethereum smart contracts [6,12]. They study the security vulnerabilities in the Ethereum smart contracts and classify different leaks that occur in smart contracts posing threats to their security into categories. The comprehensive taxonomy of vulnerabilities they present is of great assistance in identifying and studying security issues of smart contracts. Their informal analysis of possible causes under these vulnerabilities can help developers avoid such mistakes, as well as lead formal verification researches into resolving these problems.

Hirai [17] formally defines the Ethereum Virtual Machine and its operational semantics on the instruction level in Lem, so that it can be compiled to support interactive theorem proving for Ethereum bytecode in other environments. His work lays the foundations for later research into the verification of smart contracts. He also suggests that we can model the reentrancy behavior as an adversarial environment step, which is valid to change the program state of the contract only when it obeys certain invariants. The idea is similar to ours, though his work does not implement it formally.

Bhargavan et al. [8] apply the F* framework to verify the runtime safety and functional correctness of Solidity contracts. They can detect dangerous patterns, including reentrancy, only by typechecking possible reentrant methods. Grossman et al. [15] propose a notion of Effectively Callback Free (ECF) object, of which the security can be guaranteed if we can eliminate callbacks in all of its execution traces. They formalize the idea at the level of operation semantics, which bears certain similarities to our definition of the denotational semantics for the reentry call. Their work and Hirai's work [17] are delivered only at the semantic level, which may serve as great models formalizing smart contracts but would be more useful when they can reason about the correctness and safety of the contract at the logic level.

To assist researchers to approach the functional correctness of smart contracts at the logic level, Ahrendt et al. [2] outline a research agenda for the deductive verification of smart contracts at the source code level. The authors admit the difficulty of reasoning about security when dealing with reentrancy attacks that use non-functional aspects.

Building on the existing EVM model [17], Amani et al. [3] develops a program logic for reasoning about smart contracts in the EVM bytecode form. But they do not explore the reentrancy bug in detail and they do not analyze smart contracts at the source code level.

Nielsen and Spitters [23] formalize the blockchain along with smart contracts deployed on it in Coq as abstract models, and they can reason about the specification of a contract at bytecode level. But they do not provide a program logic for source code level reasoning.

Kalra *et al.* [19] make analyzing source code of smart contracts available by demonstrating Zeus, a framework for verifying the correctness and validating the fairness of smart contracts presented in high-level languages. They also formulate strategies for detecting reentry bugs. Liu *et al.* [22] propose the ReGaurd, a fuzzing-based analyzer that targets the detection of reentrancy bugs. However, these strategies are independent of the functional verification of the contract.

Another source-level verification tool for smart contracts is the SOLC-VERIFY devised by Hajdu *et al.* [16]. Users may write specifications as annotations in the code, and the verifier will verify whether the program states are consistent with specifications. However, the tool uses SMT-solver based methods for verification, so it cannot handle higher-order cases. Furthermore, it does not provide a clear program logic like ours. Although detection for reentrancy bugs is also available in this system, they fail to show the soundness of their approaches.

As for the analysis of reentrancy bugs, we can also model them as their counterparts in the concurrent programs. Sergey and Hobor [24] identify the similarity between the smart contract with conventional concurrent programs and seek to understand the behavior of smart contracts by considering them as concurrent objects. In this way, many loopholes in smart contracts can be analyzed based on formal verification techniques for analyzing concurrent programming context. Nevertheless, their research provides no formalization of the idea, which might be worthy of further development.

A different approach to deal with the security of smart contracts is runtime loophole detection and protection. Cook *et al.* [14] elaborate on a real-time monitoring and protecting system for Solidity smart contracts that collect information from the blockchain network and tracks potential attacks to the contract. When establishing the concept of ECF, Grossman *et al.* [15] also invent an algorithm for the online detection of ECF and evaluated it on the history of the blockchain. These systems are of great aid to the protection of deployed contracts, but it is not for identifying and locating loopholes in the contract beforehand. Since we can not recall contracts deployed on the blockchain, the detection of bugs before deployment is considered more economical.

Our contribution in this paper is mainly theoretical but we also show how to formalize these results (about a toy language that can simulate real contracts) in a theorem prover. In order to establish end-to-end functional correctness of real Solidity contracts, an interactive verification tool should contain the followings:

- A formalized semantics for real Solidity language;
- A formalized semantics for Etheurem VM bytecode;
- A verified compiler from solidity to Etheurem VM bytecode;

- A coarse-grained logic and fine-grained logic for Solidity, which is formally proved sound w.r.t. Solidity's semantics;
- A verified symbolic execution library, which is based on logics above and can provide some proof automation support.

We believe that all of these components above can be developed by a reasonable amount proof engineering, according to our results in this paper and successful experience of previous program verification projects. On one hand, the famous CompCert [21] project provides a general framework to define formal small step semantics for realistic programming languages (e.g. C and assembly), to develop a verified compiler, and to connect a small step semantics with a big step semantics (like our denotational semantics in this paper). This is a great guideline of how to build the first three components above. On the other hand, the VST project [11] shows how to formally prove a program logic sound (whose proof would be concise and elegant on toy languages) w.r.t. a realistic programming language (while all language subtleties are taken into consideration), and how to implement a verified symbolic execution system based on such logics above and based on a theorem prover's tactic system. Their experience will be very helpful when building the last two components above.

7   Conclusion

In this paper, we have presented two program logics about reentrancy behaviors. Our coarse-grained logic can prove coarse-grained specifications and is both sound and complete. However, its triple lacks expressiveness when we want fine-grained function specifications to connect execution results with other hyper-parameters of reentrancy (e.g. the number of times reentry call happens, the order of different reentry calls and the parameters of reentry calls). In comparison, our fine-grained logic can use relatively complicated quintuples to specify not only preconditions and postconditions of functions, but also assertions of program state at each reentry point. These reentry assertions include the effect of reentrancy hyper-parameters into function specifications. Nevertheless, we sometimes would need several complex quintuples to cover specifications for a function thoroughly.

Acknowledgement. This research is sponsored by Shanghai Pujiang Program and National Natural Science foundation of China (NSFC) Grant No. 61902240.

References

1. Solidity - Solidity 053 documentation. https://solidity.readthedocs.io/en/v0.5.3/
2. Ahrendt, W., Pace, G.J., Schneider, G.: Smart contracts: a killer application for deductive source code verification. Principled Software Development, pp. 1–18. Springer, Cham (2018). https://doi.org/10.1007/978-3-319-98047-8_1

3. Amani, S., Bégel, M., Bortin, M., Staples, M.: Towards verifying ethereum smart contract bytecode in Isabelle/HOL. In: Proceedings of the 7th ACM SIGPLAN International Conference on Certified Programs and Proofs, pp. 66–77. ACM (2018)
4. Appel, A.W.: Verified software toolchain. In: Barthe, G. (ed.) ESOP 2011. LNCS, vol. 6602, pp. 1–17. Springer, Heidelberg (2011). https://doi.org/10.1007/978-3-642-19718-5_1
5. Apt, K., De Boer, F.S., Olderog, E.R.: Verification of Sequential and Concurrent Programs. Springer, London (2010). https://doi.org/10.1007/978-1-84882-745-5
6. Atzei, N., Bartoletti, M., Cimoli, T.: A survey of attacks on ethereum smart contracts (SoK). In: Maffei, M., Ryan, M. (eds.) POST 2017. LNCS, vol. 10204, pp. 164–186. Springer, Heidelberg (2017). https://doi.org/10.1007/978-3-662-54455-6_8
7. Barras, B., et al.: The Coq Proof Assistant reference manual. Technical report, INRIA (1998)
8. Bhargavan, K., et al.: Formal verification of smart contracts: short paper. In: Proceedings of the 2016 ACM Workshop on Programming Languages and Analysis for Security, pp. 91–96. ACM (2016)
9. Buterin, V., et al.: A next-generation smart contract and decentralized application platform. white paper, vol. 3, p. 37 (2014)
10. Cao, Q., Wang, Z.: Reentrancy? Yes. Reentrancy bug? No (2020). https://archive.org/details/paper_reentry
11. Cao, Q., Beringer, L., Gruetter, S., Dodds, J., Appel, A.W.: VST-Floyd: a separation logic tool to verify correctness of C programs. J. Autom. Reason. **61**, 367–422 (2018)
12. Chen, H., Pendleton, M., Njilla, L., Xu, S.: A survey on ethereum systems security: Vulnerabilities, attacks and defenses. arXiv preprint arXiv:1908.04507 (2019)
13. ConsenSys. https://consensys.github.io/smart-contract-best-practices/known_attacks/ (Ethereum Smart Contract Best Practices: Known Attacks)
14. Cook, T., Latham, A., Lee, J.H.: DappGuard: Active monitoring and defense for solidity smart contracts (2017). Accessed 18 July 2018
15. Grossman, S., Abraham, I., Golan-Gueta, G., Michalevsky, Y., Rinetzky, N., Sagiv, M., Zohar, Y.: Online detection of effectively callback free objects with applications to smart contracts. In: Proceedings of the ACM on Programming Languages, vol. 2, no. POPL, p. 48 (2017)
16. Hajdu, Á., Jovanović, D.: solc-verify: A modular verifier for solidity smart contracts. arXiv preprint arXiv:1907.04262 (2019)
17. Hirai, Y.: Defining the ethereum virtual machine for interactive theorem provers. In: Brenner, M., et al. (eds.) FC 2017. LNCS, vol. 10323, pp. 520–535. Springer, Cham (2017). https://doi.org/10.1007/978-3-319-70278-0_33
18. Hoare, C.A.R.: An axiomatic basis for computer programming. Commun. ACM **12**(10), 578–580 (1969)
19. Kalra, S., Goel, S., Dhawan, M., Sharma, S.: Zeus: analyzing safety of smart contracts. In: NDSS (2018)
20. Krebbers, R., Timany, A., Birkedal, L.: Interactive proofs in higher-order concurrent separation logic. In: Castagna, G., Gordon, A.D. (eds.) Proceedings of the 44th ACM SIGPLAN Symposium on Principles of Programming Languages, POPL 2017, Paris, France, 18–20 January 2017, pp. 205–217. ACM (2017). http://dl.acm.org/citation.cfm?id=3009855
21. Leroy, X.: Formal verification of a realistic compiler. Commun. ACM **52**(7), 107–115 (2009)

22. Liu, C., Liu, H., Cao, Z., Chen, Z., Chen, B., Roscoe, B.: ReGuard: finding reentrancy bugs in smart contracts. In: Proceedings of the 40th International Conference on Software Engineering: Companion Proceeedings, ICSE 2018, pp. 65–68. ACM, New York (2018). http://doi.acm.org/10.1145/3183440.3183495
23. Nielsen, J.B., Spitters, B.: Smart contract interactions in coq. Submitted to FMBC19 (2019)
24. Sergey, I., Hobor, A.: A concurrent perspective on smart contracts. In: Brenner, M., et al. (eds.) FC 2017. LNCS, vol. 10323, pp. 478–493. Springer, Cham (2017). https://doi.org/10.1007/978-3-319-70278-0_30
25. Siegel, D.: Understanding the DAO attack (2016). Accessed 13 June 2018
26. Szabo, N.: Formalizing and securing relationships on public networks. First Monday **2**(9) (1997)
27. Tan, G., Appel, A.W.: A compositional logic for control flow and its application in foundational proof-carrying code. Princeton University (2005)
28. Wloka, J., Sridharan, M., Tip, F.: Refactoring for reentrancy. In: Proceedings of the the 7th Joint Meeting of the European Software Engineering Conference and the ACM SIGSOFT Symposium on The Foundations of Software Engineering, pp. 173–182. ACM (2009)

Graph Transformation Systems: A Semantics Based on (Stochastic) Symmetric Nets

L. Capra[✉]

Dipartimento di Informatica, Università degli Studi di Milano, Milan, Italy
capra@di.unimi.it

Abstract. Graph transformation systems (GTS) and Petri nets (PN) are central formal models for concurrent/distributed systems. PN are usually considered as instances of GTS, due to the lack of ability to dynamically adapt their structure. Reversing this perspective, a formal encoding of GTS was recently defined using Symmetric Nets (SN), a High-Level PN formalism which syntactically highlights system behavioural symmetries. This makes it possible reusing the efficient analysis techniques and tools available for SN, e.g., new achievements in SN structural analysis, which are exploited to characterize valid transformation rules. This paper is on the same line, but follows a very different approach. Instead of directly formalizing GTS in terms of SN, a SN semantics is provided for the classical double-pushout approach, by constructively translating DPO rules to equivalent SN subnets. Using the native stochastic extension of SN (SSN) permits a for free encoding of stochastic GTS.

1 Introduction and Related Work

Graph transformation (or rewriting) [13], introduced around fifty years ago [15], has been successfully proposed as a general, flexible, theoretically sound model for concurrent systems with a dynamical structure. Many foundational papers describe/compare different models of graph transformation, using the category theory as a unifying framework [11,16]. Many others present applications, e.g., in the area of software engineering [13], networking, biology [12].

The relationship with other formalisms for concurrent systems, in particular Petri nets (PN) [25] and process algebra [17,26], have been deeply studied. Petri nets (PN) [25], on the other side, are a central model for concurrent or distributed systems, and represent a reference for any formalism meant to describe concurrent or distributed systems, including Graph transformation systems (GTS).

PN have been often considered as instances of GTS, due to the lack of ability to adapt/reconfigure their structure. The idea, shown by Kreowsky in its seminal work [22], is to represent a marked PN as a graph with three different types of nodes (for places, transitions, and tokens) and describe the firing of a PN transition thorough a rule. We refer to [10] for a survey of the earliest woks, and

© Springer Nature Switzerland AG 2020
J. Pang and L. Zhang (Eds.): SETTA 2020, LNCS 12153, pp. 35–51, 2020.
https://doi.org/10.1007/978-3-030-62822-2_3

to [2,14] for more recent ones. Some PN extensions have been equipped with dynamical reconfiguration features [24], somehow inspired to Graph transformation rules.

To cope with non-functional aspects of distributed systems, such as performance and dependability, *stochastic* graph transformation systems (SGT) are introduced [18]. In analogy with Stochastic PN, each rule is associated with the rate of an exponential pdf. A continuous time Markov chain is thus derived from a SGT, and a (timed) logic is given to formally check properties.

In [5], we consider the relationship between GTS and PN from a new perspective. Graph transformation rules are directly formalized in terms of Symmetric Nets (SN) [8], a class of Coloured Petri nets [19,20] showing an acceptable trade-off between expressivity and analysis capability. A GTS rule matches a SN subnet whose marking encodes a graph. The advantages are numerous: the SN structured syntax, which outlines model symmetries, is exploited in efficient analysis techniques integrated in the GreatSPN package [1]; the interleaving semantics for a GTS is given by the state-transition system of a SN; its symbolic version [9] provides an abstraction for graph isomorphism; and above all, a new tool [7] (www.di.unito.it/~depierro/SNex) for symbolic structural analysis of SN [3,4], allows an effective validation of rules, and verification of GTS properties.

This paper is complementary to [5]. We formalize SGT in terms of stochastic Symmetric Net (SSN), the native extension of SN. We refer to the classical, algebraic double-pushout model (DPO) [11]. We do not use the categorical notions, but we follow an operational, though rigorous, approach. Differently from [5], we constructively translate any DPO rules to equivalent SSN subnets. The intent is twofold: provide a semantic characterization of the SN approach to graph rewriting, and promote the interoperability among different formalisms/tools.

Below is the balance of the paper: Sect. 2 introduces SN, GTS, and DPO rules; Sect. 3 formalizes the SN-based encoding of directed (multi-)graphs, and shortly discusses about the graph isomorphism abstraction provided by the SN Symbolic Reachability Graph; Sect. 4 describes the steps for translating injective, stochastic, DPO rules into corresponding, elementary (S)SN rules, first considering injective rule matches, then non-injective ones; Sect. 5 draws some conclusion and outlines ongoing work.

The proofs of the main statements (properties/corollaries), along with all the examples used in the paper (in GreatSPN format), are available as additional material at github.com/lgcapra/GTS-SN.

2   Background

This section describes the formalisms used in the rest of the paper. We refer to [25] and [8] for a detailed description of classical Petri nets and SNs.

2.1   Symmetric Nets

(Stochastic) Symmetric Nets (SSN) (iso.org/standard/43538.html), in origin, Well-formed Nets [8], are a High-Level PN formalism [19] featuring a syntax which highlights the *behavioural symmetries* of systems. Like any (High Level) PN, SSN are a kind of finite, bipartite graph, whose elements are annotated.

A SSN is a 10-tuple $(P, T, \mathcal{C}, \mathcal{D}, g, \mathrm{I}, \mathrm{O}, \mathrm{H}, \pi, \rho)$, where P and T are non-empty, disjoint sets holding the *places* and *transitions*. The former, drawn as circles, represent state variables, whereas the latter, events causing local state changes. There are two kinds of transitions: *timed* (drawn as rectangles), having an associated random firing delay, and *immediate* (drawn as tiny bars), representing non-observable events, firing in zero time and with priority over the formers.

$\mathcal{C} = \{C_i, i : 1 \ldots, \mathrm{n}\}$ holds the *basic color classes*, finite, pair-wise disjoint sets representing system entities of a certain kind. A class *may* be either *partitioned* into *static subclasses* $C_{i,j}$, or (circularly) *ordered* (this feature is not used). The static partition of classes determines the symmetry of a SN model, in fact, only the colors of a subclass are meant to denote equivalently behaving components.

$\mathcal{D}$ maps each $v \in P \cup T$ to a *color domain*, defined as Cartesian products of classes: $\mathcal{D}(v) = \prod_i C_i^{e_i}$, where $e_i \in \mathbb{N}$ is repetitions of class C_i. A place's color domain, $\mathcal{D}(p)$, defines the type of *tokens* (color tuples from $\mathcal{D}(p)$) place p may hold; a transition's color domain, $\mathcal{D}(t)$, defines the possible *firing instances* of t. Typed variables $(Var(t))$ are used to refer to the elements of a color tuple in $\mathcal{D}(t)$: for each C_i, there are e_i distinct type-C_i variables. An instance of t, denoted (t, b), $b \in \mathcal{D}(t)$, may be seen as a binding of colors to variables in $Var(t)$.

Henceforth, color classes are denoted by capital letters, e.g., N, L. The ith static subclass of a class, if any, is denoted by a subscripted capital letter, e.g., L_i. Variables in $Var(t)$ are denoted by lower-case letters, e.g. n_i, which refer to the variable's type (e.g., N), with a subscript ranging in $1 \ldots e^{\mathrm{N}}$, e^{N} being the repetitions of N in $\mathcal{D}(t)$ (it may be omitted if $e^{\mathrm{N}} = 1$). This outlines the real semantics of variables: $n_i \in Var(t)$ is a function $\mathcal{D}(t) \rightarrow Bag[\mathrm{N}]$ that maps a color-tuple b to the set-type bag holding the i-th occurrence of color N in b.

g maps each $t \in T$ to a boolean function, $g(t) : \mathcal{D}(t) \rightarrow Bool$, called *guard*, defined in terms of *basic predicates*: the only used here are (in)equalities, e.g., $[n_1 = (\neq)n_2]$, which is *true* when n_1 and n_2 are bound to the same/a different color; memberships, e.g., $[l_1 \in L_2]$, which is *true* when the color bound to l_i belongs to subclass L_2. An instance (t, b), is said *valid* if and only if $g(t)(b) = true$. With $\mathcal{D}(t)$ we shall refer to its *restriction* (assumed non-empty) to valid instances of t. The default, implicit guard is the constant *true*.

$\mathrm{I}[p, t]$, $\mathrm{O}[p, t]$, $\mathrm{H}[p, t]$, are families of arc-functions, $\mathcal{D}(t) \rightarrow Bag[\mathcal{D}(p)]$, defined $\forall p \in P, t \in T$, annotating input (from p to t), output (from t to p), and inhibitor arcs (ending with a small circle), respectively.

π is a map $T \rightarrow \mathbb{N}$, associating priorities with transitions (instances). t is said *timed* if and only if $\pi(t) = 0$, *immediate* otherwise.

ρ is a map $T \rightarrow \mathbb{R}^+$, which associates each transition (instance) a stochastic parameter.

Semantics. PN are equipped with a distributed state notion called *marking*, a P-indexed vector $\mathbf{m}$ such that $\mathbf{m}[p] \in Bag[\mathcal{D}(p)]$. The dynamics of a SN is defined by the *firing rule*. An instance (t, b) has *concession* in $\mathbf{m}$ if and only if:

- $\forall p \in P$: $\mathrm{I}[p, t](b) \leq \mathbf{m}[p]$

– $\forall p \in P$, $x \in \mathrm{H}[p,t](b)$: $\mathrm{H}[p,t](b)(x) > \mathbf{m}[p](x)$

(t,b) is *enabled* in $\mathbf{m}$ if and only if it has concession in $\mathbf{m}$ and there is no higher priority transition's instance having concession. If enabled, (t,b) may *fire*, leading to a marking $\mathbf{m}'$ such that: $\forall p\, \mathbf{m}'[p] = \mathbf{m}[p] - \mathrm{I}[p,t](b) + \mathrm{O}[p,t](b)$. $\mathbf{m}'$ is said *reachable* from $\mathbf{m}$ through (t,b), and this is denoted $\mathbf{m}[t,b\rangle\mathbf{m}'$.

A marking $\mathbf{m}$ is said *vanishing* if there are some immediate transition instances enabled in $\mathbf{m}$, *tangible* otherwise. A SN *model* is a SN with a *tangible initial marking* $\mathbf{m}_0$. If there are no cyclic paths of immediate transition instances, it is possible to build the (tangible) *reachability graph* (TRG) of a SN model, an edge-labelled, directed multi-graph (V,E) whose nodes are tangible markings: $\mathbf{m}_0 \in V$; if $\mathbf{m} \in V$, and there exists a possibly *empty* sequence $\{(t_i,b_i), \pi(t_i) > 0\}$, $i : 1\ldots n \in \mathbb{N}$, such that $\mathbf{m}[t,b\rangle\mathbf{m}_1[t_1,b_1\rangle \ldots \mathbf{m}_n[t_n,b_n\rangle\mathbf{m}'$, with $\mathbf{m}'$ tangible, then $\mathbf{m}' \in V$, $\mathbf{m} \xrightarrow{t,b} \mathbf{m}' \in E$.

If t is timed, then $\rho(t)$ is the *rate* of a non-negative exponential pdf from which the firing delay of any instance of t is sampled. If t is immediate, $\rho(t)$ is a weight used to probabilistically solve conflicts among enabled transition instances. As a result, the timed semantics of a SSN model is a Continuous Time Markov Chain (CTMC) whose states are the TRG nodes. The $[i,j]$ entry of the generator matrix $(i \neq j)$ is the sum of rates of transition instances leading from $\mathbf{m}_i$ to $\mathbf{m}_j$. Vanishing paths are assigned a probability, according to immediate transition weights. A *lumped* CTMC is automatically derived from to the *SRG*.

Arc function syntax Formally, an arc function is a linear combination:

$$\sum_k \lambda_k.T_k[g_k], \ \lambda_k \in \mathbb{Z}, \tag{1}$$

where T_k is a tuple (Cartesian product) $\langle f_1, \ldots, f_h \rangle$ of *class-functions*, possibly suffixed by a guard on $\mathcal{D}(t)$: if $g_k(b) = true$, then $T_k[g_k](b) = f_1(b) \times \ldots f_h(b)$, otherwise, $T_k[g_k](b) = \epsilon$. Scalars in (1) must be such that the linear combination is well-defined.

A class-C function f_i is a *type-set* map $\mathcal{D}(t) \to Bag[\mathrm{C}]$, defined in terms of *elementary functions* $\mathcal{E}_\mathrm{C} = \{c_j, ++c_j, --c_j, \mathrm{C}_q, All\}$:

– c_j (variable, or *projection*) maps a color-tuple $b \in \mathcal{D}(t)$ to the jth occurrence of color C in b; if C is ordered, $++c_j, --c_j$ yield the $\mathrm{mod}_{|\mathrm{C}|}$ successor/predecessor of the color bound to $c_j{}^1$;
– C_q (defined only if C is partitioned) and All are *constant* maps to C_q and C, respectively.

Formally, a class-function f_i is recursively defined:

$$f_i = \begin{cases} e, & e \in \mathcal{E}_\mathrm{C} \\ e \pm f_i, & e \in \mathcal{E}_\mathrm{C} \end{cases} \tag{2}$$

---

[1] In this paper only unordered classes are used.

where in (2) $\pm$ are meant as *set-operations*. This syntax/semantics is fully in accordance with that of GreatSPN package [1], and is slightly different (even if equivalent) from that used in legacy papers on SNs, where class-functions are defined in turn as linear combinations. It will be exploited when modelling non-injective graph morphisms.

For example, consider the function-tuple $\langle n_1, n_2 + n_3, L_1 \rangle : N^k \to N^2 \times L$, $k > 2$: when evaluated on a color-tuple $\langle v_1, v_2, v_3 \rangle$, it yields the type-set bag $1 \cdot \langle v_1, v_2, lb_1 \rangle + 1 \cdot \langle v_1, v_3, lb_1 \rangle$, instead, when evaluated on a color-tuple $\langle v_1, v_2, v_2 \rangle$, yields $1 \cdot \langle v_1, v_2, lb_1 \rangle$. Its semantics is thus different from $\langle n_1, n_2, L_1 \rangle + \langle n_1, n_3, L_1 \rangle$, which, when evaluated on $\langle v_1, v_2, v_2 \rangle$ results in $2 \cdot \langle v_1, v_2, lb_1 \rangle$.

It is sometimes convenient to rewrite arc functions, according with:

Property 1. Any SN arc function can be equivalently expressed as $\sum_i \lambda_i T_i[g_i]$, $\lambda_i \in N$, where function-tuples $T_i[g_i]$ are (type-set and) pairwise disjoint.

For example, $\langle 2 \cdot All - n_1, n_2 \rangle + 2 \cdot \langle n_2, n_2 \rangle : N^k \to N^2$, $k > 1$, may be rewritten as $2 \cdot \langle All, n_2 \rangle [n_1 = n_2] + 2 \cdot \langle All - n_1 - n_2, n_2 \rangle [n_1 \neq n_2] + 3 \cdot \langle n_2, n_2 \rangle [n_1 \neq n_2]$.

We henceforth assume that arc-functions are expressed as in terms of pairwise disjoint (guarded) tuples.

2.2   Graph, Graph Morphisms, Gluing (Pushout), DPO Rule

We consider a quite general class of graphs, i.e, directed, edge-labelled, multi-graphs (with parallel edges). Let Λ be the fixed set of labels.

Graph. A graph G is a 5-tuple $G = (N, E, s, t, l)$ where

- N is a set of nodes, E is a set of edges, $N \cap E = \emptyset$
- $s : E \to N$ is the *source* function; $t : E \to N$ is the *target* function
- $l : E \to \Lambda$ is the *labelling* function

The components of a graph will be subscripted by the graph's name, if needed. The source and target nodes of $e \in E$ are said *incident* to e.

Graph morphism. Let G, H be graphs. A (total) graph morphism $\phi : G \to H$ is a pair of functions $\phi_N : N_G \to N_H$, $\phi_E : E_G \to E_H$, such that $\forall e \in E_G$:

$$s_H(\phi_E(e)) = \phi_N(s_G(e)), t_H(\phi_E(e)) = \phi_N(t_G(e)), l_H(\phi_E(e)) = l_G(e)$$

A morphism preserves graph structure and edge labelling. $\phi : G \to H$ is said *injective (surjective)* if both ϕ_N and ϕ_E are. If ϕ is both injective and surjective ϕ is said an *isomorphism*, written $G \cong H$. Morphisms are used to match the left-hand side of a rule in a host graph.

Another key concept is that of graph *gluing* (*pushout* in the categorical setting). If G and H have a common interface I, then gluing G and H through I, results in a graph, denoted $G +_I H$, obtained by "joining" G and H via their overlap I. The embedding of I into G and H is described by two morphism $\phi_H : I \to H$, $\phi_G : I \to G$. The explanation above is valid only if both ϕ_H, ϕ_G are injective, otherwise, there may be some merge effect of graph elements.

Given a set A, and an equivalence relation $\equiv$ on A, the set of equivalence classes is denoted $A / \equiv$, whereas the equivalence class of $a \in A$ is denoted $[a]_\equiv$. In all subsequent definitions, we assume that all node and edge sets are disjoint.

Graph Gluing. Let I, G, H, be graphs, and $\phi_H : I \to H$, $\phi_G : I \to G$ be graph morphism (I is called *interface*). Let $\equiv$ be the smallest equivalence relation on $E_G \cup N_G \cup E_H \cup N_H$ such that $\forall x \in N_I \cup E_I$ $\phi_H(x) = \phi_G(x)$. The gluing of G, H, over I, (denoted $G +_I H$ or $G +_{\phi_H, \phi_G} H$) is a graph X such that

$$N_X = (N_G \cup N_H)/\equiv \quad E_X = (E_G \cup E_H)/\equiv$$

$$s_X([e]_\equiv) = \begin{cases} [s_G(e)]_\equiv & \text{if } e \in E_G \\ [s_H(e)]_\equiv & \text{if } e \in E_H \end{cases} \quad t_X([e]_\equiv) = \begin{cases} [t_G(e)]_\equiv & \text{if } e \in E_G \\ [t_H(e)]_\equiv & \text{if } e \in E_H \end{cases}$$

$$l_X([e]_\equiv) = \begin{cases} l_G(e) & \text{if } e \in E_G \\ l_H(e) & \text{if } e \in E_H \end{cases}$$

$G +_I H$ is obtained by juxtaposing the parts of G, H which are not in the images of ϕ_H, ϕ_G, and merging the elements of G, H with a common pre-image.

DPO Rule. A graph transformation rule r is composed of three graphs, L, I, R (left-hand side, interface, right-hand side) and two morphisms: $L \xleftarrow{\phi_L} I \xrightarrow{\phi_R} R$.

The elements of L which do not belong to the image of ϕ_L are said *obsolete*, whereas the elements of R not in the image of ϕ_R are said *fresh*. A rule is said *injective* if both ϕ_L and ϕ_R are. The application of an injective rule is intuitive: once a match of the rule's left-hand side is found in a host graph G, the obsolete nodes/edges are removed and the fresh elements are added, while preserving I.

If ϕ_L or ϕ_R are not injective, this interpretation is incorrect, because of some merge/split effect (depending on whether ϕ_R or ϕ_L is not injective). The general semantics of a rule application (i.e., a graph transformation) may be given using the graph gluing concept previously introduced.

Graph transformation Given $r = (L \xleftarrow{\phi_L} I \xrightarrow{\phi_R} R)$, a graph G is transformed by r into a graph H (written $G \xRightarrow{r} H$) if there is a graph C (context) and a morphism $\nu : I \to C$, such that $G \cong L +_{\phi_L, \nu} C$ and $H \cong R +_{\phi_R, \nu} C$.

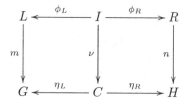

This is illustrated by the DPO diagram above, where the morphisms m and n are called match and co-match, respectively. In other words, we search for an unknown graph C (*context*) such that G is the gluing of L and C over I. If there is a context, G is rewritten to the graph obtained by gluing C and R over I.

Most papers deal with injective rules, extending this assumption to the match (ϕ_L is almost always assumed injective). We relax these constraints, considering first injective rules/ matches, then non-injective matches m and right morphisms ϕ_R. It is reasonable to assume that m_E, ν_E are injective (whereas m_N, ν_N need not), i.e., edges cannot be identified by a match.

Two conditions ensure that, given a match m, a rule can apply: the sum of the two is called *gluing* condition.

Property 2. Let $r = (L \xleftarrow{\phi_L} I \xrightarrow{\phi_R} R)$ be a rule and $m : L \to G$ be a graph morphism, such that m_E is injective. A context C and a morphism $\nu : I \to C$ such that $G \cong L +_{\phi_L, \nu} C$ do exist if and only if

- $\forall v \in N_L$ such that $m(v)$ is incident to $e \in E_G - m_E(E_L)$: $v \in \phi_L(N_I)$
- $\forall v_1, v_2 \in N_L$, $v_1 \neq v_2 : m(v_1) = m(v_2) \Rightarrow v_1, v_2 \in \phi_L(N_I)$

The dangling condition (the 1st one) says that every node of L whose image is incident to an edge of G which is not in the image of m, is not obsolete (if a node is removed, also all linked edges contextually are). The identification condition (the 2nd one) says a match may only identify elements which are retained.

If ϕ_L is injective, and m satisfies the gluing condition, the context C and the morphism ν are unique (up to isomorphism), thus r deterministically applies.

A *Graph transformation system* (GTS) is a pair $(G_0, \mathcal{R})$, where G_0 is the *initial graph* and $\mathcal{R}$ a set of rules. Starting from G_0 we may build the associated state-transition system, whose nodes include G_0 and the graphs reachable from G_0 by applying $\mathcal{R}$ rules. According with [18], each rule is associated with the rate of an exponential pdf governing the delay of its application.

An example of injective DPO rule is given in Fig. 1. By convention, a morphism $f : G_1 \to G_2$ is described by associating identifiers 1 through $|N_{G_1}|$ with nodes of the source graph (so we may speak of ith node), and pair-wise disjoint, non-empty sets of values in the same range to nodes belonging to the image of G_1. In the case of an injective morphism, these are singletons.

3   Graph Encoding in SN

A graph is encoded by a pair of SN places, Node and Edge, that any transition (subnet) representing a rule has to be linked to.

Two basic color classes are used: $N = \{v_i, i : 1 \ldots |N|\}$, holding node descriptors, and large enough to cover the possible rewritings of a graph; $L = L_1 \cup L_2 \cup \ldots L_m$, holding label descriptors, represented by singleton subclasses $L_i = \{lb_i\}$. The place color domains are: $\mathcal{D}(\text{Node}) = N$, $\mathcal{D}(\text{Edge}) = N^2 \times L$.

A graph $G = (N, E, s, t, l)$ is encoded as a marking, $\mathbf{m}_G$: whenever possible, we use the same symbols for graph nodes, labels, and corresponding colors of N and L; otherwise, the color-descriptor of node $x \in N$ is denoted by an injective map $c(x) \in N$. We assume $|N| \leq |N|$, $|\Lambda| = |L|$ (we may write $N \subseteq N$, $\Lambda \cong L$).

$$\mathbf{m}_G[\text{Node}] = \sum_{v_i \in N} v_i \qquad \mathbf{m}_G[\text{Edge}] = \sum_{e \in E} \langle s(e), t(e), l(e) \rangle.$$

$\mathbf{m}_G[\texttt{Node}]$ is a *type-set* bag (bag's elements have multiplicity one), whereas the elements of $\mathbf{m}_G[\texttt{Edge}]$ may have a multiplicity greater than one (parallel edges).

Vice-versa, the conditions under which a SN marking encodes a graph are set by the following (n_1, n_2 are projections)

Definition 1. $\mathbf{m}$ *is a graph-encoding if and only if*

- $\mathbf{m}[\texttt{Node}]$ *is set-type*
- $(n_1 + n_2)(\mathbf{m}[\texttt{Edge}]) \subseteq \overline{\mathbf{m}[\texttt{Node}]}$

The 2nd condition means that there are no *dangling edges*, i.e., edges with non-encoded, incident nodes. The graph corresponding to a graph-encoding $\mathbf{m}$ is denoted $G_{\mathbf{m}}$ (its formalization is trivial). This kind of graph-encoding allows isolated nodes to be efficiently managed in a dynamic context.

In [5] graph transformation rules are *directly* expressed in terms of SN. *Elementary* rules consist of (timed) transitions linked to places $\texttt{Node}$ and $\texttt{Edge}$, whereas, *composite* rules are described by subnets containing one timed transition triggering a sequence of immediate transitions. General *structural* conditions are given, preserving Definition 1, verifiable with the $\texttt{SNexpression}$ tool.

We here follow a completely different approach: starting from (stochastic) DPO rules, we formally show how to encode them in terms of SSN subnets.

Coherently with a base encoding of graphs, edge labels are elementary objects, denoted by singleton subclasses of L. To enhance expressivity, we may use a richer labelling, where a label is a color-tuple of an arbitrary color domain, on which all available SN functions apply. This goes in the direction of attributed-graph rewriting [21,23], and is part of our ongoing work.

Graph Isomorphism Abstraction: The Symbolic Marking. In GTS context, all considerations are done up to graph isomorphism. SN are provided with a *syntactical* state-equivalence notion, called *symbolic marking* (SM). Let us just recall a few basic concepts, referring to [9] for the details. Two SN markings $\mathbf{m}_1$, $\mathbf{m}_2$ belong to the same SM $\widehat{\mathbf{m}}$ if and only if there is a permutation s on color classes *preserving static subclasses*, such that $\mathbf{m}_2 = s(\mathbf{m}_1)$ (we write $\mathbf{m}_1 \equiv \mathbf{m}_1$). An immediate consequence is the following.

Property 3. $G \cong G'$ if and only if there exists a permutation s of class-N colors such that $\mathbf{m}_{G'} = s(\mathbf{m}_G)$.

By setting an *initial* SM, $\widehat{\mathbf{m}}_0$, we can automatically generate a quotient graph, called Symbolic Reachability Graph (SRG), which retains all the information (in the strong bisimulation sense) of the TRG. A SM is defined using *dynamic subclasses* in place of colors. Dynamic subclasses represent a *parametric* partition of color classes: each dynamic subclass refers to a colour class (a subclass, if the class is partitioned), and has a *size* indicating a set colors evenly distributed over the SN places. Given a graph-encoding $\mathbf{m}_G$, the corresponding SM $\widehat{\mathbf{m}}_G$ is straightforwardly derived by replacing each color-token $v_i \in$ N with a cardinality-one dynamic subclass zv_i. The SRG is *directly* built through a

Table 1. Symbolic Expressions used in DPO rule mapping.

Symbol	Definition/Description
$\mathcal{D}(t) \rightarrow Bag[\mathcal{D}(p)]$	
$W^+[p, t]$	$O[p, t] - I[p, t]$ bag of colors put in place p by an instance of t
$W^-[p, t]$	$I[p, t] - O[p, t]$ bag of colors removed from p by an instance of t
$\mathcal{D}(t) \rightarrow Bag[\mathcal{D}(\text{Edge})]$	
T^*	$\langle W^-[\text{Node}, t], All, All \rangle + \langle All - W^-[\text{Node}, t], W^-[\text{Node}, t], All \rangle$ "set" of edges incident to any node removed by an instance of t
$W^-[\text{Edge}, t]^*$	$\sum_i \lambda_i \cdot T_i \cap T^*$, where $W^-[\text{Edge}, t] = \sum_i \lambda_i \cdot T_i$ bag of edges removed by an instance of t incident to withdrawn nodes

symbolic firing mechanism. When huge graphs are encoded, the achieved isomorphism abstraction may be effective. A *canonical representative* for SM is used to syntactically compare SM. Bringing a SM to a canonical form has the same complexity as checking graph isomorphism, so the state/edge reduction is paid in terms of execution time. Improving the efficiency of the legacy SRG builder of GreatSPN is a part of ongoing work.

4   Mapping Injective DPO Rules to SN Transitions

Given an "injective" DPO rule r, we formally show hot to map r to a single SN timed transitions, t_r, whose firing delay has the same exponential rate as the rule. The expressions in Table 1 are used.

4.1   The Procedure Translating an Injective DPO Rule (and Match)

Let t_r denote the SN transition corresponding to $r = L \xleftarrow{\phi_L} I \xrightarrow{\phi_R} R$. The following steps formalize the definition of the functions annotating the arcs linking t_r to places Node, Edge, and the guard $g(t_r)$. In the sequel, an empty summation (of bag-functions) is equivalent to ϵ, whereas an empty conjunctive form is equivalent to *true*.

1. The set of type-N variables n_i (projection functions) used in arc functions, denoted $Var(t_r)$, is composed of three *pair-wise disjoint* parts:

$$Var(t_r) = Var_I \cup Var_{obs} \cup Var_{fresh}$$

$Var_I = \{n_i, i : 1 \ldots |N_I|\}$ corresponds to the set of interface's nodes, whereas Var_{obs} and Var_{fresh} are isomorphic to $N_L - \phi_L(N_I)$ and $N_R - \phi_R(N_I)$, respectively (the *obsolete* and *fresh* nodes). Two bijections var_o, var_f, arbitrarily defined, map any obsolete/fresh node to the corresponding variable; by convention, if $n_i \in Var_{obs}$ and $n_j \in Var_{fresh}$, then $i < j$.

2. The arc functions involving place Node are

$$I[\text{Node}, t_r] = \sum_{n_i \in Var_I \cup Var_{obs}} \langle n_i \rangle \qquad O[\text{Node}, t_r] = \sum_{n_i \in Var_I \cup Var_{fresh}} \langle n_i \rangle$$

$$H[\text{Node}, t_r] = \sum_{n_i \in Var_{fresh}} \langle n_i \rangle$$

3. Having associated graph nodes with variables, edges in I, L, R, are consequently identified by tuples $\langle n_i, n_j, L_k \rangle$, where $n_i, n_j \in Var_{t_r}$ and L_k is the static subclass holding label lb_k. Since we are considering multi-graphs, we can represent the edge sets E_I, E_L, E_R as bags[2]: $bag_{E_I} \in Bag[Var_I{}^2 \times L]$, $bag_{E_L} \in Bag[(Var_I \cup Var_{obs})^2 \times L]$, $bag_{E_R} \in Bag[(Var_I \cup Var_{fresh})^2 \times L]$. If ϕ_R, ϕ_L are injective, then $bag_{E_I} \leq bag_{E_L} \wedge bag_{E_I} \leq bag_{E_R}$.

4. The arc functions involving place Edge are:

$$I[\text{Edge}, t_r] = \sum_{T \in bag_{E_L}} bag_{E_L}(T) \cdot T \qquad O[\text{Edge}, t_r] = \sum_{T \in bag_{E_R}} bag_{E_R}(T) \cdot T$$

$$H[\text{Edge}, t_r] = (T^* - W^-[\text{Edge}, t]) + (W^-[\text{Edge}, t]^* + 1)$$

5. $g(t_r)$ is a conjunctive form which contains these predicates:

$$\forall n_i, n_j \in Var_{fresh}, i \neq j : n_i \neq n_j.$$
$$\forall n_i \in Var_{obs}, n_j \in Var_{obs} \cup Var_I, i \neq j : n_i \neq n_j.$$

The SN in Fig. 2 has been obtained from rule in Fig. 1 by mechanically applying the procedure above: $Var_I = \{n_1, n_2\}$, $Var_{obs} = \emptyset$, $Var_{fresh} = \{n_3\}$.

Definition 2 (SN Graph-Transformation).
A transition t is a Graph-Transformation if and only if, for any graph-encoding $\mathbf{m}$, $\forall b \in \mathcal{D}(t)$: $\mathbf{m}[t, b\rangle \mathbf{m}' \Rightarrow \mathbf{m}'$ is a graph-encoding.

Property 4. Any t_r defined according to Steps 1. through 6. is a SN Graph-Transformation.

Since the marking of place Node is assumed type-set, there are some implicit predicates: $\forall n_i, n_j \in Var_I$, $i \neq j$: $n_i \neq n_j$. As for the fresh variables (due to $H[\text{Node}, t_r]$): $\forall n_i \in Var_{fresh}, n_j \in Var_I \cup Var_{obs} : n_i \neq n_j$. This suggests a rewriting of t_r in a possibly simpler form.

Let $Var_I^* \subseteq Var_I$ include all the variables occurring on $I[\text{Edge}, t_r]$.

Corollary 1. *Let t_r be the transition obtained according to steps 1. through 5. If we erase Var_I^* from $I[\text{Node}, t_r]$ and $O[\text{Node}, t_r]$, and include in $g(t_r)$ an inequality $n_i \neq n_j$, $\forall n_i, n_j \in Var_I^*$, $i \neq j$, we get an equivalent SN rule.*

The rewriting of the SN in Fig. 2(a), according to Corollary 1, is shown in Fig. 2 (b) ($Var_I^* = \{n_1, n_2\}$).

---

[2] They can be seen both as bags of functions and bag-functions.

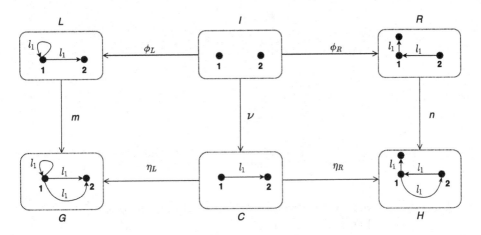

Fig. 1. Injective DPO rule and graph transformation

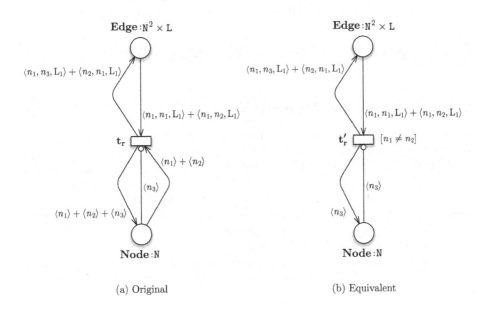

(a) Original   (b) Equivalent

Fig. 2. SN Translation(s) of DPO rule in Fig. 1

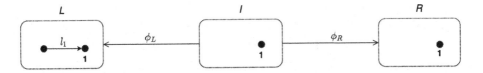

Fig. 3. DPO rule removing a node

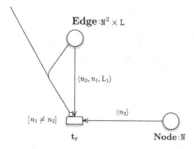

Fig. 4. SN translation of rule in Fig. 3

Another example of translation of an injective DPO rule, involving a node's removal, is shown Fig. 3: $Var_I = Var_I^* = \{n1\}$, $Var_{obs} = n_2$, $Var_{fresh} = \emptyset$. The inhibitor arc-function ensures the dangling-edge condition (Fig. 4).

We may trace a parallelism between a (injective) DPO rule $r: L \xleftarrow{\phi_L} I \xrightarrow{\phi_R} R$ and the corresponding SN transition t_r through the diagram below.

$$\begin{pmatrix} \text{I}[\text{Node}, t_r] \\ bag_{E_L} \end{pmatrix} \geq \begin{pmatrix} \text{I}[\text{Node}, t_r] \cap \text{O}[\text{Node}, t_r] \\ bag_{E_I} \end{pmatrix} \leq \begin{pmatrix} \text{O}[\text{Node}, t_r] \\ bag_{E_R} \end{pmatrix}$$

4.2 Graph Match and Transformation

In order to define the semantics of a transition t_r representing a rule r, we need to formalize a match $m : L \to G$ in terms of t_r.

We establish an intuitive relationship between $m : L \to G$ and a class of instances of t_r, i.e., elements of $\mathcal{D}(t_r) = \mathbb{N}^{|Var_I| + |Var_{obs}| + |Var_{fresh}|}$ (in the context of $\mathbf{m}_G$), which holds independently on whether m is injective or not.

Given m, we say that $b \in \mathcal{D}(t_r)$ is a *corresponding instance* if b is such that $\forall n_i \in Var_I \cup Var_{obs}: n_i = c(m(x))$, where x is the ith node in N_L and c is the color-descriptor map for G ($c(m(x))$ may be a color or a dynamic subclass) [3].

The other way round, let $b \in \mathcal{D}(t_r)$ be such that $\text{I}[\text{Node}, t_r](b) \leq \mathbf{m}_G(\text{Node})$ and $\text{I}[\text{Edge}, t_r](b) \leq \mathbf{m}_G(\text{Edge})$. The *corresponding morphism* $m : L \to G$ ($\cong \mathbf{m}_G$) is defined as: [4]

- $\forall n_i \in Var_I \cup Var_{obs}: m_N(n_i) = n_i(b)$
- Let E_L be formally defined as: $\forall T = \langle n_i, n_j, L_k \rangle \in bag_{E_L}$, there are $bag_{E_L}(T)$ edges $e \in E_L$, such that $s(e) = n_i$, $t(e) = n_j$, $l(e) = L_k$: the image of e in G, $m_E(e)$, is the colour tuple $\langle n_i(b), n_j(b), lb_k \rangle$.

Lemma 1. *Let* $r = L \xleftarrow{\phi_L} I \xrightarrow{\phi_R} R$ *be an injective rule and* t_r *its translation.*

---

[3] Given a transition instance b, we may equivalently write $b : n_i = v_i, \dots$ or $n_i(b) = v_i$.

[4] L may be seen as a graph whose nodes are $Var_I \cup Var_{obs}$, and whose edges are represented by the symbolic bag bag_{E_L}.

If match $m : L \rightarrow G$ is injective and satisfies the gluing condition (Property 2), then there exists a corresponding instance b_m of t_r which is enabled in $\mathbf{m}_G$.

Vice-versa, if b is an instance of t_r which is enabled in $\mathbf{m}_G$, then the corresponding morphism m_b satisfies the gluing condition.

The parallelism between DPO rules and their SN translation is complete observing that, given a rule r, a match $m : L \rightarrow G$ satisfying a gluing condition and a corresponding instance of t_r have the same effect. It comes from this explanation of a rule application, valid for whichever m, ϕ_R:

1. the image of obsolete elements, $m(L - \phi_L(I))$, is removed from G, to obtain the context C; the morphism ν is directly derived from m
2. the target graph H is obtained as gluing of C and R over I ($H \cong R +_{\phi_r,\nu} C$): elements of R, C with a common pre-image in I are *merged*, whereas all the other elements of R and C are included, separately.

If ϕ_R is injective no merge of graph elements is done. In such a case, if also m is injective (this restriction will be relaxed) and satisfies the gluing condition, and b_m is an instance of t_r corresponding to m, the two steps above may be exactly reproduced by the SN firing rule: let $p \in \{\mathtt{Node}, \mathtt{Edge}\}$

$$1. \ \mathbf{m}_C[p] = \mathbf{m}_G[p] - \mathrm{W}^-[p, t_r](b_m) \qquad 2. \ \mathbf{m}_H[p] = \mathbf{m}_C[p] + \mathrm{W}^+[p, t_r](b_m)$$

Corollary 2. *Let $r = L \xleftarrow{\phi_L} I \xrightarrow{\phi_R} R$ be an injective rule and t_r its SN translation. If $m : L \rightarrow G$ is an injective match of r satisfying the gluing condition, and b_m a corresponding instance of t_r enabled in $\mathbf{m}_G$, such that $\mathbf{m}_G[t_r, b_m\rangle \mathbf{m}_{G'}$, then the graph H obtained by applying r is isomorphic to G'.*

4.3   Non-injective Match

The translation of an injective DPO rule r in a transition t_r formalized in the previous section, implicitly deals with injective matches of rule's left-hand side. If we want to consider non-injective matches, we have just to integrate the procedure with a simple rewriting of t_r arc functions. All definitions/outcomes presented in Sect.4.2 extend as well. We consider a possibly non-injective, node map m_N, instead, we assume that the edge map m_E is injective, being non-injective edge-maps of null practical interest.

A non-injective match m for the rule in Fig. 1 identifies nodes 1, 2 of L in G. The reason why the rule's translation (Fig. 2), in either form (a) or (b), is not able to include such a match, is that a corresponding instance b_m of t_r binds variables $n_1, n_2 \in Var_I$ to the same color v_h (associated to the node of G that the two nodes of L map to). In the original form of t_r, the instance b_m is not enabled, because $\mathrm{I}[\mathtt{Node}, t_r](b_m)$ doesn't result in a type-set bag; in the equivalent form, b_m is not even a valid instance, due to t_r's guard.

The workaround for considering injective matches is unexpectedly simple, and consists of writing the function $\mathrm{I}[\mathtt{Node}, t_r]$ ($\mathrm{O}[\mathtt{Node}, t_r]$) as a (elementary) tuple with an inner summation, instead of a sum of tuples, in order to exploit the "type-set" semantics of class-functions.

An example is shown in Fig. 5. The input function $I[\texttt{Node}, t_r]$, according to the translation procedure (Sect. 4.1), and Corollary 1 ($Var_I^- = \{n_1, n_2\}$), is $\langle n1 \rangle + \langle n_2 \rangle$. But, if we (re)write $I[\texttt{Node}, t_r]$ as:

$$\langle n1 \rangle + \langle n_2 \rangle \rightarrow \langle n_1 + n_2 \rangle$$

we get a non-equivalent expression, which evaluates like the original if n_1, n_2 are bound (map) to different colors, but that correctly represents non-injective morphisms, i.e., t_r instances where n_1 and n_2 are bound (map) to the same color. Note that this is the semantics used in $\texttt{SNexpression}$ for function-tuples.

Obviously, this solution doesn't work for the SN in Fig. 2(b), where both $I[\texttt{Node}, t_r]$ and $O[\texttt{Node}, t_r]$ are null ($Var_I^- = \emptyset$). In that case, however, we only need to remove the inequality $n1 \neq n_2$ from t_r's guard: an instance b of t_r would in fact represent an injective match, or a non-injective one, depending on whether $b(n_1) \neq b(n_2)$ evaluates to $true$ or $false$.

Based on the above remarks, Step 2 of the procedure described in Sect. 4.1 has to be slightly modified.

Step 2 of the procedure translating an injective DPO rule (Sect. 4.1) to a SN Graph-Transformation, revised to include non-injective matches (the function $H[\texttt{Node}, t_r]$ is defined as before)

$$I[\texttt{Node}, t_r] = \langle \sum_{n_i \in Var_I^- \cup Var_{obs}} n_i \rangle \qquad O[\texttt{Node}, t_r] = \langle \sum_{n_i \in Var_I^- \cup Var_{fresh}} n_i \rangle$$

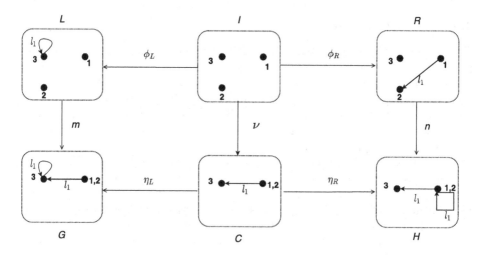

Fig. 5. DPO rule with non-injective m_N

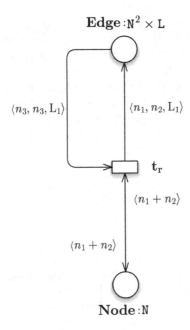

Edge:$\mathbb{N}^2 \times L$

$\langle n_3, n_3, L_1 \rangle$ $\langle n_1, n_2, L_1 \rangle$

t_r

$\langle n_1 + n_2 \rangle$

$\langle n_1 + n_2 \rangle$

Node:$\mathbb{N}$

Fig. 6. SN translation of DPO rule in Fig. 5

Figure 6 illustrates the translation of the rule in Fig. 5, when considering also non-injective matches.

All notions and outcomes previously presented are fully valid. In particular, the gluing condition is still ensured, since the changes to the translation procedure of DPO rules do not affect it in any way. Note that the arc-function rewriting due to Corollary 1 are embedded in revised Step 2.

5   Conclusions and Ongoing Work

We have provided a semantic characterization of the (S)SN-based graph transformation approach, by mapping the classical, algebraic, DPO approach to (S)SN. We have shown in a constructive way that any injective, stochastic, DPO rule maps to a corresponding, elementary SSN rule. Both injective and non-injective matches of a rule are considered. Edge-labelled, multi-graphs are treated. Throughout the paper, we have used simple but significant examples.

Ongoing/Future Work. The theoretical work is being completed by considering non-injective DPO rules, which are mapped to SSN subnets composed of one timed transition, and a sequence of immediate ones. We are extending the SN-based graph transformation by encoding Place/Transitions (P/T) Petri nets enriched with inhibitor arcs. A SN emulator for P/T nets (encoded as a marking) has been defined in [6] We aim at integrating the SN emulator with the theoretically sound, flexible graph transformation approach presented in this paper. More general classes of graphs, in particular hypergraphs, cannot simply encoded with SN, due to the SN low data abstraction ability. On the other side, for the same reason, graph transformations with a richer (typed, constrained) labelling mechanism, generally known as Attributed graph rewriting [21,23], are hardly translatable into SN. To cover more complex graph encodings and graph transformation approaches, Algebraic (or Spec-inscribed) Petri nets [20] may be more conveniently used. Unfortunately this formalism pays its expressivity with less analysis capability than SN, so its use deserves deeper investigations.

References

1. Baarir, S., Beccuti, M., Cerotti, D., De Pierro, M., Donatelli, S., Franceschinis, G.: The GreatSPN tool: recent enhancements. SIGMETRICS Perform. Eval. Rev. **36**(4), 4–9 (2009)
2. Baldan, P., Corradini, A., Gadducci, F., Montanari, U.: From petri nets to graph transformation systems. ECEASST **26**, 01 (2010)
3. Capra, L., De Pierro, M., Franceschinis, G.: Computing structural properties of symmetric nets. In: Campos, J., Haverkort, B.R. (eds.) QEST 2015. LNCS, vol. 9259, pp. 125–140. Springer, Cham (2015). https://doi.org/10.1007/978-3-319-22264-6_9
4. Capra, L., De Pierro, M., Franceschinis, G.: A high level language for structural relations in well-formed nets. In: Ciardo, G., Darondeau, P. (eds.) ICATPN 2005. LNCS, vol. 3536, pp. 168–187. Springer, Heidelberg (2005). https://doi.org/10.1007/11494744_11
5. Capra, L.: An operational semantics of graph transformation systems using symmetric nets. Electron. Proc. Theor. Comput. Sci. **303**, 107–119 (2019)
6. Capra, L., Camilli, M.: Towards evolving Petri nets: a symmetric nets-based framework. IFAC-PapersOnLine **51**(7), 480–485 (2018). 14th IFAC Workshop on Discrete Event Systems, WODES 2018
7. Capra, L., De Pierro, M., Franceschinis, G.: SNexpression: a symbolic calculator for symmetric net expressions. In: Janicki, R., Sidorova, N., Chatain, T. (eds.) PETRI NETS 2020. LNCS, vol. 12152, pp. 381–391. Springer, Cham (2020). https://doi.org/10.1007/978-3-030-51831-8_19
8. Chiola, G., Dutheillet, C., Franceschinis, G., Haddad, S.: Stochastic well-formed colored nets and symmetric modeling applications. IEEE Trans. Comput. **42**(11), 1343–1360 (1993)
9. Chiola, G., Dutheillet, C., Franceschinis, G., Haddad, S.: A symbolic reachability graph for coloured Petri nets. Theoret. Comput. Sci. **176**(1), 39–65 (1997)
10. Corradini, A.: Concurrent graph and term graph rewriting. In: Montanari, U., Sassone, V. (eds.) CONCUR 1996. LNCS, vol. 1119, pp. 438–464. Springer, Heidelberg (1996). https://doi.org/10.1007/3-540-61604-7_69
11. Corradini, A., Montanari, U., Rossi, F., Ehrig, H., Heckel, R., Löwe, M.: Algebraic Approaches To Graph Transformation - Part I: Basic Concepts and Double Pushout Approach, pp. 163–245 (1996)
12. Danos, V., et al.: Graphs, rewriting and pathway reconstruction for rule-based models. In: DŚouza, D., Kavitha, T., Radhakrishnan, J., (eds.) IARCS Annual Conference on Foundations of Software Technology and Theoretical Computer Science, FSTTCS 2012, Hyderabad, India, vol. 18 of LIPIcs, pp. 276–288 (December 2012). Schloss Dagstuhl Leibniz-Zentrum fuer Informatik

13. Ehrig, H., Engels, G., Kreowski, H.-J., Rozenberg, G. (eds.): Handbook of Graph Grammars and Computing by Graph Transformation: Vol. 2: Applications, Languages, and Tools. World Scientific Publishing Co., Inc., USA (1999)

14. Ehrig, H., Padberg, J.: Graph grammars and Petri net transformations, pp. 496–536 (2003)

15. Ehrig, H., Pfender, M., Schneider, H.J.: Graph-grammars: an algebraic approach. In: Proceedings of the 14th Annual Symposium on Switching and Automata Theory, SWAT 1973, USA, pp. 167–180. IEEE Computer Society (1973)

16. Ehrig, H., Ehrig, K., Prange, U., Taentzer, G.: Fundamentals of Algebraic Graph Transformation. Springer, Berlin (2006). https://doi.org/10.1007/3-540-31188-2

17. Fokkink, W.: Introduction to Process Algebra. Texts in Theoretical Computer Science. An EATCS Series. Springer, Berlin (2000). https://doi.org/10.1007/978-3-662-04293-9

18. Heckel, R., Lajios, G., Menge, S.: Stochastic graph transformation systems. Fundam. Inform. **74**, 63–84 (2004)

19. Jensen, K.: Basic Concepts. Coloured Petri Nets Basic Concepts, Analysis Methods and Practical Use. Monographs in Theoretical Computer Science, vol. 1. Springer, Heidelberg (1997). https://doi.org/10.1007/978-3-662-03241-1. 2nd corrected printing. ISBN: 3-540-60943-1, 1997

20. Jensen, K., Rozenberg, G. (eds.): High-level Petri Nets: Theory and Application. Springer, London (1991). https://doi.org/10.1007/978-3-642-84524-6

21. König, B., Kozioura, V.: Towards the verification of attributed graph transformation systems. In: Ehrig, H., Heckel, R., Rozenberg, G., Taentzer, G. (eds.) ICGT 2008. LNCS, vol. 5214, pp. 305–320. Springer, Heidelberg (2008). https://doi.org/10.1007/978-3-540-87405-8_21

22. Kreowski, H.J.: A comparison between petri-nets and graph grammars. In: Noltemeier, H. (ed.) WG 1980. LNCS, vol. 100. Springer, Heidelberg (1981). https://doi.org/10.1007/3-540-10291-4_22

23. Orejas, F.: Symbolic graphs for attributed graph constraints. J. Symb. Comput. **46**(3), 294–315 (2011)

24. Padberg, J., Kahloul, L.: Overview of reconfigurable Petri nets, pp. 201–222 (2018)

25. Reisig, W.: Petri Nets: An Introduction. Monographs in Theoretical Computer Science. An EATCS Series. Springer, New York (1985). https://doi.org/10.1007/978-3-642-69968-9

26. Sangiorgi, D., Walker, D.: The π-calculus: a theory of mobile processes. Cambridge University Press, Cambridge (2001)

Modelling and Implementation of Unmanned Aircraft Collision Avoidance

Weizhi Feng[1,2], Cheng-Chao Huang[3], Andrea Turrini[1,3(✉)] (iD), and Yong Li[1] (iD)

[1] State Key Laboratory of Computer Science, Institute of Software,
Chinese Academy of Sciences, Beijing, China
{fengwz,turrini,liyong}@ios.ac.cn
[2] University of the Chinese Academy of Sciences, Beijing, China
[3] Institute of Intelligent Software, Guangzhou, Guangzhou, China
huangchengchao@gziis.org

Abstract. With the increasing application of unmanned aircraft in civil airspace, collision avoidance systems for unmanned aircraft are becoming more and more important and valuable. An ideal collision avoidance system gives the aircraft an optimal strategy for choosing flight actions to avoid collision risks when it detects other aircraft nearby. Currently the general approach to generating collision avoidance logics is to model the problem as a partially observable Markov decision process (POMDP), and then synthesize an optimal policy. However, the existing systems require the precise position information of the intruder aircraft to generate the avoidance actions and ignore the effects of the flight path changes, which may result in its lower robustness or a wasting of flying resources.

In this paper, we construct a collision avoidance system based on limited information that reduces the variations from the original flight path. We use POMDPs to model the collision avoidance system with only the destination information of our own aircraft and rough information about the intruder position and generate the collision resolution logic. We implement the collision avoidance module, embed it into the real unmanned aircraft system over PX4 flight control platform and demonstrate the effectiveness of our system by flight simulation.

1 Introduction

Safety is a core requirement for aviation. In order to increase safety, modern aviation involves pilots that are periodically trained on the airplane types they are qualified for, air-traffic controllers that instruct pilots about what route and altitude to keep and what ground movements to perform, and more and more advanced computerized control systems on board of the aircraft to help pilots to control their airplane. One of the most dangerous situations during a flight is the possibility to have a mid-air collision. The standard way for avoiding a collision is to implement a strict and effective air traffic control, where pilots adapt route and altitude as instructed by the air-traffic controller. When this is

J. Pang and L. Zhang (Eds.): SETTA 2020, LNCS 12153, pp. 52–69, 2020.
https://doi.org/10.1007/978-3-030-62822-2_4

not possible, e.g., in the middle of a trans-oceanic flight, pilots are assisted by aircraft on-board automation.

1.1   Airborne Collision Avoidance System

As air travel became commonplace, the risk of a mid-air collision increased; the research on automatic aircraft collision avoidance systems gained attraction. In the late 1960s and early 1970s, several manufacturers developed prototype aircraft collision avoidance systems, like the Beacon Collision Avoidance System (BCAS). BCAS uses reply data from the Air Traffic Control Radar Beacon System transponders to determine an intruder's range and altitude. In 1978, FAA started the development of Traffic alert and Collision Avoidance System (TCAS) [9,10] widely used nowadays. As an improvement over BCAS, TCAS can issue a resolution advisory, including a suggested "climb" or "descent" rate, to the pilot to reduce the collision risk when other aircraft are detected nearby. After decades of development, TCAS is currently mandated on board of all large passenger and cargo aircraft worldwide.

TCAS uses an on-board beacon radar to monitor the local air traffic and logic to determine when to alert pilots to potential near mid-air collision (NMAC). The logic is specified using pseudocode that has been validated through simulation studies to ensure the system safety while remaining operationally acceptable. This decision logic was the result of decades of experience which, however, also limits its robustness. For instance, it does not consider the scenario where pilots do not follow the suggested collision avoidance manoeuvre. Due to the high complexity of the TCAS pseudocode, it is hard to fully understand the overall TCAS logic, let alone modify it. See [9] for more details about TCAS and the development of airborne collision avoidance systems.

1.2   Towards Collision Avoidance in Unmanned Aircraft

In recent years, a new collision avoidance system—Airborne Collision Avoidance System X (ACAS X) [8]—has been proposed and started to be investigated by many researchers. The approach currently implemented in ACAS X is to model the aircraft nearby aviation environment as a partially observable Markov decision process (POMDP), and use dynamic programming algorithms to solve the POMDP model to get the optimal control policy ensuring as much as possible that a collision does not occur. The collision avoidance system then stores the policy as a lookup table, queries the table and chooses the optimal action to avoid the collision when other aircraft are detected. It has been shown in [8] that ACAS X outperforms TCAS in terms of the robustness, efficiency and flexibility of the generated threat resolution logic.

ACAS Xu, the version of ACAS X specifically tailored for unmanned aircraft, is still under development. In fact, in recent years aviation safety needed to consider not only human-piloted airplanes, but also unmanned ones. Unmanned aircraft are becoming more and more common in several scenarios: from military service where they are used in several types of missions due to their lightness, hiding ability, and safety of the pilot, to civil service where unmanned aircraft can be used for aerial photography, resource exploration, express delivery, plant protection, and so on. With the increasing number of unmanned aircraft used in public airspace, the safety of unmanned aircraft has begun to attract attention. In particular, for mid-air collision avoidance, unmanned aircraft need to have the ability to sense other aircraft and be able to enforce the flight corrections needed to preserve the aircraft integrity.

Compared to the passenger and cargo aircraft, the design of a collision avoidance system for unmanned aircraft faces a lot of new challenges, such as more complex flying environments, weaker sensor capabilities and tight time limit to react to avoid other aircraft, which make it difficult to ensure the correctness of the collision avoidance systems for unmanned aircraft. In particular, differently from large transport aircraft [12], unmanned aircraft collision avoidance has to consider the following challenges: 1) unmanned aircraft need to sense non-cooperative traffic and tend to use cheaper, lighter, but noisier sensors due to sensor cost and payload; 2) aircraft flying in controlled airspace have similar performances while unmanned aircraft have a larger range of performances. The resolution logic has to support more complex situations; 3) ACAS X only provides resolution in the vertical plane for manned aviation, but unmanned aircraft need both vertical and horizontal resolutions for safety reasons.

There are various previous works on collision avoidance systems for unmanned aircraft [1,5,20]. [20] modeled the collision avoidance system using POMDPs under limited observation capabilities, applied algorithms in discrete state space to get the policy, and performed experiments in a simulator with parameters taken from the unmanned aircraft Global Hawk. [1] directly solved continuous-sate POMDPs to handle high-dimensional state space situations. [5] used a deep neural network to learn an approximation of the lookup table. However they do not implement the obtained avoidance logic on real flight systems, as we do in this work. Also, their simulation results usually do not consider the impact of the generated logic on the flight path, which we also analyze.

These works are usually rather dependent on the precise detection information of the intruder aircraft (e.g. position, distance from own aircraft, etc.), as obtained from the sensors, to generate the avoidance actions. In practice, however, due to the weak sensor capabilities and complex flying environments, it is often very difficult to obtain such a detailed information about the intruder, as well as about our own aircraft, which may result in lower robustness of the system or waste of flying resources.

1.3   Contribution of the Paper

To address the problems described above, in this paper we construct a collision avoidance system working with limited information and minimizing the corrections to the original flight path in order to save flying resources. We use POMDPs to model the collision avoidance system with only the destination information of our own aircraft and rough direction information of the intruder aircraft and then generate the collision resolution logic. We evaluate the effectiveness of our proposal by implementing the collision avoidance module and running it in a Pixhawk simulator, as well as embedding it into the Pixhawk unmanned aircraft system running the PX4 flight control platform, which has been widely used for both customer drones and industrial applications, such as boats and under water vehicles. As our experiment on flying a real Pixhawk unmanned aircraft shows (cf. Sect. 4.4), the generated avoidance logic performs well in avoiding the intruder also in real world situations.

2   Partially Observable Markov Decision Processes

In this section we briefly recall POMDP formulation and solution methods for unmanned aircraft collision avoidance as given in [1].

Consider an agent (for example, a robot in the robotic navigation problem, or the unmanned aircraft in our setting) operating in a stochastic environment. The agent together with the environment represent our system, which keeps information about the state of the agent and of the environment. At each time step the agent, based on its view of the system state, decides what action to perform; this results in a change of the agent (and system) state, change that can be governed by a probability measure to model uncertainty in the outcome of the action. When the agent has a perfect knowledge of the state of the system, it can be modeled by means of a Markov decision process [15]; when the knowledge is only partial, partially observable MDPs allow for a better modeling of the system: in the context of unmanned aircraft equipped with noisy sensors, the exact position of an intruder is not known exactly, but only a coarse observation about its position (like: being on the left/front/right) is available.

POMDPs augment MDPs by hiding the actual states and providing an observation process that generates observations probabilistically based on the underlying state. A POMDP models an agent decision process taking a sequence of actions to maximize the total reward obtainable from the underlying system. The agent, however, is not able to know precisely the underlying system state, but only gets some observations about it; different underlying system states can result in the same observation. The agent keeps a belief over the system state according to the actions performed and the observations seen so far, where a belief is usually a probability measure over the system's states.

2.1   POMDP Formulation

Formally, a POMDP is a 7-tuple $(S, A, O, T, Z, R, \gamma)$ where S, A, O denote the state, action, and observation spaces of the system; $T\colon S \times A \times S \to [0, 1]$ and $Z\colon S \times A \times O \to [0, 1]$ are the transition and observation functions, respectively, such that for each $s \in S$ and $a \in A$, and $s' \in S$ and $o \in O$, $T(s, a, s') = p_S(s'|s, a)$ and $Z(s, a, o) = p_O(o|s, a)$ for appropriate probability measures p_S and p_O modelling the system's dynamics and observations, respectively; $R\colon S \times A \to \mathbb{R}$ is the reward function; and $\gamma \in [0, 1)$ is the discount factor balancing the trade-off between immediate and future rewards. In the remainder of the paper, we assume that both A and O are finite sets.

At each step, the POMDP evolves as follows: when the system is in state $s \in S$ and action $a \in A$ is performed, the system 1) gets the reward $r = R(s, a)$ for having performed action a in s, 2) moves to state s' with probability $T(s, a, s')$, 3) and generates the observation $o \in O$ for s' with probability $Z(s', a, o)$. Note that the observation depends on the states reached after the transition.

Since the agent has only a belief over the system state, it needs to update its belief according to the performed action a and the observed observation o. Let $\mathcal{B}$ denote the set of beliefs, i.e., the set of probability measures over S. Given $b \in \mathcal{B}$, after taking action a and observing o, the agent updates its belief about the system's next state s' as follows:

$$b_a^o(s') = \eta Z(s', a, o) \int_{s \in S} T(s, a, s') b(s) \, ds, \tag{1}$$

where η is a normalization factor ensuring $\int_{s \in S} b_a^o(s) = 1$. To simplify the notation, we may just write b' instead of b_a^o when a and o are clear from the context. This process of updating the belief state follows directly from Bayes' rule and is known as state estimation or filtering [7].

2.2 Solution Methods

POMDPs, like MDPs, exhibit both probabilistic and nondeterministic behaviors. The nondeterminism existing between the different actions available in a system state is resolved by a policy π representing the agent's choice, i.e., a function $\pi: \mathcal{B} \to A$ that specifies which action to perform based on the current belief.

The execution process of the agent alternates between action selection and belief update. Given π and the agent's current belief b, the control of the agent takes the action $a = \pi(b)$. Then the belief is updated according to Eq. (1).

The goal of solving a POMDP is to synthesize an optimal policy π^* maximizing the agent's expected total reward $\mathbb{E}(\sum_{n=0}^{\infty} \gamma^n R(s_n, a_n))$, where s_n and a_n denote the system's state and chosen action at step n, respectively. A policy π induces a value function $V_\pi: \mathcal{B} \to \mathbb{R}$ representing the expected total reward. The value of the total reward obtained by following π from the belief b is

$$V_\pi(b) = \mathbb{E}\left(\sum_{n=0}^{\infty} \gamma^n R(s_n, a_n) | \pi, b \right). \tag{2}$$

In practice, solving POMDPs exactly is challenging due to the high computational complexity, even for relatively small-sized problems [16]. A variety of exact solution methods can be found in previous literature, see, e.g., the witness algorithm [6]. However, these exact methods are not suitable for large-sized problems. To synthesize a policy for large POMDPs, approximate solution methods have been developed [3]. Among them, point-based POMDP algorithms have achieved special success in computing approximate solutions to large discrete

POMDPs [13, 16]. Due to the fact that the optimal value function V^* satisfies the Bellman equation [4]

$$V^*(b) = H(V^*(b))$$
$$= \max_{a \in A} \left\{ \int_{s \in S} R(s,a)b(s)\,\mathrm{d}s + \gamma \sum_{o \in O} p(o|b,a)V^*(b_a^o) \right\} \tag{3}$$

where H is called the *backup* operator, most of the solution methods use it to compute the optimal V^*. Value iteration is a commonly used dynamic programming algorithm based on the Bellman equation for solving MDP problems [19]; its basic structure has also been used for developing POMDP algorithms [16].

In the value iteration process, an initial value function V is chosen so to represent the initial known information about the value; if no information is known in advance, then V is taken to be 0 for all beliefs. Then it performs backup operation H on V by repeatedly computing the Bellman equation until the iteration process converges to a fixed point. Once the iteration procedure terminates, the corresponding policy is extracted by taking, for each belief b, the action a satisfying the equality in Eq. (3).

When implemented naively, the value iteration algorithm needs to search the entire belief space $\mathcal{B}$, which will face the curse of dimensionality and exponential time complexity in large real-world-sized problems [16]. Two main ideas of point-based algorithms have brought about significant progress in improving computational efficiency [2]. First, a small set of points is sampled from the belief space $\mathcal{B}$ as an approximate representation of $\mathcal{B}$. The algorithm performs backup operations over the sampled belief points rather than the entire belief space $\mathcal{B}$ to compute the approximately optimal value function. Second, the α-vectors [11] are used to approximate the value function $V_\pi : \mathcal{B} \to \mathbb{R}$ representing the expected total reward of executing policy π starting from b. The optimal value function can be arbitrarily closely approximated by a piece-wise linear and convex function [18] of the form $V^*(b) = \max_{\alpha \in \Gamma} \alpha \cdot b$, where $\Gamma = \{\alpha_0, \alpha_1, \ldots, \alpha_m\}$ is a set of m vectors called α-vectors. Intuitively, each α-vector can be associated with an action and for the current belief, the solution policy selects the action corresponding to the best α-vector. Thus the policy can be represented by the set Γ of α-vectors [11]. By using α-vectors, we can use partial policies calculated at one belief point for other parts of the belief space $\mathcal{B}$ under appropriate conditions, thereby significantly improving the computational efficiency [16].

Point-based algorithms differ in how they sample the belief space and perform backup operations. PBVI [13] has been the first point-based algorithm to work well on large POMDPs. HSVI2 [17] uses heuristics to guide sampling from the belief space, which can reduce the gap between the upper and lower bounds of the optimal value function, thus speeding up convergence. SARSOP [11] is related to HSVI2, but it attempts to sample the optimally reachable space $\mathcal{R}^*(b_0)$ from the initial belief b_0 through learning-enhanced exploration and bounding techniques.

Though point-based algorithms have made great progress in solving discrete POMDPs, progress on continuous state space POMDPs is rather limited. Continuous POMDP models have more powerful representation capabilities for real-world systems; however, they make it hard to deal with the "curse of dimensionality". One common way is to place a regular grid over S and construct a discrete POMDP model first. Then one can solve the latter by using existing discrete POMDP algorithms. The difficulty with this approach is that the discretization of the state space often results in a number of states that is still too large. One idea to avoid this is to use a particular parametric form to represent beliefs and value functions of states, e.g., a linear combination of Gaussian distributions [14]. Another idea is to use particle filters to represent beliefs, like in MC-POMDP [21]. MCVI (Monte Carlo Value Iteration) [2] combines the method of particle-based belief representation and the key idea of discrete point-based POMDP algorithms: the α-vectors. MCVI represents the solution policy by means of a policy graph G [2], that is, a directed graph that encodes the optimal policy by labeling each node of the graph with an action and each edge with an observation; beliefs are not stored explicitly in the graph. Given a belief b, MCVI synthesizes the policy from a policy graph by starting from some appropriate node v of G. The action chosen by the policy is the one labeling v; then the agent receives an observation o and moves to the successor node v' by following the edge (v, v') labeled by o. This process is repeated to get the policy.

For each node v of the policy graph G, we can define the α-function α_v: $\alpha_v(s)$ is the expected total reward of executing $\pi_{G,v}$ from the current state s:

$$\alpha_v(s) = \mathbb{E}\left(\sum_{n=0}^{\infty} \gamma^n R(s_n, a_n) | \pi_{G,v}, s\right). \tag{4}$$

Then the value of b with $\pi_{G,v}$ is defined by the α-functions associated with G:

$$V_G(b) = \max_{v \in G} \int_{s \in S} \alpha_v(s) b(s) \, \mathrm{d}s. \tag{5}$$

The policy graph is constructed by approximate dynamic programming techniques and MCVI performs Monte Carlo (MC) simulation to sample the state space and the corresponding belief space. The optimal POMDP value function V^* is computed iteratively according to the backup operation in Eq. (3), i.e., by the Bellman equation, on each belief b in the reachable belief set. Each backup can choose an action that maximizes the sum of the expected immediate reward and the expected total reward at the next belief. Then the action is added to the policy graph to make it closer to the optimal policy. The reachable belief set is sampled from the whole belief space as an approximate representation of the belief space. The MCVI method performs well in dealing with integral calculations in continuous state problems, thus avoiding to discretize the state space as a grid and improving its efficiency. For more details, see [2].

3   Collision Avoidance Models

To the best of our knowledge, the algorithms and models used in the latest versions of ACAS X and ACAS Xu are not publicly accessible. Therefore, we

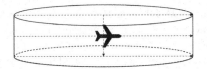

Fig. 1. Threshold range for starting the system in 3D

define our model based on the early published version of ACAS X [8] and ACAS Xu [1]. In our implementation, the aircraft model is parametric and can be easily modified to fit different types of aircraft. In this work, we use the parameter values from Pixhawk[1] and build the model with PX4[2].

In our model, we consider a simple encounter situation between two aircraft, our own aircraft and an intruder aircraft. Our own aircraft has no prior knowledge about the flight path of the intruder aircraft, when an encounter happens. During this period, our own aircraft can only get information about the intruder aircraft's elevation and bearing by sensors onboard. The collision avoidance system is responsible to control our own aircraft so to keep a safe distance from the intruder by choosing appropriate actions to avoid collision.

We will describe the state-transition, observation and reward modeling in our model in detail, similarly to the modeling proposed in [1].

3.1   State-Transition Modeling

The position of a flying aircraft can be represented as a point in the 3-dimensional space. The collision avoidance system needs to intervene when the horizontal and vertical distances of two aircraft are less than the given thresholds, which depend on the type of the aircraft and other parameters; this can be represented as the cylinder shown in Fig. 1.

Similarly to other works on collision avoidance [8,20], in order to simplify the model's state space and make verification more practical, we omit the altitude and consider only the latitude/longitude of the aircraft. So when an intruder is detected, the system tries to avoid the collision by banking left or right, i.e., by changing our aircraft's direction.

State Space. Since we ignore the aircraft altitude in our model, we let (x, y) be the position of the aircraft with respect to the Earth coordinate system, where the positive x-direction points East and the positive y-direction points North. Let θ be the heading angle of the aircraft with respect to East and u the aircraft's horizontal forward speed. The state information of each aircraft is then (x, y, θ, u). By combining the information about our aircraft and the intruder, a state in the POMDP representing our model is a 7-tuple $(x_1, y_1, \theta_1, x_2, y_2, \theta_2, u)$, where (x_1, y_1, θ_1, u) stands for the state of our own aircraft while (x_2, y_2, θ_2, u) is the intruder's state, by assuming that both aircraft have the same speed.

---

[1] https://pixhawk.org/.
[2] https://dev.px4.io/master/en/index.html, PX4 Development Guide.

The state space of the POMDP is continuous, given the nature of the aircraft information. In order to compute the next action for our own aircraft, traditional methods have to first discretize the state space by means of a grid, where each grid cell becomes a state of the discrete POMDP [9]. In our model, we will directly work in the continuous state space instead. In this way, we can apply Monte Carlo methods to improve efficiency of the computation of the policy.

Action Space. Now we introduce our modeling of actions. In order to avoid a collision in an encounter situation, we can change our aircraft direction by changing its forward angle, that is, we bank the aircraft. Thus we can represent the angular velocity $\omega \in \{-\omega_m, 0, \omega_m\}$ as an action in our model, where ω_m is the maximum input value for the banking rate. Consequently, if at step t the heading angle is θ_t and we take the action ω, then the heading angle will become $\theta_{t+1} = \theta_t + \omega \Delta t$ at step $t + 1 = t + \Delta t$ after a small duration of time Δt.

Transition Dynamics. Now we are ready to give the state-transition dynamics of an aircraft in an encounter situation. Recall that in our model, a state consists of the information about both aircraft. Let s_t be the state at step t and s_{t+1} the new state at step $t + 1$ after a small duration of time Δt, where Δt is the sum of two small durations Δt_h and Δt_f, i.e., $\Delta t = \Delta t_h + \Delta t_f$. In order to avoid a collision, our own aircraft first changes the heading angle by banking ω degrees for a small amount of time Δt_h and then goes forward at the constant speed u. After a small amount of time Δt_u, our own aircraft will reach the new position (x_{t+1}, y_{t+1}) from (x_t, y_t). This transition dynamics is formalized as follows.

$$\theta_{t+1} = \theta_t + \omega \Delta t_h,$$
$$x_{t+1} = x_t + u \Delta t_f \cos \theta_{t+1}, \tag{6}$$
$$y_{t+1} = y_t + u \Delta t_f \sin \theta_{t+1}.$$

Note that at the same time, the intruder will also change its flight state (x_2, y_2, θ_2, u) in a similar way by following the action $\omega_{intruder}$. Since our own aircraft does not know the action of the intruder, we can model it in different ways: for instance, the action $\omega_{intruder}$ can be chosen between bank-left, go-forward, and bank-right with equal probability of $\frac{1}{3}$. Other policies can be used to represent different flight plans for the intruder, such as always banking left or right, to represent an intruder flying in circle; we can also consider policies where the intruder tries to intercept our aircraft. We leave the analysis of such policies to the extended version of this paper.

3.2   Sensor Modeling

The threat resolution logic behind a collision avoidance system relies on the aircraft on-board sensors to detect intruders. Electro-optical/infrared (EO/IR) sensors and passive radars are two types of sensors commonly used on large aircraft. On smaller aircraft, the on-board sensors usually have limited accuracy;

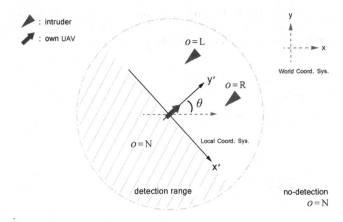

Fig. 2. Observation model

to model this scenario, we use as possible observations $\{N, L, R\}$, which stand for the fact that no intruder is detected, it is detected on the left of the aircraft, or on the right, respectively. Figure 2 shows the observation values corresponding to the possible positions of the intruder with respect to our own aircraft.

By following the state modeling introduced in Sect. 3.1, we can let (x_1, y_1) be the coordinates of our aircraft in the Earth coordinate system and θ its heading angle with respect to East. Let (x_2, y_2) be the coordinates of the intruder in the Earth coordinate system and (x'_2, y'_2) be the corresponding coordinates in the local coordinate system of our own aircraft, which is represented in Fig. 2 by the $x'y'$-coordinate system whose origin coincides with our aircraft. In order to get the position of the intruder with respect to our own aircraft, we convert the coordinates of the intruder into our local coordinate system as follows:

$$x'_2 = (x_2 - x_1)\sin\theta - (y_2 - y_1)\cos\theta,$$
$$y'_2 = (x_2 - x_1)\cos\theta + (y_2 - y_1)\sin\theta. \tag{7}$$

We let d denote the horizontal relative distance of two aircraft and o denote the observation value of the intruder; the value d can be computed as

$$d = \sqrt{(x_1 - x_2)^2 + (y_1 - y_2)^2} = \sqrt{{x'_2}^2 + {y'_2}^2}, \tag{8}$$

while the value for o, for a given detection range r, is

$$o = \begin{cases} N & \text{if } y'_2 < 0 \vee d > r, \\ L & \text{if } y'_2 \geq 0 \wedge d \leq r \wedge x'_2 < 0, \text{ and} \\ R & \text{if } y'_2 \geq 0 \wedge d \leq r \wedge x'_2 \geq 0. \end{cases} \tag{9}$$

3.3 Reward Modeling

As we have seen in Sect. 2.2, a solution for a POMDP is a policy that maximizes the expected total reward. In order to synthesize a policy piloting our own air-

Table 1. Aircraft action rewards

Condition on distance d and banking angle ω	Reward value
$d \leq$ NMAC	-100
$d >$ NMAC, $\omega \neq 0$	-1
$d >$ NMAC, $\omega = 0$	0
$d >$ NMAC, at destination	100

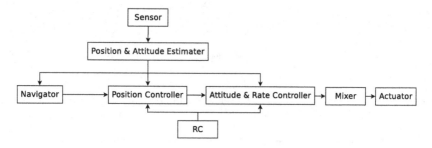

Fig. 3. Overview of the PX4 flight stack

craft to its destination while avoiding collisions, we use rewards to compute a policy that fulfills our requirements.

When at state s and the policy chooses to take action a, a penalty value (i.e., a negative value) $r = R(s, a)$ is computed: it depends on the distance between our aircraft and the intruder, as well as the chosen action.

Since we only consider the 2-D space, we use NMAC to represent the minimum horizontal distance between the two aircraft so that they are considered to be near collision. We give the large penalty of -100 to each action performed when the two aircraft are closer than the NMAC distance, as shown in Table 1. When the aircraft are enough far away, we give a penalty of -1 when the action ω of our own aircraft is not zero, i.e., the aircraft changes direction, and of 0 if it goes straight. This allows us to reduce non-necessary actions taken by our own aircraft. Finally, when our aircraft reaches its destination, a reward of 100 is given to each action, as long as the intruder is not closer than NMAC.

Regarding the discount factor for the expected reward (cf. Eqs. (3) and (4)), we use $\gamma = 0.95$ as discount factor. This values ensures that it is better to immediately avoid the intruder than eventually reach the destination; however, reaching the destination is still taken into account rather strongly (cf. [19]).

4   Experimental Evaluation

We based our experiments on the implementation of MCVI [1] publicly available in https://github.com/bhy/mcvi: it takes as input a POMDP model (coded in C++) and produces as output a policy graph file. We have created our own POMDP model of the collision avoidance problem by extending functions of the

MCVI source code and generated the corresponding collision avoidance policy graph. We then extended the PX4 flight stack by adding a collision avoidance module implementing the policy synthesized by MCVI. The performance of the collision avoidance module has then been evaluated on two scenarios.

PX4 is an open source flight control platform that is supported by the Pixhawk flight control board, an independent open-hardware project for drones and other unmanned vehicles developed by Computer Vision and Geometry Laboratory at ETH Zurich. Due to the clear structure of PX4 flight stack, shown in Fig. 3. it is easy for developers to add their own flight mode on Pixhawk hardware board with PX4 software, or in the jMAVSim tool that is a simulator for PX4-controlled unmanned aircraft. We integrated the collision avoidance module we developed into the PX4 flight stack by adding it in the position controller, the PX4 component responsible for the flight trajectory.

4.1   Experiments Configuration

In the experiments, since our Pixhawk drone has no sensors for detecting an intruder, we have created synthetic encounter situations where our own aircraft detects an intruder while performing a flight mission, so there may be a collision. The flight mission of our own aircraft is to reach the destination placed at 30 m North of the initial position. The intruder aircraft starts from our destination and its goal is to reach our initial position. When an encounter occurs, the intruder aircraft is designed to fly according to two predefined policies, introduced later in Sects. 4.2 and 4.3. By following the sensor modeling given in Sect. 3.2, our own aircraft makes a detection every second, and the detection radius is set to 10 m. That is, our own aircraft gets one observation per second about the presence and position of an intruder aircraft; it can be sensed when the distance between the two aircraft is below 10 m. After getting the observation about the intruder aircraft, our own aircraft will react according to the two different collision avoidance methods introduced below.

Simple Rule-Based Collision Avoidance Scenario. In the simple rule-based collision avoidance scenario, our own aircraft reacts to observations as follows: if L or R is observed (i.e., the intruder aircraft is in the detection range on the left or right of our aircraft), then bank to the opposite direction by $\frac{\pi}{6}$ and fly forward by 1 m; otherwise N is observed, so fly towards to destination.

MCVI-Based Collision Avoidance Scenario. In the collision avoidance scenario using the MCVI synthesized policy, our own aircraft reacts to observations as follows: as soon as an intruder aircraft is detected (observations L and R), bank according to the policy as long as the intruder is detected or the graph terminal node is reached. If the intruder aircraft is not detected or the policy graph terminal node is reached, fly towards the destination. The banking angle and step length are the same as those of the simple rule-based method. Note that after the controller stops to follow the policy, if the intruder aircraft is detected again, the controller restarts to follow the policy.

Fig. 4. One flight simulation for the opposite flight experiment. Blue line: MCVI flight path; white line: simple flight path (Color figure online)

Experiments Setting. Finally, we implemented the above two collision avoidance methods in the PX4 platform. Supported by the Software In the Loop (SITL) simulation of the PX4 platform, we used jMAVSimto simulate our experiments. jMAVSim supports the multirotor simulation and allows us to fly drones running PX4 in a synthetic world. To compare the effectiveness of two collision avoidance methods, we recorded the following measure data (with the meter as the length unit) to indicate the performance: the number *actNum* of banking performed to reach the destination, the minimum distance *minDis* between our own aircraft and the intruder aircraft, the maximum deviation distance *maxDvtDis* from the designed mission flight path, and the increased flight distance *incFltDis* from the original mission flight distance.

4.2 Simulated Intruder's Opposite Flight Experiment

In the first simulated experiment, we assume that the intruder aircraft starts from the destination of our own aircraft (viz. 30 m North of the starting place of own aircraft) and flies straight towards the starting place of our own aircraft. The flight paths of the mission while avoiding a collision are shown in Fig. 4 and the average experimental results are summarized in Table 2.

Table 2. Opposite flight results; in bold, the best results

	Rule-based	MCVI-based
actNum	**4**	5
minDis	2.51	**2.95**
maxDvtDis	9.69	**5.88**
incFltDis	14.83	**9.67**

Table 3. Random interfering flight results; in bold, the best results

	Average value		Median value	
	Rule-based	MCVI-based	Rule-based	MCVI-based
actNum	**3.82**	4.96	**2.5**	4
minDis	5.54	**6.06**	5.88	**6.04**
maxDvtDis	8.85	**5.40**	7.50	**5.60**
incFltDis	9.14	**7.10**	**6.67**	6.87

Based on the jMAVSim simulation, depicted in Fig. 4, we can see the flight path of own aircraft in the simulated map, where the blue solid line represents the flight path induced by the MCVI method while the white dashed line tracks the flight path given by the simple rule-based method. It can be intuitively seen from the figure that the MCVI method can reduce the useless avoidance distance of our own aircraft, and avoid the collision risk more effectively.

Table 2 gives more details about the flight paths: we note that although the logic generated by MCVI based on the POMDP model takes 5 actions instead of 4 to reach the destination while avoiding the intruder aircraft, it does not results in an increase of the flight distance. On the contrary, as shown in Fig. 4 by the MCVI method's blue solid line being closer to the straight line between the terminal points than the simple method's white dashed line, the flight distance is increased by just 9.67 m, about 5 m less than the 14.83 m of the simple method. Furthermore, the MCVI-based approach increases the minimum distance (2.95 vs. 2.51 m) from the intruder aircraft while deviating less (5.88 vs. 9.69 m) from the optimal path without intruders than the simple method; this guarantees a higher safety level while decreasing the maximum deviation distance from the new flight path to the original mission flight path.

4.3   Simulated Intruder's Random Interfering Flight Experiment

In the second simulated experiment, we assume that the intruder aircraft takes off from the midway between the start place and destination of our own aircraft (viz. 15 m North of the starting place of our own aircraft). This time the intruder aircraft chooses randomly an action between bank-left, go-forward and bank-right, i.e., each one with probability $\frac{1}{3}$. Since the flight behavior of the intruder aircraft in this experiment is randomized, we repeated the simulation 50 times and then considered the average outcomes of the two scenarios against the same intruder's random choices, which can be reproduced by fixing the same random seed for the two scenarios.

The statistics for this experiment are presented in Table 3; as we can see, we have a behavior similar to the opposite flight experiment: although the logic generated by MCVI on the POMDP model banks on average one time more to avoid the intruder than the simple rule-based method, it is able to reduce the increased flight distance. Furthermore, it increases the minimum distance between the two aircraft, which implies that the MCVI method gives a higher safety level when dealing with the random behavior of the intruder aircraft. It is particularly noteworthy that when compared with the simple rule-based method, MCVI-based collision avoidance is able to save about 40% of the maximum deviation distance between the actual flight path and the original mission flight path, which is a straight line between the designed takeoff and landing coordinates.

We now give some more details about the safety level achieved by the two collision avoidance scenarios introduced in Sect. 4.1. Out of the 50 simulations for each of the two scenarios, both scenarios ensure that there is no collision since in none of the simulations the minimum distance was below 2 m, the value we set for NMAC; the minimum distance has been at least 2.5 m. There have been few simulations where the distance was about 3 m and the majority above 4 m, with the MCVI-based scenario usually keeping a larger distance. This is reflected also by the average *minDis* values reported in Table 3, where the rule-based *minDis* value is lower than the one for MCVI, which means that the former control policy got closer to the intruder than the latter one.

From these experiments, we obtain that the MCVI-based collision avoidance controller provides a better safety level, since it keeps a larger distance between our aircraft and the intruder than the rule-based controller. This comes at the cost of banking the aircraft few more times, which still allows for reducing the increased flown distance. The flown distance is also an aspect to be considered for drones and other unmanned aircraft, since the increased flight distance reduces the actual operative range of the aircraft, given the limited amount of energy stored in the batteries that can be used to power the aircraft.

While the experiments give a good indication about the safety level provided by the MCVI-based collision avoidance controller, there is no guarantee that it always avoids collisions. We leave the formal analysis of its safety as future work.

4.4   Actual Pixhawk Drone Flight Experiment

In the third experiment, we have taken the PX4 MCVI-based collision avoidance module we developed and uploaded it on a real Pixhawk drone we assembled ourselves. The flight mission is the same as for the previous experiments. The Pixhawk drone communicates to its ground station several data about the position and flight attitude. Since the Pixhawk drone has no sensors for detecting intruders, we used the ground station to inject in the drone's PX4 control system the synthetic intruder from the opposite flight experiment presented in Sect. 4.2.

We show in Fig. 5 the actual flight path flown by our drone as registered by the ground control station and superimposed on the map.

As we can see, the MCVI-based collision avoidance module works well not only in a synthetic environment, but also in the real world. This suggests that the policy synthesis for specifically crafted POMDPs can improve the safety of unmanned aircraft equipped with a collision avoidance module basing its decisions on the synthesized policy.

Fig. 5. The actual Pixhawk drone flight path registered by the ground control station

5   Conclusion

We have constructed a collision avoidance system working with limited information, which also tried to save flying resources by means of reducing the change of the original flight path. Our approach used a POMDP to model the collision avoidance system with only the destination information of our own aircraft and rough direction information of the intruder and then generated the collision resolution logic that maximizes the expected sum of rewards of selected actions. We have implemented the collision avoidance module and embedded it into the PX4 flight control platform that can control real unmanned aircraft systems. The effectiveness of our system is witnessed by the experimental evaluation in both a simulated environment and a real world scenario using a Pixhawk drone.

As future work, we consider to study the scalability of the MCVI approach to more detailed flight scenarios, such as the ones with the 3D environment, different aircraft speeds, more accurate observations given by better sensors, and so on. Also, we plan to apply machine learning algorithms to improve the efficiency of the algorithm for searching an optimal policy. Moreover, we also consider the use of rigorous methods, such as model checking, to ensure the correctness of the collision avoidance system.

Acknowledgments. The authors are very thankful to Xuechao Sun and Junwen Li for helpful discussion and the assembly of the Pixhawk drone. This work has been supported by the Guangdong Science and Technology Department (grant no. 2018B010107004), the Natural Science Foundation of Guangdong Province (grant no. 2019A1515011689), and the National Natural Science Foundation of China (grant nos. 61761136011, 61532019, 61836005).

References

1. Bai, H., Hsu, D., Kochenderfer, M.J., Lee, W.S.: Unmanned aircraft collision avoidance using continuous-state POMDPs. In: Durrant-Whyte, H.F., Roy, N., Abbeel, P. (eds.) Robotics: Science and Systems VII, University of Southern California, Los Angeles, CA, USA, 27–30 June 2011 (2011). https://doi.org/10.15607/RSS.2011.VII.001. http://www.roboticsproceedings.org/rss07/p01.html
2. Bai, H., Hsu, D., Lee, W., Vien, N.: Monte Carlo value iteration for continuous-state POMDPs. Algorithmic Found. Robot. IX **68**, 175–191 (2010). https://doi.org/10.1007/978-3-642-17452-0_11
3. Hauskrecht, M.: Value-function approximations for partially observable Markov decision processes. J. Artif. Intell. Res. **13**, 33–94 (2000). https://doi.org/10.1613/jair.678
4. Hazeghi, K., Puterman, M.: Markov decision processes: discrete stochastic dynamic programming. J. Am. Stat. Assoc. **90**, 392 (1995). https://doi.org/10.2307/2291177
5. Julian, K.D., Lopez, J., Brush, J.S., Owen, M.P., Kochenderfer, M.J.: Policy compression for aircraft collision avoidance systems. In: 2016 IEEE/AIAA 35th Digital Avionics Systems Conference (DASC), pp. 1–10 (2016)
6. Kaelbling, L., Littman, M., Cassandra, A.: Planning and acting in partially observable stochastic domains. Artif. Intell. **101**, 99–134 (1998). https://doi.org/10.1016/S0004-3702(98)00023-X
7. Kamen, E.W., Su, J.K.: Optimal estimation. In: Grimble, M.J., Johnson, M.A. (eds.) Introduction to Optimal Estimation. Advanced Textbooks in Control and Signal Processing, Springer, London (1999). https://doi.org/10.1007/978-1-4471-0417-9_3
8. Kochenderfer, M., Chryssanthacopoulos, J.: Robust airborne collision avoidance through dynamic programming (2011)
9. Kochenderfer, M., Holland, J., Chryssanthacopoulos, J.: Next generation airborne collision avoidance system. Lincoln Lab. J. **19**, 17–33 (2012)
10. Kuchar, J., Drumm, A.: The traffic alert and collision avoidance system. Lincoln Lab. J. **16**(2), 277–296 (2007)
11. Kurniawati, H., Hsu, D., Lee, W.S.: SARSOP: efficient point-based POMDP planning by approximating optimally reachable belief spaces. In: Robotics: Science and Systems IV (2008)
12. Manfredi, G., Jestin, Y.: An introduction to ACAS Xu and the challenges ahead. In: DASC, pp. 1–9 (2016). https://doi.org/10.1109/DASC.2016.7778055
13. Pineau, J., Gordon, G., Thrun, S.: Point-based value iteration: an anytime algorithm for POMDPs. In: IJCAI, pp. 1025–1032 (2003)
14. Porta, J., Vlassis, N., Spaan, M., Poupart, P.: Point-based value iteration for continuous POMDPs. J. Mach. Learn. Res. **7**, 2329–2367 (2006)

15. Puterman, M.L.: Markov Decision Processes: Discrete Stochastic Dynamic Programming. Wiley Series in Probability and Statistics, vol. 594. Wiley, Hoboken (2005)
16. Shani, G., Pineau, J., Kaplow, R.: A survey of point-based POMDP solvers. Auton. Agent. Multi-Agent Syst. **27**, 1–51 (2013). https://doi.org/10.1007/s10458-012-9200-2
17. Smith, T., Simmons, R.: Point-based POMDP algorithms: improved analysis and implementation. In: UAI, pp. 542–549 (2005)
18. Sondik, E.J.: The optimal control of partially observable Markov processes over the infinite horizon: discounted costs. Oper. Res. **26**(2), 282–304 (1978). https://doi.org/10.1287/opre.26.2.282
19. Sutton, R.S., Barto, A.G.: Reinforcement Learning - An Introduction. Adaptive Computation and Machine Learning. MIT Press, Cambridge (1998). http://www.worldcat.org/oclc/37293240
20. Temizer, S., Kochenderfer, M., Kaelbling, L., Lozano-Perez, T., Kuchar, J.: Collision avoidance for unmanned aircraft using Markov decision processes. In: AIAA Guidance, Navigation, and Control Conference (2010). https://doi.org/10.2514/6.2010-8040
21. Thrun, S.: Monte Carlo POMDPs. In: NIPS, pp. 1064–1070 (1999)

Randomized Refinement Checking
of Timed I/O Automata

Andrej Kiviriga[✉], Kim Guldstrand Larsen, and Ulrik Nyman

Aalborg University, Selma Lagerløfs Vej 300, 9220 Aalborg, Denmark
{kiviriga,kgl,ulrik}@cs.aau.dk

Abstract. To combat the *state-space explosion* problem and ease system development, we present a new refinement checking (falsification) method for Timed I/O Automata based on random walks. Our memoryless heuristics *Random Enabled Transition* (RET) and *Random Channel First* (RCF) provide efficient and highly scalable methods for counterexample detection. Both RET and RCF operate on concrete states and are relieved from expensive computations of symbolic abstractions. We compare the most promising variants of RET and RCF heuristics to existing symbolic refinement verification of the ECDAR tool. The results show that as the size of the system increases our heuristics are significantly less prone to exponential increase of time required by ECDAR to detect violations: in very large systems both "wide" and "narrow" violations are found up to 600 times faster and for extremely large systems when ECDAR timeouts, our heuristics are successful in finding violations.

Keywords: Model-checking · Timed I/O automata · Randomized · State-space · Refinement

1 Introduction

Model-checking has been established as a useful technique for verifying properties of formal system models. The most notable obstacle in this field, *state-space explosion*, relates to the exponential growth of the state-space to be explored as the size of models increases. Over the last three decades a vast amount of research has attempted to combat this problem resulting in a plethora of techniques that reduce the number of states to be explored [1, 4, 28]. Various symbolic and reduction techniques (e.g. [3, 9, 23, 25, 34]) have become a ground for implementation of verification tools (CADP, NuSMV, KRONOS, SPIN, UPPAAL, etc.), allowing them to handle a much larger domain of finite state and timed systems; however, for all cases symbolic and exhaustive verification still remains an expensive approach.

Counterexample detection techniques (e.g. [22]) can be used to even further avoid state-space explosion and facilitate a more efficient process of model

Supported by the ERC Advanced Grant Project: LASSO: Learning, Analysis, Synthesis and Optimization of Cyber-Physical Systems.

J. Pang and L. Zhang (Eds.): SETTA 2020, LNCS 12153, pp. 70–88, 2020.
https://doi.org/10.1007/978-3-030-62822-2_5

verification. A prominent example in this area is the Counterexample-Guided Abstraction Refinement (CEGAR) [12] technique which has been intensely studied and applied to a variety of systems in model-checking including probabilistic systems [21], hybrid automata [31,37], Petri net state equations [35] and timed automata [20,27,29]. The core idea is to automatically generate *abstraction models* (e.g. by reducing the amount of clocks), which may have a substantially smaller state-space, and verify them in a traditional model-checker to generate counterexamples if a property is not satisfied. The counterexamples are in turn used to refine the abstraction models.

On the other hand, some counterexample detection techniques give up on the requirement of completeness and only explore part of the state-space, which no longer allows to guarantee correctness but provides a powerful mechanism for fault detection if one exists in the model. This is similar in approach to using the QuickCheck tool [11] for testing of Haskell program properties. Therefore, we believe a productive *development method* should consist of two steps: running multiple cheap and approximate counterexample detection algorithms early in the development for quick violation discovery and performing an expensive and exhaustive symbolic model-checking at the very end.

A very promising approach in counterexample detection methods is based on employing randomness. The first steps in that direction were made by [19,30] where the state-space is explored by means of repeatedly performing *random walks*. With a sufficient amount of such walks an existing violation will eventually be found; nonetheless, designing efficient methods that excel at counterexample detection is not a trivial task. The difficulty lies in unintentional probabilities in the exploration methods that may lead to uneven coverage of the models' state-space. A recent example in the domain of *untimed systems* was done by [24] where the authors study verification of LTL properties and compare their random walk tactics, namely *continue walking* and *only accepting* and respective memory-efficient variants of those, to the tactics of [19].

A first attempt to use randomness in the setting of *timed systems* was made by [18], where a *Deep Random Search* (DRS) algorithm, which explores the state-space of a simulation graph of a *timed automaton* (TA) [2] in a symbolic manner, was presented. DRS performs an exhaustive exploration by means of random walks in a depth-first manner until a specified *cutoff* depth. Even though DRS conducts a complete search of the state-space, its computational advantage relies on detecting existing counterexamples quickly. In some sense DRS conforms to both steps of the above-mentioned *development method* - either counterexamples are detected potentially early in the search or, if none exist, the entire state-space is explored. DRS has been experimentally shown to outperform Open-Kronos and UPPAAL model-checkers; however, the experiments do not compare DRS with UPPAAL's *Random Depth First Search* (RDFS) - a powerful method for TA with strong fault detection potential.

In this paper we focus on carrying out random walks on networks of *timed I/O automata* (TIOA) for refinement checking as a quick and efficient falsification method. To improve performance we intend to work with the concrete

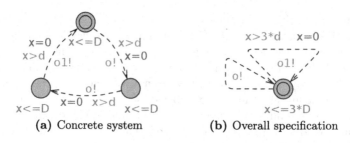

(a) Concrete system   (b) Overall specification

Fig. 1. Detailed automaton (a) refines overall specification (b).

semantics which relieves us from expensive computations of symbolic abstractions based on such data structures as *Difference Bounded Matrices* (DBM) [17]. The refinement verification helps to determine if a system specification can be successfully replaced by a single or even a number of other systems. Figure 1 shows a common refinement application example where a detailed system (a) refines a more general specification of desired behavior (b). The detailed system models a token being passed around a ring. The clock x ensures that the token is passed within the time bounds of x>d and x<=D. The overall specification requires the whole loop to be completed within x<=3*D.

An easy way to perform randomized exploration is to exploit the stochastic semantics of TIOA allowing the use of existing Statistical Model Checking (SMC) techniques [33,36]. The idea of SMC is to produce a number of *sample traces* from a stochastic model, that are then statistically analyzed to estimate a probability that a random run of the model will satisfy a given property. Moreover, the estimate comes with a level of confidence which requires more sample traces for higher precision. The SMC method has been implemented in a number of tools, including UPPAAL SMC [13] which uses stochastic timed automata (STA). For more details of this stochastic semantics see [8,13]. Due to its simplicity, SMC is widely accepted in industrial applications where exhaustive model-checking is not feasible.

Fig. 2. Timed I/O Automaton. Difficult case for SMC.

For the purpose of violation discovery however, SMC simulation techniques may not be a productive approach. Figure 2 shows a trivial, yet very difficult case for SMC to detect if an ErrorLoc is ever reached. Due to the stochastic semantics SMC operates on, a delay is uniformly chosen between 0 and 10^6 making it nearly impossible to traverse "narrow guard" edges. The probability of reaching ErrorLoc in one step is $\frac{1}{2} * 10^{-6}$, thus it requires in average $2 * 10^6$ steps to reach that location. While such stochastic semantics allows for a model to mimic the behavior of a real system, counterexample detection methods require different heuristics in order to be efficient.

In this paper we present two lightweight, randomized and memory-less techniques for refinement checking of Timed I/O Automata: *Random Enabled Transition* (RET) and *Random Channel First* (RCF). Similarly to UPPAAL SMC and existing randomized techniques, our methods operate on concrete states and perform random walks through systems to detect violations. We show experimentally the potential of these algorithms on Milner's scheduler and Leader Election protocol with a varying number of nodes and compare their performance to those of existing symbolic and discrete state-space exploration methods - ECDAR and SMC for Timed I/O Automata. Our heuristics detect violations of the overall specification up to 600 times faster than ECDAR and scale better.

2   TIOA, Composition and Refinement

We now introduce key definitions of the formalism based on [16]. Let Clk be a finite set of clocks. A clock valuation over Clk is a mapping $u \in [Clk \mapsto \mathbb{R}_{\geq 0}]$. A guard is represented as a finite conjunction of expressions of the form $x \prec n$, where $x \in Clk$, $\prec$ is a relational operator $(<, \leq, >, \geq, =, \neq)$ and $n \in \mathbb{N}$. A set of such *guards* over Clk is denoted as $\mathcal{B}(Clk)$, whereas $\mathcal{P}(Clk)$ is used to denote a powerset of the clock set.

Definition 1 (Timed I/O Automaton). *A Timed I/O Automaton (TIOA) is represented as a tuple $A = (Loc, q_0, Clk, E, Act, Inv)$ where Loc is a finite set of locations, $q_0 \in Loc$ is the initial location, Clk is a finite set of clocks that represent time, $E \subseteq Loc \times Act \times \mathcal{B}(Clk) \times \mathcal{P}(Clk) \times Loc$ is a set of edges, $Act = Act_i \oplus Act_o$ is a finite set of actions, partitioned into inputs and outputs respectively, and $Inv: Loc \rightarrow \mathcal{B}(Clk)$ is a set of location invariants.*

An edge is a tuple $(q, a, \varphi, c, q') \in E$ where the source location is q, the action label is a, the constraint over clocks to be satisfied is φ, the clocks to be reset are c, and the target location is q'. The semantics of TIOA is given by a Timed I/O Transition System $S = (St, s_0, \Sigma, \rightarrow)$, where St is an infinite set of states, $s_0 \in St$ is the initial state, $\Sigma = \Sigma_i \oplus \Sigma_o$ is a finite set of actions and $\rightarrow: St \times (\Sigma \cup \mathbb{R}_{\geq 0}) \times St$ is a transition relation (see [16] for complete definition).

An example of **Researcher** TIOA, shown in Fig. 3, contains three locations - id0, id1 and id2. Input and output actions are denoted by ? and ! respectively. A **Researcher** can do some work w! (e.g. research) with at least **8** and at most **10** time units required to finish the job, defined as constraints on clock x: the guard x>=8 on edge from id0 to id2 and invariant x<=10 at location id0, respectively. Alternatively, if a researcher receives a cup of tea (tea ?) the work can be done faster - between **6** and **7** time units. However, for now this TIOA has

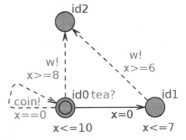

Fig. 3. Researcher automaton.

a flaw in that the initial work progress, if any, is lost (due to the update x=0) when a researcher gets a cup of tea.

A run within TIOA is a sequence of *concrete states* defined as (l, u), where l is a location and u is a function that assigns values to all clocks. The following gives two sample runs ρ_1 and ρ_2 of the **Researcher**:

$$\rho_1 \equiv (\text{id0}, \text{x=0}) \xrightarrow{9.27} (\text{id0}, \text{x=9.27}) \xrightarrow{\text{w!}} (\text{id2}, \text{x=9.27})$$

$$\rho_2 \equiv (\text{id0}, \text{x=0}) \xrightarrow{1.14} (\text{id0}, \text{x=1.14}) \xrightarrow{\text{tea?}} (\text{id1}, \text{x=0}) \xrightarrow{4.91} (\text{id1}, \text{x=4.91}) \xrightarrow{\text{w!}}$$
$$(\text{id2}, \text{x=4.91})$$

Fig. 4. Machine specification.   **Fig. 5. SlowMachine** specification.

Parallel composition, a feature allowing to combine specifications, is an important aspect of refinement verification. An overall specification is often challenged to be refined by a number of parallelly composed systems. Consider a simplistic **Machine** component, shown in Fig. 4, which is responsible for providing tea immediately after the payment (**coin**) is received. It can be run in parallel (i.e. composed) with previously seen **Researcher** (Fig. 3) where both components are able to interact with each other and altogether act as a single system. To avoid state-space unfolding, composition is usually not constructed, but its behavior is deduced based on transition synchronization rules (see [16] for formal definition). For illustration purposes, the automaton which captures the overall behavior of parallelly composed **Machine** and **Researcher** components is given in Fig. 6(a).

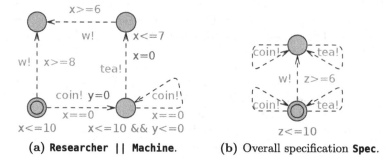

(a) **Researcher || Machine.**   (b) Overall specification **Spec.**

Fig. 6. Composition (a) refines overall specification (b).

Note that only automata whose output action sets are disjoint may be composed. Moreover, input and output edges that synchronize on identical signatures become output edges in a resulting composition (e.g. **coin** and **tea**). Such *internal synchronization* reflects both components advancing to new locations simultaneously. Since the composition component is now in control of when the tea is received, the work progress of a researcher can no longer be lost.

To capture the desired behavior of components a notion of *specification* is introduced. Its concept of *input-enabledness* reflects a belief that an input cannot be prevented from being sent to the system and thus requires an explicitly modelled behavior. To improve the modelling process, model-checking tools such as ECDAR treat unspecified behavior for inputs as location loops in the automaton.

Definition 2 (Specification). *A TIOTS $S = (St, s_0, \Sigma, \rightarrow)$ is a specification if each of its states $s \in St$ is input-enabled: $\forall i? \in \Sigma_i. \exists s' \in St. \; s \xrightarrow{i?} s'$.*

The specification theory of TIOA supports a notion of *refinement* which if satisfied allows to replace a specification with another one in every environment and obtain an equivalent system. For a specification S to refine specification T, both outputs and delays done by S must be matched by T, leading to a new pair of states in the refinement relation. Moreover, all inputs of T are required to be matched by S, which is always the case due to input-enabledness of specifications.

Definition 3 (Refinement). *A specification $S = (St^S, s_0, \Sigma, \rightarrow^S)$ refines a specification $T = (St^T, t_0, \Sigma, \rightarrow^T)$, written $S \leq T$, iff there exists a binary relation $R \subseteq St^S \times St^T$ containing (s_0, t_0) such that for each pair of states $(s, t) \in R$ we have:*

Input rule: *whenever $t \xrightarrow{i?}^T t'$ for some $t' \in St^T$ then $s \xrightarrow{i?}^S s'$
             and $(s', t') \in R$ for some $s' \in St^S$*

Output rule: *whenever $s \xrightarrow{o!}^S s'$ for some $s' \in St^S$ then $t \xrightarrow{o!}^T t'$
             and $(s', t') \in R$ for some $t' \in St^T$*

Delay rule: *whenever $s \xrightarrow{d}^S s'$ for $d \in \mathbb{R}_{\geq 0}$ then $t \xrightarrow{d}^T t'$
             and $(s', t') \in R$ for some $t' \in St^T$*

Figure 6 shows a refinement example where a **Researcher || Machine** composition (a) is challenged to refine a more general desired behavior specification **Spec** (b). Since the composition requires between **6** to **10** time units to perform the work, which is what the overall specification expects, the refinement relation holds. However, if the **Researcher** is composed with the **SlowMachine** from Fig. 5 instead, the tea is no longer provided immediately but requires up to **4** time units to be prepared. Performing the work after getting the tea altogether now requires **11** time units at most. This is not allowed by the overall specification with invariant **z<=10** and thus refinement fails.

The refinement in the ECDAR tool is handled by using the UPPAAL-TIGA engine [5] for verification of timed games. This engine searches for a winning strategy by playing a turn-based game between two players using the on-the-fly algorithm proposed in [10]. The first player, being the attacker, plays outputs of the left side and inputs of the right side of the refinement, while the second player, the defender, plays inputs of the left side and outputs of the right side. The refinement fails if the defender cannot match either a delay or an action performed by the attacker. The underlying data structure for the algorithm of [10] is based on *zones* which provides a *zone-based* symbolic abstraction, allowing to effectively store and manipulate states. Zones represent sets of clock valuations, defined as lower and upper bound constraints on clocks and on differences between each of the clocks. Unlike reachability analysis, refinement verification requires keeping track of a pair of states - one for each refinement side, which includes a single zone containing the union of clocks from both sides of the refinement relation. All newly discovered state pairs and already verified ones are stored in the *waiting* and *passed* data structures respectively, the latter of which allows to guarantee termination and avoid repeated exploration of states.

3   Random Walk Heuristics

Conducting concrete-state based random walks means that we are no longer able to verify refinement but are rather looking for violations of one of the refinement rules. Verification of the delay rule is similar to the symbolic approach. Following the definition, it suffices to check if the refinement right side allows delaying at least as much as the left side. With a concrete state as a starting point it is easy to compute the *maximal delay* available for that state by selecting the smallest difference between the upper bound specified by the invariant and the current value for each individual clock. Since such computations are also necessary for determining transition's availability, for each encountered state pair we check if the maximal delay on the right side is at least as big as on the left side, thus potentially capturing more delay rule violations at a small cost.

To maintain quick state-space exploration, our random walks are completely memory free, i.e. no state pairs are stored in memory except for the current one. When a transition is taken, we advance to the target state pair and verify either input or output rule based on the action type of the transition. Due to input-enabledness, an input transition may only result in the discovery of a new state pair, whereas an output transition on the left side, if not followed by the right side, can provide a counterexample. Moreover, not storing any information about already visited states introduces two issues: termination guarantee and repeated exploration of the states.

Termination. In the setting of concrete-state random walks, revisiting already explored state pairs is not necessarily a bad thing; in fact, it can be beneficial as it may lead to traversal of other, yet unseen, transitions. Termination on the other hand requires certain conditions. Upon reaching a state with either no outgoing transitions or no eventually enabled (after performing a delay) transitions we terminate the random walk and issue a new one. This, however, becomes a problem for cyclic systems where above-mentioned conditions may never occur, resulting in an infinite exploration. We approach the termination problem in a straightforward way by supplying random walks with a parameter of *steps* (number of transitions) that can be taken before a walk is terminated. Ideally, this parameter should be dynamically adapted to the target system; however, finding the optimal value is far beyond from trivial (e.g. see [7]). Therefore, we limit ourselves to a predefined (static) number of steps.

3.1   Selecting Transition

During a random walk through the model, the actions of both delaying and traversing transition are made in sequence. We, however, reverse the process such that the concrete delay is selected after the target transition is chosen. As a result, not only do delays not determine transition choice, but a delay is no longer made if there are no transitions available. Given that the delay rule is checked by comparison of *maximal delays* of refinement sides, this strategy (of choosing transition first) makes sense as with no available transitions no other refinement rules can be violated. We propose two heuristics for selecting transitions.

The idea of the *Random Enabled Transition* (RET) heuristic is to first compute all eventually enabled transitions, i.e. transitions which are either currently available or will become such after a delay, for a given state of the refinement left side. Contrary to the refinement input rule, we consider input transitions starting from the left side as due to input-enabledness they can never violate refinement relation, but can only lead to new, potentially unexplored, state pairs. Next, we uniformly choose one of the computed transitions as a target for traversal. The counterexample is found when the right side cannot match an output transition.

Profiling has shown that computing eventually enabled transitions is the most resource demanding operation in our random walks. It needs to consider all parallelly composed automata and construct transitions on the fly. Given a concrete state it is necessary to check potential availability, i.e. if guards are satisfied, for each edge by computing lower and upper bounds that correspond to minimal and maximal delays after which a transition is enabled. To reduce the total amount of such computations we propose an alternative heuristic for choosing transitions - *Random Channel First* (RCF). It chooses a random channel (same as action) from the list of all channels and computes enabled transitions only for that channel. If none exist, the selected channel is removed from the list. The process is repeated until either transitions are found or the list of channels is exhausted, where the latter option leads to *termination* of the random walk. If transitions are discovered, a random one is uniformly chosen for traversal.

3.2   Selecting Delay

Next, we need to select a concrete delay, i.e. value to increase all clocks by, before traversing a transition as it potentially affects further choices. With target transition being selected first, the choice of delay is made within availability bounds of the transition which are computed during transition selection. This keeps the process lightweight as no additional computations are required. Choosing a target transition prior to delaying also allows to exclude the width (size) of the edge's guard from affecting the probability for that edge to be explored. A delay for the automaton from Fig. 2 would therefore depend on a chosen transition and be in either of the two ranges - $[0; 10^6]$ or $(10^6 - 1; 10^6]$. In comparison to SMC our heuristics have a probability of $\frac{1}{2}$ to traverse the edge leading to ErrorLoc thus requiring 2 runs in average to discover the error. This leads to a better state-space coverage and increases the chance to detect counterexamples since "narrow" and "wide" edges become equally easy to traverse.

Initially, we selected the delay uniformly from the transition's range of available delays. We believe however that selecting lower bound (LB) or upper bound (UB) is often more efficient for violation detection. This is because the prevailing amount of practical model-checking applications is concerned with either meeting deadlines, i.e. something that has an upper limit, or satisfying minimal requirements, i.e. something that cannot be done faster than specified. For example, the overall specification from Fig. 6(b) ensures both upper and lower time limits to be followed by a more concrete system. Similarly in QuickCheck [11] the random selection of datatype values is biased towards base-elements (empty list, empty tree, etc.) because they are more likely to be the source of errors. Thus, we expect a more corner-case oriented delay choice distribution (e.g. 40% LB, 20% uniform, 40% UB) to show better results at violation detection.

3.3   RET vs RCF

Since the RCF heuristic partitions the computation of eventually enabled transitions into smaller chunks, which are based on channel, and chooses a target transition as soon as one of these chunks yields a result, it is less computationally demanding than RET. For models with outdegree of at least two edges with different channels, RCF in average will perform fewer expensive operations to compute transitions which implies a faster exploration of the state-space; however, due to underlying probabilities this is not always the case.

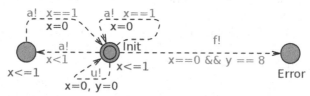

Fig. 7. Difficult case for RCF.

Consider the automaton from Fig. 7 where the `Error` location represents a counterexample. At the initial location `Init` both the values of clocks x and y are set to 0 and the output edge with action f is not available until x==0 and y==8. Moreover, the invariant (x<=1) on `Init` restricts us from directly delaying until the f edge becomes available. This leaves three enabled edges: two of action a, both of which increase the clock y by 1 unit upon returning to `Init`, and one of action u, which is "undesired" in a sense that it prohibits the walk from reaching `Error` by resetting clock y and must therefore be avoided during exploration.

While clock y is less than 8, only channels a and u can yield a result for a target transition. The probabilities for RCF and RET to choose edges for these channels is shown in Table 1. RCF heuristic randomly chooses one of two channels at a 50% probability, leaving a 50% chance to traverse either one of the a! edges or the only existing edge for channel u, which "resets" the model back to its initial state. On the other hand, choosing randomly amongst all eventually enabled transitions regardless of channel, RET selects any of the three edges at a probability of 33%. To reach the `Error` location either of the two `a!` edges must be taken 8 times in a row, followed by the `f!` edge. The probability of doing so in one *attempt* for RET is $0.67^8 * 0.25 \approx \frac{102}{10000}$, whereas for RCF it is $0.5^8 * 0.33 \approx \frac{13}{10000}$. After traversing the "undesired" edge, a random walk continues making new *attempts* until either the violation is found or the number of allowed steps is made. Given the probabilities, RCF requires 769 attempts in average to reach `Error` compared to an average of 98 attempts for RET.

Table 1. RET and RCF probabilities to traverse edges while `y<8`.

Action	RET	RCF
a! (x<1)	33.3%	50%
a! (x==1)	33.3%	
u!	33.3%	50%

3.4 Delay Probability Distribution Changes

The drawback of the static delay choice proposed in Sect. 3.2 is that such (or any) static distribution (40% LB, 20% uniform, 40% UB) naturally favors some models more than others in terms of error detection. In fact, some sophisticated systems might benefit the most from delaying only LB or UB; however, it might be impossible to derive this knowledge from a static analysis of the system.

Algorithm 1. Check refinement

```
1: function CHECKREFINEMENT
2:     chanceUB ← 0.5, chanceLB ← 0.5
3:     while violation not found do
4:         perform random walk with chanceLB and chanceUB
5:         if violation found then return false
6:         else
7:             chanceUB += 0.1;                    ▷ Increase UB by 10%
8:             if (chanceUB > 1) then chanceUB = 0;
9:             chanceLB = 1 − chanceUB;
```

To fight this, we propose a strategy where each random walk has a different delay choice distribution, as shown in Algorithm 1. First, a random walk is executed where all the delays follow 50% LB/50% UB distribution. If a violation is not found, a new random walk is issued where the probability to delay LB is decreased and probability to delay UB is increased by 10%, resulting in 40% LB/60% UB. Upon reaching a probability distribution which guarantees the choice of an upper bound value (0% LB/100% UB), the next random walk has its probabilities "flipped", s.t. only the lower bound value is chosen for the delay. The process continues until the violation is found. Naturally, if a random walk with the most efficient probability distribution for a target model is unsuccessful at finding a violation, it will take another 11 random walks to reach that probability distribution again. However, the main drawback of this strategy is its inability to detect the "in between" violations as only bounds of the potential delay range are considered; nonetheless, while always missing a particular kind of violation, we believe this technique will often be substantially more efficient than others.

4 Test Setting

The experiments are performed on the models of Milner's scheduler [26] and Leader Election protocol [14], which operate on a ring topology and can be instantiated for an arbitrary number of nodes that communicate in sequence.

4.1 Milner's Scheduler

We analyze a real-time version of Milner's scheduler [15], where each node N_i can perform two actions in parallel: do some work by outputting on $\mathbf{w}_i!$ and pass the token to the next node N_{i+1} in the sequence by outputting on $\mathbf{rec}_{i+1}!$. Figure 8 shows a node template (a) and a template for the overall specification (b) that a ring of nodes has to refine. Templates allow multiple instances of the same model as also used in UPPAAL [6]. Each node starts at a location where it waits to receive a token before any actions can be taken. As soon as the token is received clocks are reset and all further actions are limited by a lower bound of d and an upper bound D represented by guards and invariants respectively.

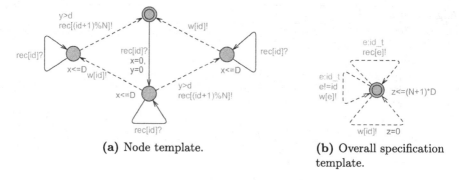

(a) Node template.

(b) Overall specification template.

Fig. 8. Real-time version of Milner's Scheduler. Templates for the ECDAR tool.

Note that the first node of the system has to be instantiated with a different initial location (bottom one) to represent the initial ownership of the token. The overall specification on the other hand only ensures that w0!, i.e. work done by initial node, requires at most (N+1)*D time units. Later in our experiments, we modify the overall specification such that it is violated in order to create counterexamples that can be detected by RET, RCF and SMC. To do so, we modify the invariant of the overall specification to be z<=(N+1)*D*(1-v), s.t. $\{v \in \mathbb{R}: 0 \leq v \leq 1\}$ where v is the desired violation size in percentage. The higher the value of v the wider, and therefore easier to detect, violation is created. Apart from different node amounts, we also manipulate the lower bound variable on guards (d), the smaller values of which drastically increase the state-space.

4.2   Leader Election Protocol

The Leader Election protocol has each of its nodes assigned a unique *priority* in addition to *id*. The goal of the protocol is to elect a leader with the highest *priority* by having nodes pass their current *priority* to the next node in sequence. If the *priority* received by a node is higher than its own, the node records that *priority* and further only sends it to the next node instead of its own *priority*. Otherwise, the received *priority* is discarded. Upon receiving its own *priority* the node knows it can claim the leadership since that *priority* has travelled one full round without being discarded and is thus the highest.

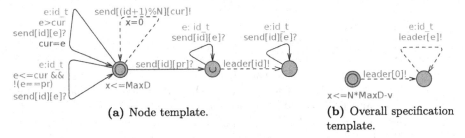

(a) Node template.

(b) Overall specification template.

Fig. 9. Leader Election protocol templates for the ECDAR tool.

The templates for this protocol are shown in Fig. 9. The overall specification (b) ensures that only the correct node (a) can declare itself a leader, and only within N*MaxD-v time units, s.t. $\{v \in \mathbb{Z}: 0 \leq v \leq N*MaxD\}$, where v is used to modify specification to introduce refinement violations. Here, two-dimensional channel arrays, e.g. send[id][pr], are used as way of value passing, where the first and the second indices represent node *id* and *priority* respectively. The cur variable, representing the highest received priority, is initialized to pr (own priority) for each node. Contrary to Milner's scheduler, this protocol does not constrain nodes to acting only after having received the token; instead, any node is free to send its priority at all times.

4.3   Implementation

We have implemented a Java prototype of both the RET and RCF heuristics for refinement checking of TIOA. For a more fair comparison of our heuristics with SMC, we reimplemented SMC in Java for the network of TIOA with the stochastic semantics. Table 2 gives an overview on performance differences between Java and that of UPPAAL C++ implementation of SMC. Surprisingly, Java SMC appeared to be faster, however this is most likely due to it being a prototype which does not retain all the features of UPPAAL SMC. For the rest of the paper we will be using Java SMC as it is not substantially different.

Table 2. Average time (in seconds) to detect violation for Milner's scheduler.

Settings	Java SMC	Uppaal SMC
$N=8,\ d=20,\ v=6\%$	1.720	3.413
$N=12,\ d=20,\ v=6\%$	33.869	57.762

To use SMC in a refinement setting, we transform refinement into a reachability problem by constructing a *complement* automaton of the refinement right side and composing it with the left side.

5   Experiments

To understand how delay choice influences violation detection, we compare the performance of three variants of each heuristic and the SMC approach. The results are reported in Table 3 for Milner's scheduler where each case ran for 60 min. RET-U and RCF-U did a *uniform* delay choice, RET-PD and RCF-PD delayed based on a *predefined distribution* of 40% LB, 20% uniform, 40% UB, and RET and RCF had changing probability distributions, but could miss violations requiring "intermediate delays", as described in Sect. 3.4.

Table 3. Each cell represents an average time (in sec) to discover a violation calculated over all discovered violations within 60 min in Milner's scheduler. Not found (nf) cells represent no discovered violations.

Settings		RET-U	RET-PD	RET	RCF-U	RCF-PD	RCF	SMC
$N=8$ $d=20$	$v=2\%$	nf	0.042	0.011	nf	0.024	**0.007**	nf
	$v=4\%$	21.577	0.008	0.003	12.590	0.005	**0.002**	50.832
	$v=6\%$	0.558	0.004	0.003	0.361	0.003	**0.002**	1.720
$N=8$ $d=4$	$v=2\%$	nf	0.078	0.010	nf	0.043	**0.005**	nf
	$v=4\%$	491.800	0.044	0.010	1506.872	0.026	**0.005**	891.425
	$v=6\%$	*58.688*	0.033	0.010	42.996	0.017	**0.005**	96.811
$N=12$ $d=20$	$v=2\%$	nf	0.655	0.030	nf	0.336	**0.017**	nf
	$v=4\%$	2770.389	0.082	0.017	1376.237	0.043	**0.010**	2882.110
	$v=6\%$	26.082	0.021	0.008	13.564	0.012	**0.005**	33.869
$N=12$ $d=4$	$v=2\%$	nf	2.056	0.032	nf	0.886	**0.017**	nf
	$v=4\%$	nf	0.851	0.031	nf	0.440	**0.017**	nf
	$v=6\%$	nf	0.501	0.031	nf	0.254	**0.017**	nf

It is clear that delay choice strategies have a large impact on the efficiency of random walks. Both the SMC approach and our heuristics with uniform delay choice (RET-U, RCF-U) have the weakest potential in terms of counterexample detection and are strongly affected by the size of the violation. While "wide" violations are found relatively quickly, "narrow" counterexamples ($v=2\%$) were not discovered at all. Therefore, the low efficiency of SMC, RET-U and RCF-U approaches makes their practical application not feasible for a number of nodes higher than 12. On the other hand, RET-PD, RET, RCF-PD and RCF are significantly quicker at discovering violations and less sensitive to increasing the number of nodes or decreasing the d variable, both of which explode the state-space. The delay choice based on the predefined distribution (RET-PD and RCF-PD) was, as expected, superior to uniform choice and enabled detection of even "narrow" violations. The most efficient appears to be RET and RCF heuristic variants with changing probabilities, which have also shown the smallest difference in time for detection of "wide" and "narrow" violations.

Table 4. Each cell represents an average time (in sec) to discover a violation calculated over all discovered violations within 60 min in Milner's Scheduler. The $v = 0\%$ case can only be verified by the complete exploration of ECDAR.

Settings		ECDAR	RET	RCF	Settings		ECDAR	RET	RCF
	$v{=}0\%$	**0.619**	-	-		$v{=}0\%$	**3.622**	-	-
$N{=}50$	$v{=}2\%$	0.686	0.638	**0.314**	$N{=}100$	$v{=}2\%$	4.050	2.791	**1.304**
$d{=}20$	$v{=}4\%$	0.688	0.487	**0.249**	$d{=}20$	$v{=}4\%$	3.942	2.206	**1.024**
	$v{=}6\%$	0.689	0.360	**0.176**		$v{=}6\%$	3.974	1.701	**0.776**
	$v{=}0\%$	**1.576**	-	-		$v{=}0\%$	**9.510**	-	-
$N{=}50$	$v{=}2\%$	2.252	0.692	**0.326**	$N{=}100$	$v{=}2\%$	13.367	2.873	**1.302**
$d{=}10$	$v{=}4\%$	2.208	0.613	**0.291**	$d{=}10$	$v{=}4\%$	13.252	2.686	**1.194**
	$v{=}6\%$	2.182	0.547	**0.255**		$v{=}6\%$	12.832	2.383	**1.080**
	$v{=}0\%$	**160.015**	-	-		$v{=}0\%$	**2631.751**	-	-
$N{=}50$	$v{=}2\%$	224.724	0.688	**0.322**	$N{=}100$	$v{=}2\%$	693.688	2.856	**1.279**
$d{=}4$	$v{=}4\%$	274.632	0.621	**0.292**	$d{=}4$	$v{=}4\%$	695.181	2.721	**1.231**
	$v{=}6\%$	295.818	0.576	**0.268**		$v{=}6\%$	689.754	2.490	**1.102**

We further compare the most promising RET and RCF heuristics with ECDAR on a large number of nodes and report results in Table 4. Increasing the number of nodes or especially decreasing d significantly increases time needed by ECDAR for verification. Contrary to that, RET and RCF are not so sensitive to the change of d which shows that due to probability changes our heuristics perform almost equally well on "narrow" and "wide" edge systems. For $N = 100$ and $d = 4$ ECDAR takes more than 10 min to detect the violation, whereas RET and RCF require just under 3 and 1.3 s respectively. Surprisingly, complete symbolic refinement verification in ECDAR in case of $v = 0\%$ is still feasible on such high number of nodes as 50 and 100. Thus, the use of our proposed development method is supported: first RET and RCF can be used to quickly detect possible violations, and once no further violations are found using our heuristics an expensive and complete verification by ECDAR is to be conducted.

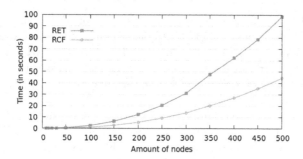

Fig. 10. RET and RCF comparison on Milner's scheduler with $d = 4$ and $v = 2\%$

In Fig. 10 the performance of RET and RCF for Milner's scheduler increasing number of nodes is compared in the difficult setting of $d = 4$ and $v = 2\%$ which significantly reduces chances to detect violations. The results are very encouraging: even for 500 nodes RET and RCF manage to discover violations in an average of under 100 and 50 s respectively.

We now compare most promising variants of RET and RCF (with changing probabilities) against ECDAR on a much heavier, non tokenized Leader Evaluation protocol. The results (shown in Table 5) demonstrate a severe state-space explosion: even for 7 nodes ECDAR is not able to conclude verification within an hour. On the positive note, RET and RCF are able to handle up to 10 nodes; however, in comparison to Milner's scheduler, here the "width" of the violation has a much stronger impact on the performance. Moreover, the exponential growth of channels (`send[id][e]`) makes the RCF heuristic much more favorable.

Table 5. Each cell represents an avg. time (in sec) to discover a violation calculated over all discovered violations within 60 min in Leader Election protocol. The $v = 0$ case can only be verified by the complete exploration of ECDAR. Not found (nf) cells represent no discovered violations.

Settings		ECDAR	RET	RCF	Settings		ECDAR	RET	RCF
$N=5$	$v=0$	**0.103**	-	-	$N=6$	$v=0$	**17.190**	-	-
	$v=2$	**0.127**	1.411	0.403		$v=2$	18.170	11.392	**2.916**
	$v=4$	0.130	0.080	**0.024**		$v=4$	15.952	0.576	**0.138**
	$v=6$	0.085	0.009	**0.003**		$v=6$	8.695	0.059	**0.015**
$N=7$	$v=0$	nf	-	-	$N=8$	$v=0$	nf	-	-
	$v=2$	nf	102.653	**26.617**		$v=2$	nf	**170.782**	172.880
	$v=4$	nf	4.140	**0.722**		$v=4$	nf	38.217	**5.166**
	$v=6$	nf	0.345	**0.073**		$v=6$	nf	2.113	**0.340**

To further examine the efficiency of our heuristics to quickly detect violations during iterative development, we perform mutation testing on Leader Election protocol. Table 6 reports the results where either one ($M^{\exists}_{1-4}$) or all ($M^{\forall}_{1-4}$) nodes have been replaced with a certain type of mutant, s.t. the refinement relation is violated. We have tried a mutant with the initial location's invariant bound doubled (M_1), a mutant that always sends its own *priority* instead of the recorded one (M_2), a mutant that forgets to record the received *priority* (M_3) and a mutant that records its own *id* instead of the received *priority* (M_4).

Table 6. Mutation testing for Leader Election protocol. Each cell represents an avg. time (in sec) to discover a violation calculated over all discovered violations within 60 min. Not found (nf) cells represent no discovered violations.

Settings		ECDAR	RET	RCF		Settings		ECDAR	RET	RCF
	$M_1^\exists$	38.204	51.704	**11.697**			$M_1^\exists$	nf	563.254	**125.991**
$N{=}6$	$M_2^\exists$	25.183	0.002	**0.001**		$N{=}7$	$M_2^\exists$	nf	0.005	**0.001**
	$M_3^\exists$	19.709	0.002	**0.001**			$M_3^\exists$	nf	0.005	**0.001**
	$M_4^\exists$	18.007	0.002	**0.001**			$M_4^\exists$	687.573	0.005	**0.001**
	$M_1^\forall$	12.592	0.077	**0.016**			$M_1^\forall$	nf	0.054	**0.011**
$N{=}6$	$M_2^\forall$	11.452	0.006	**0.001**		$N{=}7$	$M_2^\forall$	nf	0.007	**0.001**
	$M_3^\forall$	10.643	0.003	**0.001**			$M_3^\forall$	nf	0.006	**0.001**
	$M_4^\forall$	11.183	0.005	**0.001**			$M_4^\forall$	35.230	0.001	**0.001**

The time to discover violation with mutants M_2-M_4 is surprisingly small, which persists for even higher amount of nodes with very small increments in time. This occurs due to the modifications in these mutants in different ways leading to an overall inability of the "node ring" to elect a leader, which most of the time can be detected with only a single random walk. Mutant M_1 on the other hand does not prevent leadership from being correctly declared, but creates the possibility of it happening too late, i.e. violating the time requirement imposed by the overall specification. In cases where only one such mutant is present in the "ring" ($M_1^\exists$) it is significantly harder to detect violation for both ECDAR, due to the state-space growth, and our heuristics, due to decreasing underlying probabilities to find a violation.

Overall, for both of the models RCF appears to be noticeably faster than RET. This is caused by frequently occurring states with the outdegree of at least 2 transitions for different channels, which helps RCF to avoid a lot of expensive transition computations. This difference is especially large for Leader Election protocol, where the amount of channels grows exponentially to the amount of nodes. The general tendency is such that our heuristics are much less affected by state-space explosion than symbolic verification using ECDAR.

The complete model, test results and Java prototype code are available at http://www.cs.aau.dk/~ulrik/submissions/982983/SETTA2020.zip.

6   Conclusions and Future Work

We have presented what we believe to be the first randomized technique for refinement checking of Timed I/O Automata by means of random walks. Our two heuristics RET and RCF provide a fast and scalable way of detecting counterexamples, the benefits of which are most noticeable in large systems where the memory demands of symbolic verification are high. Such techniques are best used for quick falsification to save time during development of large and industrial sized systems. If no errors are found, a long and expensive complete symbolic verification can be conducted.

The experiments have shown that the choice of delays can strongly influence the efficiency of the technique. The most efficient and scalable variations of RET and RCF heuristics appeared to be the ones based on the adaptive approach, s.t. the delay choice distribution changes based on the outcome of the previous run. We anticipate that some models may even require the delay choice heuristic to be different for each state while for other systems it might suffice delaying according to the same distribution. Therefore, we believe that as more techniques appear, a successful violation detection strategy will be to run multiple heuristics in parallel (see e.g. [32]).

The direction for the future work is to test RET and RCF on more models to see if these heuristics are efficient or different strategies are required. Our methods can also be applied for real time model-checking of other analysis problems than refinement. Furthermore, a better performance of the heuristics can potentially be achieved by supplying random walks with the dynamic number of steps based on a static analysis of the model and/or certain heuristics that manipulate the depth of each walk based on the outcome of the previous one.

References

1. Alur, R., Brayton, R.K., Henzinger, T.A., Qadeer, S., Rajamani, S.K.: Partial-order reduction in symbolic state space exploration. In: Grumberg, O. (ed.) Computer Aided Verification, pp. 340–351. Springer, Heidelberg (1997). https://doi.org/10.1007/3-540-63166-6_34

2. Alur, R., Dill, D.: The theory of timed automata. In: de Bakker, J.W., Huizing, C., de Roever, W.P., Rozenberg, G. (eds.) REX 1991. LNCS, vol. 600, pp. 45–73. Springer, Heidelberg (1992). https://doi.org/10.1007/BFb0031987

3. Behrmann, G., Larsen, K.G., Pearson, J., Weise, C., Yi, W.: Efficient timed reachability analysis using clock difference diagrams. In: Halbwachs, N., Peled, D. (eds.) CAV 1999. LNCS, vol. 1633, pp. 341–353. Springer, Heidelberg (1999). https://doi.org/10.1007/3-540-48683-6_30

4. Behrmann, G., Bouyer, P., Larsen, K.G., Pelánek, R.: Lower and upper bounds in zone based abstractions of timed automata. In: Jensen, K., Podelski, A. (eds.) TACAS 2004. LNCS, vol. 2988, pp. 312–326. Springer, Heidelberg (2004). https://doi.org/10.1007/978-3-540-24730-2_25

5. Behrmann, G., Cougnard, A., David, A., Fleury, E., Larsen, K.G., Lime, D.: UPPAAL-Tiga: time for playing games!. In: Damm, W., Hermanns, H. (eds.) CAV 2007. LNCS, vol. 4590, pp. 121–125. Springer, Heidelberg (2007). https://doi.org/10.1007/978-3-540-73368-3_14

6. Behrmann, G., David, A., Larsen, K.G.: A tutorial on Uppaal. In: Bernardo, M., Corradini, F. (eds.) SFM-RT 2004. LNCS, vol. 3185. Springer, Heidelberg (2004). https://doi.org/10.1007/978-3-540-30080-9_7

7. Behrmann, G., Larsen, K.G., Pelánek, R.: To store or not to store. In: Hunt, W.A., Somenzi, F. (eds.) CAV 2003. LNCS, vol. 2725, pp. 433–445. Springer, Heidelberg (2003). https://doi.org/10.1007/978-3-540-45069-6_40

8. Bertrand, N., Bouyer, P., Brihaye, T., Carlier, P.: When are stochastic transition systems tameable? J. Log. Algebraic Meth. Program. **99**, 41–96 (2018)
9. Burch, J., Clarke, E., McMillan, K., Dill, D., Hwang, L.: Symbolic model checking: 1020 states and beyond. Inf. Comput. **98**(2), 142–170 (1992)
10. Cassez, F., David, A., Fleury, E., Larsen, K.G., Lime, D.: Efficient on-the-fly algorithms for the analysis of timed games. In: Abadi, M., de Alfaro, L. (eds.) CONCUR 2005. LNCS, vol. 3653, pp. 66–80. Springer, Heidelberg (2005). https://doi.org/10.1007/11539452_9
11. Claessen, K., Hughes, J.: QuickCheck: a lightweight tool for random testing of Haskell programs. SIGPLAN Not. **46**(4), 53–64 (2011)
12. Clarke, E., Grumberg, O., Jha, S., Lu, Y., Veith, H.: Counterexample-guided abstraction refinement. In: Emerson, E.A., Sistla, A.P. (eds.) CAV 2000. LNCS, vol. 1855. Springer, Heidelberg (2000). https://doi.org/10.1007/10722167_15
13. David, A., Larsen, K.G., Legay, A., Mikucionis, M., Poulsen, D.B.: Uppaal SMC tutorial. Int. J. Softw. Tools Technol. Transf. **17**(4), 397–415 (2015)
14. David, A., Larsen, K.G., Legay, A., Møller, M.H., Nyman, U., Ravn, A.P., Skou, A., Wasowski, A.: Compositional verification of real-time systems using Ecdar. Int. J. Softw. Tools Technol. Transf. **14**, 703–720 (2012)
15. David, A., Larsen, K.G., Legay, A., Nyman, U., Wąsowski, A.: ECDAR: an environment for compositional design and analysis of real time systems. In: Bouajjani, A., Chin, W.-N. (eds.) ATVA 2010. LNCS, vol. 6252, pp. 365–370. Springer, Heidelberg (2010). https://doi.org/10.1007/978-3-642-15643-4_29
16. David, A., Larsen, K.G., Legay, A., Nyman, U., Wasowski, A.: Timed I/O automata: a complete specification theory for real-time systems. In: Proceedings of the 13th ACM International Conference on Hybrid Systems: Computation and Control, HSCC 2010, pp. 91–100. Association for Computing Machinery, New York (2010)
17. Dill, D.L.: Timing assumptions and verification of finite-state concurrent systems. In: Sifakis, J. (ed.) CAV 1989. LNCS, vol. 407. Springer, Heidelberg (1990). https://doi.org/10.1007/3-540-52148-8_17
18. Grosu, R., Huang, X., Smolka, S.A., Tan, W., Tripakis, S.: Deep random search for efficient model checking of timed automata. In: Kordon, F., Sokolsky, O. (eds.) Monterey Workshop 2006. LNCS, vol. 4888. Springer, Heidelberg (2008). https://doi.org/10.1007/978-3-540-77419-8_7
19. Grosu, R., Smolka, S.A.: Monte Carlo model checking. In: Halbwachs, N., Zuck, L.D. (eds.) TACAS 2005. LNCS, vol. 3440, pp. 271–286. Springer, Heidelberg (2005). https://doi.org/10.1007/978-3-540-31980-1_18
20. He, F., Zhu, H., Hung, W.N., Song, X., Gu, M.: Compositional abstraction refinement for timed systems. In: 2010 4th IEEE International Symposium on Theoretical Aspects of Software Engineering, pp. 168–176. IEEE (2010)
21. Hermanns, H., Wachter, B., Zhang, L.: Probabilistic CEGAR. In: Gupta, A., Malik, S. (eds.) CAV 2008. LNCS, vol. 5123. Springer, Heidelberg (2008). https://doi.org/10.1007/978-3-540-70545-1_16
22. Kupferschmid, S., Wehrle, M., Nebel, B., Podelski, A.: Faster than Uppaal? In: Gupta, A., Malik, S. (eds.) CAV 2008. LNCS, vol. 5123. Springer, Heidelberg (2008). https://doi.org/10.1007/978-3-540-70545-1_53
23. Larsen, K.G., Larsson, F., Pettersson, P., Yi, W.: Efficient verification of real-time systems: compact data structure and state-space reduction. In: Proceedings Real-Time Systems Symposium, pp. 14–24 (1997)

24. Larsen, K., Peled, D., Sedwards, S.: Memory-efficient tactics for randomized LTL model checking. In: Paskevich, A., Wies, T. (eds.) VSTTE 2017. LNCS, vol. 10712. Springer, Cham (2017). https://doi.org/10.1007/978-3-319-72308-2_10

25. Lind-Nielsen, J., Andersen, H.R., Behrmann, G., Hulgaard, H., Kristoifersen, K., Larsen, K.G.: Verification of large state/event systems using compositionality and dependency analysis. In: Steffen, B. (ed.) TACAS 1998. LNCS, vol. 1384. Springer, Heidelberg (1998). https://doi.org/10.1007/BFb0054173

26. Milner, R.: A Calculus of Communicating Systems. LNCS, vol. 92. Springer, Heidelberg (1982). https://doi.org/10.1007/3-540-10235-3

27. Nagaoka, T., Okano, K., Kusumoto, S.: An abstraction refinement technique for timed automata based on counterexample-guided abstraction refinement loop. IEICE Trans. Inf. Syst. **93**–**D**(5), 994–1005 (2010)

28. Norris IP, C., Dill, D.L.: Better verification through symmetry. Form. Meth. Syst. Des. **9**(1), 41–75 (1996)

29. Okano, K., Bordbar, B., Nagaoka, T.: Clock number reduction abstraction on CEGAR loop approach to timed automaton. In: 2011 2nd International Conference on Networking and Computing, pp. 235–241. IEEE (2011)

30. Oudinet, J., Denise, A., Gaudel, M.-C., Lassaigne, R., Peyronnet, S.: Uniform Monte-Carlo model checking. In: Giannakopoulou, D., Orejas, F. (eds.) FASE 2011. LNCS, vol. 6603, pp. 127–140. Springer, Heidelberg (2011). https://doi.org/10.1007/978-3-642-19811-3_10

31. Prabhakar, P., Duggirala, P.S., Mitra, S., Viswanathan, M.: Hybrid automata-based CEGAR for rectangular hybrid systems. Form. Meth. Syst. Des. **46**(2), 105–134 (2015). https://doi.org/10.1007/s10703-015-0225-4

32. Rasmussen, J.I., Behrmann, G., Larsen, K.G.: Complexity in simplicity: flexible agent-based state space exploration. In: Grumberg, O., Huth, M. (eds.) TACAS 2007. LNCS, vol. 4424, pp. 231–245. Springer, Heidelberg (2007). https://doi.org/10.1007/978-3-540-71209-1_19

33. Sen, K., Viswanathan, M., Agha, G.: Statistical model checking of black-box probabilistic systems. In: Alur, R., Peled, D.A. (eds.) CAV 2004. LNCS, vol. 3114, pp. 202–215. Springer, Heidelberg (2004). https://doi.org/10.1007/978-3-540-27813-9_16

34. Valmari, A.: A stubborn attack on state explosion. In: Clarke, E.M., Kurshan, R.P. (eds.) CAV 1990. LNCS, vol. 531. Springer, Heidelberg (1991). https://doi.org/10.1007/BFb0023729

35. Wimmel, H., Wolf, K.: Applying CEGAR to the Petri net state equation. In: Abdulla, P.A., Leino, K.R.M. (eds.) TACAS 2011. LNCS, vol. 6605, pp. 224–238. Springer, Heidelberg (2011). https://doi.org/10.1007/978-3-642-19835-9_19

36. Younes, H.L.S., Simmons, R.G.: Probabilistic verification of discrete event systems using acceptance sampling. In: Brinksma, E., Larsen, K.G. (eds.) CAV 2002. LNCS, vol. 2404, pp. 223–235. Springer, Heidelberg (2002). https://doi.org/10.1007/3-540-45657-0_17

37. Zutshi, A., Deshmukh, J.V., Sankaranarayanan, S., Kapinski, J.: Multiple shooting, CEGAR-based falsification for hybrid systems. In: Proceedings of the 14th International Conference on Embedded Software, EMSOFT 2014. Association for Computing Machinery, New York (2014)

Computing Linear Arithmetic Representation of Reachability Relation of One-Counter Automata

Xie Li[1,3], Taolue Chen[2], Zhilin Wu[1(✉)], and Mingji Xia[1]

[1] State Key Laboratory of Computer Science, Institute of Software,
Chinese Academy of Sciences, Beijing, China
`wuzl@ios.ac.cn`
[2] Department of Computer Science, University of Surrey, Guildford, UK
[3] University of Chinese Academy of Sciences, Beijing, China

Abstract. One-counter automata (OCA) are a well-studied automata model that extends finite-state automata with one counter. The reachability problem of OCA was shown to be NP-complete when the integers in the OCA are encoded in binary. In this paper, we study the problem of computing the reachability relation of OCA. We show that, for each OCA, an existential Presburger arithmetic (EPA) formula of polynomial size can be computed in polynomial time to represent its reachability relation. This yields a polynomial-time reduction from the reachability problem of OCA to the satisfiability problem of EPA, enabling its solution via off-the-shelf SMT solvers. We implement the algorithm and provide the first tool OCAREACH for the reachability problem of OCA. The experimental results demonstrate the efficacy of our approach.

1 Introduction

Counter automata have been extensively studied in computer science and have found numerous applications, notably in formal verification. Some examples include verification of programs with lists [7] and recursive or multi-threaded programs [22], XML query validation [8], parameterized hardware verification [29], and decision procedures for separation logics with data [30], to name a few. Historically, counter automata were introduced by Minsky as a formal model of computation. It is well-known that two counters are already sufficient for counter automata to simulate Turing machines, rendering almost all decision problems about them undecidable. In particular, this includes the reachability problem, arguably the most fundamental problem in verification.

This work is supported by Guangdong Science and Technology Department grant (No. 2018B010107004), Overseas Grant (KFKT2018A16) from the State Key Laboratory of Novel Software Technology, Nanjing University, China, the NSFC grants (No. 61872340), Natural Science Foundation of Guangdong Province, China (No. 2019A1515011689), the Open Project of Shanghai Key Laboratory of Trustworthy Computing (No. 07dz22304201601), and the INRIA-CAS joint research project VIP.

© Springer Nature Switzerland AG 2020
J. Pang and L. Zhang (Eds.): SETTA 2020, LNCS 12153, pp. 89–107, 2020.
https://doi.org/10.1007/978-3-030-62822-2_6

To tame the undecidability, numerous restrictions on counter automata have been proposed, which were the subject of thorough investigation in the past 40 years. These restrictions include, for instance, the types of allowable tests on the counters (e.g., in Petri nets zero tests are disallowed), the set of paths under consideration (e.g., reversal boundedness [23]), the underlying structure of the automaton (e.g., flatness [27]). Probably the simplest restriction is to allow only one counter, giving rise to one-counter automata (OCA). We are primarily interested in the reachability problem of OCA. From a certain perspective, this is simple since OCA can be considered a special case of pushdown automata where the stack alphabet is a singleton. Indeed, Lafourcade et al. [26] showed that reachability in OCA in NL-compete, namely, it is no harder than the reachability in directed graphs. However, this result must be stated with caveat that it assumes that the updates in OCA are encoded in *unary*. On the contrary, we note that these updates involve integers which are most naturally encoded in *binary*. When this encoding is adopted, the NL-completeness does not hold any more, and it has been shown [20] that the reachability problem becomes NP-complete. Technically, for an OCA $\mathcal{A}$ the reachability problem is to decide, when given two configurations (q, n) and (q', n'), whether there exists a run of $\mathcal{A}$ from the configuration (q, n) to (q', n'). Note that in OCA all the counter values along the path must be nonnegative, which is the main source of the complication.

The formulation of reachability as a decision problem may not be sufficient for verification purposes from a practical perspective. Instead, one needs a characterization of the *reachability relation*, viz. the relation $R_{\mathcal{A},q,q'}$ comprising the pairs (n, n') of natural numbers such that there exists a run of $\mathcal{A}$ from (q, n) to (q', n'). Such a characterization turns out be possible in the existential fragment of Presburger arithmetic (EPA). That is to say, one can construct an EPA formula $\psi(x, y)$ such that $(n, n') \in R_{\mathcal{A},q,q'}$ if and only if $\psi(n, n')$ holds. Such a construction is important for at least two reasons: (1) one can feed the generated formula to, e.g., an off-the-shelf SMT solver to facilitate the reachability checking, especially when it is required as part of the decision procedure as in [30]; (2) it entails the NP membership of the reachability problem, since it is well-known that the satisfiability of EPA is NP-complete. Indeed, Haase [18] has shown the existence of such a formula. He gave an algorithm to generate an EPA formula ψ from the OCA and a pair of states. However, the algorithm therein runs in *nondeterministic* polynomial time. Whilst this may be sufficient for the purpose (2), it is not amenable to the purpose (1), because one needs to "guess" an EPA formula, rendering the algorithm implementation-unfriendly and inefficient.

In this paper, we provide a *deterministic* polynomial-time algorithm to construct an EPA formula to characterize the reachability relation in OCA, which enables us to utilize the off-the-shelf SMT solvers (e.g., Z3) to decide the reachability problem of OCA. The main idea is to utilize the existential quantifiers and arithmetic operations available in EPA to encode the nondeterministic guessing of the reachability certificates in [18]. For example, to account for the existence of a simple path, we introduce existentially quantified integer variables to index the edges along the path and specify that the indices of the edges are mutually distinct, and for any two edges sharing a common vertex, their indices must be consecutive. Moreover, we show that even more involved graph-theoretical concepts (e.g., edge decompositions and positive cycle templates [18]), can still be encoded by polynomial-sized EPA formulas. The new encoding yields a more direct, conceptually simpler approach to obtain an EPA formula for the reachability relation of OCA. As a proof-of-concept, we implement the algorithm in a tool OCAReach, which, to the best of our knowledge, is the first tool that is able to decide the reachability problem of OCA. We test OCAReach on both handcrafted and random generated benchmarks. The experimental results demonstrate the potential of OCAReach to be used in solving practical verification problems related to OCA.

Related Work. There is a large body of theoretical work on OCA and its variants, a survey of which is out of the scope of the current paper. Related to verification, Demri and Gascon investigated the problem of model checking an extension of LTL against OCA [11]. Moreover, model checking CTL and its fragments against OCA was also studied [15–17]. The similarity and bisimilarity problem of OCA and its variants have also been considered in [1,4,5,24,25], to name a few.

There have also been some verification tools for counter systems. For instance, the FAST tool [2] targets flattable counter systems, whose behavior can be captured by flat path schemes, i.e., concatenations of paths and simple cycles such that no two cycles share a vertex. If a counter system is flattable, then its reachability relation can be easily captured by an EPA formula. While zero-test free OCA are known to be flattable, the resulting path schemes are of exponential length [3]. Hence, EPA formulas of polynomial size appear to be difficult to be generated to capture the reachability relation via flattening. We instead utilize the polynomial-size reachability certificate [18], which is more involved than the flat path schemes, to construct a polynomial-size EPA formula.

An automata model closely related to counter automata is timed automata (TA), which equip finite-state automata with real-valued clocks rather than integer-valued counters. The relationship between reachability problems of TA and bounded counter automata (where counters take values from an arbitrary but fixed finite interval over the natural numbers) was established [21]. The reachability problem of TA is known to be PSPACE-complete, even when there are only two clocks [13]. The reachability relation of TA has also been studied. Comon and Jurski [9] first showed that the reachability relation of TA is effectively definable by a linear arithmetic formula over the integers and reals. This problem was revisited afterwards [10,12], and very recently, Fränzel et al. provided a considerably simplified proof for this fact [14].

Structure of the Paper. Preliminaries are given in Sect. 2. The algorithm to generate the EPA formula for a given OCA is presented in Sect. 3. The experimental results are given in Sect. 4. We conclude the paper in Sect. 5.

2   Preliminaries

Throughout the paper, $\mathbb{Z}$ and $\mathbb{N}$ denote the set of integers and natural numbers respectively. For a positive natural number n, $[n] := \{1, \cdots, n\}$. We also fix a set of operations $\mathsf{Op} = \{\mathsf{add}(c), \mathsf{zero} \mid c \in \mathbb{Z}\}$.

2.1   One-Counter Automata

Definition 1 (OCA). *A one-counter automaton is a tuple $\mathcal{A} = (Q, F, \Delta)$ where Q is a finite set of* control locations; *$F \subseteq Q$ is the set of* final location, *$\Delta \subseteq Q \times \mathsf{Op} \times Q$ is the (finite)* transition relation.

The transitions $(q, \mathsf{zero}, q') \in \Delta$ are referred to as zero transitions. We write $N_{\mathcal{A}}$ for the maximum absolute value of the integer constants occurring in the transitions of $\mathcal{A}$. The set of all *configurations* of $\mathcal{A}$ is denoted by $C(\mathcal{A}) = Q \times \mathbb{N}$. The transition system generated by $\mathcal{A}$ is $(S, \xrightarrow{\mathcal{A}})$ where $S = C(\mathcal{A})$ and $(q, n) \xrightarrow{\mathcal{A}} (q', n')$ iff there is $(q, op, q') \in \Delta$ satisfying (1) in case $op = \mathsf{add}(c)$, $n' = n + c$; and (2) in case $op = \mathsf{zero}$, $n' = n = 0$. We use $\overset{\mathcal{A}}{\Rightarrow}$ to denote the reflexive and transitive closure of $\xrightarrow{\mathcal{A}}$.

The *reachability* problem asks, given an OCA $\mathcal{A}$ and two configurations $C, C' \in C(\mathcal{A})$, does $C \overset{\mathcal{A}}{\Rightarrow} C'$ hold? In applications of OCA, it is usually more convenient to compute the reachability relation $R_{\mathcal{A},q,q'}$ for two given control locations q, q', defined as $R_{\mathcal{A},q,q'} = \{(n, n') \in \mathbb{N}^2 \mid (q, n) \overset{\mathcal{A}}{\Rightarrow} (q', n')\}$. The main purpose of the paper is to give a new representation of this relation in terms of Presburger arithmetic.

2.2   Presburger Arithmetic

Presburger arithmetic (PA) is the first-order theory of integer numbers in the structure $(\mathbb{Z}, <, +, 0, 1)$. This is a decidable first-order theory, in contrast to the Peano arithmetic where multiplication is included. Let X be a set of first-order variables. PA Formulae are defined by

$$\varphi ::= \boldsymbol{a}^T \boldsymbol{x} \bowtie b \mid \varphi \wedge \varphi \mid \neg\varphi \mid \exists x.\varphi$$

where $\boldsymbol{a}$ is a vector over $\mathbb{Z}$, $b \in \mathbb{Z}$, and $\bowtie \in \{\geq, >, <, \leq\}$.

In this paper, we are primarily interested in the existential fragment of PA (EPA, aka. quantifier-free PA), which comprises the PA formulae where each existential quantifier is under the scope of an even number of negations. All EPA formulae can be easily rewritten into the prenex normal form $\varphi = \exists \boldsymbol{x}.\ \psi(\boldsymbol{x}, \boldsymbol{y})$, where no quantifiers are allowed in ψ. It is well-known that checking the satisfiability of EPA formulae is NP-complete [6,19].

For a PA formula φ with free variables $x_1, \cdots, x_k$, we use $\varphi(x_1, \cdots, x_k)$ to highlight the free variables of φ. Moreover, we use $\varphi[n_1/x_1, \cdots, n_k/x_k]$ to denote φ under the assignment η with $\eta(x_j) = n_j$ for each $j \in [k]$.

2.3   Weighted Graphs

Definition 2 (Weighted graph). *A weighted graph is a tuple $G = (V, E)$ where V is a finite set of vertices, $E \subseteq V \times \mathbb{Z} \times V$ is a finite set of directed edges with weights.*

Let $G = (V, E)$ be a weighted graph. For an edge $e = (v, z, v') \in E$, $s(e)$ and $t(e)$ denote the source (i.e., v) and the target (i.e., v') of e respectively, and $w(e)$ denotes the weight z. For $v \in V$, we use $E_{in}(v)$ (resp. $E_{out}(v)$) to denote the set of incoming (resp. outgoing) edges of v, namely, the set of edges e such that $t(e) = v$ (resp. $s(e) = v$). A *path* in G is a sequence of edges $e_1 \cdots e_n$ for $n \geq 1$ such that $t(e_i) = s(e_{i+1})$ for each $i \in [n-1]$, where $s(e_1)$ and $t(e_n)$ are called the source and target vertex of π respectively and n is called the *length* of π. A path $\pi = e_1 \cdots e_n$ is a simple path if each vertex occurs at most once along π. Moreover, we use ε to denote the empty path, i.e., a vacuous path containing no edges. If both the source and the target vertex of a path π are v, we say π is a v-cycle. π is a simple cycle if v is the only vertex which occurs twice along a v-cycle π. A weighted graph G is a *loop* if it is strongly connected and there is exactly one simple v-cycle for any vertex v. For a path π in G, we define

- weight(G, π): the sum over all weights of the edges along π,
- drop(G, π): the *minimum* accumulated weight of all prefixes of a path π.

If G is clear from the context, we simply write weight(π) and drop(π).

Example 1. Let $\pi = v_1 \xrightarrow{2} v_2 \xrightarrow{-3} v_3 \xrightarrow{2} v_4$. Then weight$(\pi) = 2 - 3 + 2 = 1$ and drop$(\pi) = \min(2, 2 - 3, 2 - 3 + 2) = -1$.

A cycle π is said to be a *positive* (resp. *negative*, resp. *zero*) cycle if weight$(\pi) > 0$ (resp. weight$(\pi) < 0$, resp. weight$(\pi) = 0$).

For $v, v' \in V$, the reachability relation $R_{G,v,v'}$ comprises all the pairs $(n, n') \in \mathbb{N}^2$ such that there exists a path $\pi = v = v_1 \xrightarrow{z_1} v_2 \cdots v_k \xrightarrow{z_k} v_{k+1} = v'$ such that (1) weight$(\pi) = n' - n$ and (2) for all $i \in [k]$, $n + \sum\limits_{j \in [i]} z_j \geq 0$. As a convention, we assume that $(n, n) \in R_{G,v,v}$ for all $v \in V$ and $n \in \mathbb{N}$. For convenience, we use $(v, n) \overset{G}{\Rightarrow} (v', n')$ to denote $(n, n') \in R_{G,v,v'}$.

For a weighted graph $G = (V, E)$, we use $G^{op} = (V, E^{op})$ to denote the weighted graph with $E^{op} = \{e^{op} \mid e \in E\}$, where $e^{op} = (v', -z, v)$ for $e = (v, z, v')$. For a path $\pi = e_1 \cdots e_n$ in G, π^{op} denotes the path $e_n^{op} \cdots e_1^{op}$ in G^{op}.

3   The EPA Formula Generation Algorithm

Fix an OCA $\mathcal{A} = (Q, q_0, F, \Delta)$ in this section. Let $G_{\mathcal{A}} = (Q, E)$ be the corresponding weighted graph. Recall that $E = \{(q, z, q') \mid (q, \mathsf{add}(z), q') \in \Delta\}$. We shall show that, for any $q, q' \in Q$, an EPA formula $\varphi_{\mathcal{A},q,q'}$ can be computed *in polynomial time* to define the reachability relation. The crux of the algorithm is to show that the reachability relation from q to q' in the weighted graph $G_{\mathcal{A}}$

(without zero transitions) can be characterized by an EPA formula $\psi_{G_{\mathcal{A}},q,q'}$ of polynomial size. In the sequel, we first assume the existence of the EPA formula $\psi_{G_{\mathcal{A}},q,q'}$ and show how to formalize the reachability relation in EPA. We then show how the formula $\varphi_{G_{\mathcal{A}},q,q'}$ can be constructed.

3.1   Formalizing the Reachability Relation of $\mathcal{A}$ in EPA

Let $\mathsf{zt}_{\mathcal{A}}$ denote the set of zero transitions of $\mathcal{A}$. We define the *zero-transition graph* $G_{zt}[\mathcal{A}] = (\mathsf{zt}_{\mathcal{A}}, E_{zt})$ where E_{zt} comprises the pairs $((q_1, \mathsf{zero}, q_2), (q'_1, \mathsf{zero}, q'_2))$ satisfying $\psi_{G_{\mathcal{A}},q_2,q'_1}(0, 0)$, i.e., $(q'_1, 0)$ is reachable from $(q_2, 0)$ in $G_{\mathcal{A}}$. Intuitively, $G_{zt}[\mathcal{A}]$ satisfies that for $(q_1, \mathsf{zero}, q_2) \in \mathsf{zt}_{\mathcal{A}}$ and $(q'_1, \mathsf{zero}, q'_2) \in \mathsf{zt}_{\mathcal{A}}$, $(q'_1, \mathsf{zero}, q'_2)$ is reachable from $(q_1, \mathsf{zero}, q_2)$ in $G_{zt}[\mathcal{A}]$ iff the configuration $(q'_1, 0)$ is reachable from $(q_2, 0)$ in $G_{\mathcal{A}}$. Note that our algorithm does not explicitly construct the graph $G_{zt}[\mathcal{A}]$; this is for the sake of presentation.

Lemma 1. *Let (q, n) and (q', n') be two configurations of $\mathcal{A}$. Then $(q, n) \overset{\mathcal{A}}{\Rightarrow} (q', n')$ iff one of the following conditions holds: either $(q, n) \overset{G_{\mathcal{A}}}{\Rightarrow} (q', n')$; or there is a zero-transition $(p, \mathsf{zero}, p') \in \mathsf{zt}_{\mathcal{A}}$ such that $(q, n) \overset{G_{\mathcal{A}}}{\Rightarrow} (p, 0)$ and $(p', 0) \overset{G_{\mathcal{A}}}{\Rightarrow} (q', n')$; or there are zero-transitions $(p_1, \mathsf{zero}, p_2), (p'_1, \mathsf{zero}, p'_2) \in \mathsf{zt}_{\mathcal{A}}$ such that $(q, n) \overset{G_{\mathcal{A}}}{\Rightarrow} (p_1, 0)$, $(p'_1, \mathsf{zero}, p'_2)$ is reachable from $(p_1, \mathsf{zero}, p_2)$ in $G_{zt}[\mathcal{A}]$, and $(p'_2, 0) \overset{G_{\mathcal{A}}}{\Rightarrow} (t', n')$.*

The characterization of $\overset{\mathcal{A}}{\Rightarrow}$ in Lemma 1 can be specified by an EPA formula $\varphi_{\mathcal{A},q,q'}(x, y)$ defined as follows: Let $\mathsf{zt}_{\mathcal{A}} = \{\tau_1, \cdots, \tau_k\}$, where for each $i \in [k]$, $\tau_i = (p_{2i-1}, \mathsf{zero}, p_{2i})$. Then

$$\varphi_{\mathcal{A},q,q'}(x, y) \equiv \psi_{G_{\mathcal{A}},q,q'}(x, y) \vee \bigvee_{(p,\mathsf{zero},p') \in \mathsf{zt}_{\mathcal{A}}} (\psi_{G_{\mathcal{A}},q,p}(x, 0) \wedge \psi_{G_{\mathcal{A}},p',q}(0, y)) \vee$$
$$\bigvee_{i,j \in [k], i \neq j} \psi_{G_{\mathcal{A}},q,p_{2i-1}}(x, 0) \wedge \xi_{G_{zt}[\mathcal{A}]}(\tau_i, \tau_j) \wedge \psi_{G_{\mathcal{A}},p_{2j},q'}(0, y),$$

where $\xi_{G_{zt}[\mathcal{A}]}(\tau_i, \tau_j)$ specifies that τ_j is reachable from τ_i in $G_{zt}[\mathcal{A}]$,

$$\xi_{G_{zt}[\mathcal{A}]}(\tau_i, \tau_j) \equiv \exists z_1. \cdots \exists z_k. \; z_i = 1 \wedge z_j > 1 \wedge \bigwedge_{\ell \in [k]} z_\ell \geq 0 \wedge$$
$$\bigwedge_{\ell',\ell'' \in [k], \ell' \neq \ell''} ((z_{\ell'} > 0 \wedge z_{\ell''} > 0) \rightarrow z_{\ell'} \neq z_{\ell''}) \wedge$$
$$\bigwedge_{\ell \in [k]} \left(z_\ell > 1 \rightarrow \bigvee_{\ell' \in [k], \ell' \neq \ell} \left(z_{\ell'} > 0 \wedge z_{\ell'} + 1 = z_\ell \wedge \psi_{G_{\mathcal{A}},p_{2\ell'},p_{2\ell-1}}(0, 0) \right) \right).$$

Intuitively, the variables $z_1, \cdots, z_k$ in $\xi_{G_{zt}[\mathcal{A}]}(\tau_i, \tau_j)$ represent the positions of some simple path from τ_i to τ_j in $G_{zt}[\mathcal{A}]$, where τ_i is in the first position (i.e. $z_i = 1$), τ_j is in the last position (i.e., z_j is maximal), and the vertices not in the path are assigned null (i.e. $z_\ell = 0$). Moreover, for each vertex in the path, except the one in the first position, there is a vertex in the position preceding it as well as an edge between them.

3.2   Characterizing the Reachability Relation of G_A in EPA

We first recall the core concepts of the decision procedure in [18,20]. We then show how to construct the EPA formula $\psi_{G_A,q,q'}$ for $q, q' \in Q$. The main idea of the decision procedure is to characterize $\psi_{G_A,q,q'}$ by path flows satisfying some extra constraints.

Example 2 (Running example). We will use the OCA $\mathcal{A}$ in Fig. 1 as a running example, where q_0 and q_{11} are the initial and final control locations respectively.

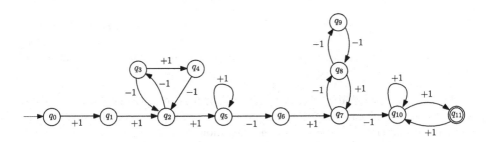

Fig. 1. G_A in the running example

Proposition 1. *Let (q, n) and (q', n') be two configurations of $\mathcal{A}$. Then (q', n') is reachable from (q, n) in G_A iff (q', n') is reachable from (q, n) through a path that contains no zero cycles.*

By Proposition 1, we will suppress zero cycles when constructing $\varphi_{G_A,q,q'}$.

Definition 3 (Flow and path flow). *Let $q, q' \in Q$. A flow from q to q' in G_A is a function $f : E \to \mathbb{N}$ such that*

- *if $q = q'$, then for all $p \in Q$,* $\displaystyle\sum_{e \in E_{in}(p)} f(e) = \sum_{e \in E_{out}(p)} f(e)$,
- *otherwise, for all $p \in Q \setminus \{q, q'\}$,*

$$\sum_{e \in E_{in}(p)} f(e) = \sum_{e \in E_{out}(p)} f(e), \text{ and}$$

$$1 + \sum_{e \in E_{in}(q)} f(e) = \sum_{e \in E_{out}(q)} f(e), \quad \sum_{e \in E_{out}(q')} f(e) = 1 + \sum_{e \in E_{in}(q')} f(e).$$

For a flow f, we use $\mathsf{weight}(f)$ to denote $\displaystyle\sum_{e \in E} f(e)\mathsf{weight}(e)$. A path flow from q to q' is a flow f corresponding to some path π from q to q', namely, $f = f_\pi$, where for each $e \in E$, $f_\pi(e)$ is the number of occurrences of e in π. In particular, for an edge e, f_e is a path flow such that $f_e(e) = 1$ and $f_e(e') = 0$ for each $e' \neq e$. Moreover, by convention, we assume that $f_\perp$ such that $f_\perp(e) = 0$ for every $e \in E$ is a path flow from q to q for each $q \in Q$.

Example 3. Let f_1 be a flow from q_0 to q_5 in $G_\mathcal{A}$ presented in Fig. 1, where $f_1((q_0, +1, q_1)) = f_1((q_1, +1, q_2)) = 1$, $f_1((q_2, -1, q_3)) = 2$, $f_1((q_3, -1, q_2)) = 1$, $f_1((q_3, +1, q_4)) = f_1((q_4, -1, q_2)) = f_1((q_2, +1, q_5)) = 1$, and $f_1(e') = 0$ for all the other edges e'. Then $f_1 = f_\pi$ where $\pi = q_0 \xrightarrow{+1} q_1 \xrightarrow{+1} q_2 \xrightarrow{-1} q_3 \xrightarrow{-1} q_2 \xrightarrow{-1} q_3 \xrightarrow{+1} q_4 \xrightarrow{-1} q_2 \xrightarrow{+1} q_5$. Therefore, f_1 is a path flow from q_0 to q_5.

Definition 4 (Support). *Given a path flow $f : E \to \mathbb{N}$, the support of f is the weighted graph $G_f = (V_f, E_f)$ with $E_f = \{e \in E \mid f(e) > 0\}$. A subgraph $F \subseteq G_\mathcal{A}$ is called a $q - q'$ support if there is a path flow f from q to q' such that $F = G_f$. In particular, the empty graph is a q-q support for each $q \in Q$.*

Example 4. Let F be the subgraph of $G_\mathcal{A}$ in Fig. 1 comprising the edges $(q_0, +1, q_1)$, $(q_1, +1, q_2)$, $(q_2, -1, q_3)$, $(q_3, -1, q_2)$, $(q_3, +1, q_4)$, $(q_4, -1, q_2)$, and $(q_2, +1, q_5)$. Then F is a q_0-q_5 support since $F = G_{f_1}$ where f_1 is the path flow from q_0 to q_5 in Example 3.

It is well-known that path flows can be captured by an EPA formula, which specifies the conditions on the incoming and outgoing flows of all vertices and the constraints that the support of the path flow is connected.

Proposition 2 ([28]). *An EPA formula $\varphi_{G_\mathcal{A}, q, q'}^{(\text{PF})}((x_e)_{e \in E})$ can be constructed, in linear time, to capture the path flows from q to q'. Namely, for each flow f from q to q', f is a path flow iff $\varphi_{G_\mathcal{A}, q, q'}^{(\text{PF})}[(f(e)/x_e)_{e \in E}]$ holds.*

Note that not all path flows correspond to runs of $G_\mathcal{A}$ since the constraints of path flows do not address the non-negativeness requirements of the counter values. In the sequel, we recall the results [18] where extra constraints (called reachability criteria) were imposed.

For a path flow f, suppose $f = f_\pi$ for some path π. We can split f into multiple path flows by dividing π into segments according to the last occurrence of each edge in π (note that an edge may occur multiple times in π). This is formalized as the concept of edge decomposition as follows.

Definition 5 (Edge decomposition). *Given a q-q' support F, an edge decomposition of F is a sequence of tuples $\{(F_i, v_i, v'_i, e_i)\}_{i \in [m]}$, where $F_i \subseteq F$, $v_1 = q$, $v'_{m+1} = q'$ such that*

1. *for each $i \in [m]$, F_i is a v_i-v'_i support, $e_i = (v'_i, z_i, v_{i+1})$ for some $z_i \in \mathbb{Z}$,*
2. *all e_i's are mutually distinct,*
3. *for each $1 \leq i < j \leq m$, $e_i \notin F_j$,*
4. *$F = \bigcup_{i \in [m]} F_i$.*

Note that if $v_i = v'_i$, then F_i may be the empty graph $\emptyset$.
Furthermore, given a path flow f, an edge decomposition of f is a sequence of tuples $\{(f_i, v_i, v'_i, e_i)\}_{i \in [m]}$, where f_i is a path flow from v_i to v'_i, $f = \sum_{i \in [m]} (f_i + f_{e_i})$, and $\{(G_{f_i}, v_i, v'_i, e_i)\}_{i \in [m]}$ is an edge decomposition of G_f.

Example 5. Let f_1 be the path flow from q_0 to q_5 and $\pi = q_0 \xrightarrow{+1} q_1 \xrightarrow{+1} q_2 \xrightarrow{-1} q_3 \xrightarrow{-1} q_2 \xrightarrow{-1} q_3 \xrightarrow{+1} q_4 \xrightarrow{-1} q_2 \xrightarrow{+1} q_5$ in Example 3 such that $f_1 = f_\pi$. The edges in G_{f_1} can be ordered according to their last occurrences in π as follows: $(q_0, +1, q_1)$, $(q_1, +1, q_2)$, $(q_3, -1, q_2)$, $(q_2, -1, q_3)$, $(q_3, +1, q_4)$, $(q_4, -1, q_2)$, $(q_2, +1, q_5)$. Note that $(q_3, -1, q_2)$ is ordered before $(q_2, -1, q_3)$ since $(q_2, -1, q_3)$ occurs twice in π and the second occurrence of $(q_2, -1, q_3)$ is after the unique occurrence of $(q_3, -1, q_2)$. Then from this ordering, we can obtain an edge decomposition $\{(f_i', v_i, v_i', e_i)\}_{i \in [7]}$ of f, where

- $(f_1', v_1, v_1', e_1) = (f_\perp, q_0, q_0, (q_0, +1, q_1))$,
- $(f_2', v_2, v_2', e_2) = (f_\perp, q_1, q_1, (q_1, +1, q_2))$,
- $(f_3', v_3, v_3', e_3) = (f_{(q_2, -1, q_3)}, q_2, q_3, (q_3, -1, q_2))$,
- $(f_4', v_4, v_4', e_4) = (f_\perp, q_2, q_2, (q_2, -1, q_3))$,
- $(f_5', v_5, v_5', e_5) = (f_\perp, q_3, q_3, (q_3, +1, q_4))$,
- $(f_6', v_6, v_6', e_6) = (f_\perp, q_4, q_4, (q_4, -1, q_2))$, and
- $(f_7', v_7, v_7', e_7) = (f_\perp, q_2, q_2, (q_2, +1, q_5))$.

The reachability criteria to guarantee the non-negativeness of counter values in path flows are classified into three types, with the first two types formalized in the following two definitions.

Definition 6 (Type-1 reachability criteria). *Let $n, n' \in \mathbb{N}$. Then a path flow f from q to q' is said to satisfy the type-1 reachability criteria for (n, n') if the following constraints hold,*

- G_f *does not contain positive cycles,*
- $\mathsf{weight}(f) = n' - n$,
- f *has an edge decomposition* $\{(f_i, v_i, v_i', e_i)\}_{i \in [m]}$ *such that* $n + \sum_{i \in [j]} (\mathsf{weight}(f_i) + \mathsf{weight}(e_i)) \geq 0$ *for all* $j \in [m]$.

Note that the condition for $\{(f_i, v_i, v_i', e_i)\}_{i \in [m]}$ in Definition 6 can be equivalently phrased as $n' - \sum_{j < i \leq m} (\mathsf{weight}(f_i) + \mathsf{weight}(e_i)) \geq 0$ for all $j \in [m]$, which intuitively explains the dual of the type-1 reachability criteria, i.e. type-2 reachability criteria in Definition 7.

Example 6. Let $(n, n') = (1, 1)$. Then the path flow f_1 from q_0 to q_5 in the Example 3 satisfies the type-1 reachability criteria for (n, n'): G_{f_1} does not contain positive cycles, $\mathsf{weight}(f_1) = 0 = 1 - 1$, f_1 has an edge decomposition $\{(f_i', v_i, v_i', e_i)\}_{i \in [7]}$ as shown in Example 5, moreover,

- $1 + \mathsf{weight}(f_1') + \mathsf{weight}(e_1) = 1 + 0 + \mathsf{weight}((q_0, +1, q_1)) = 2 \geq 0$,
- $1 + \sum_{j \in [2]} (\mathsf{weight}(f_j') + \mathsf{weight}(e_j)) = 2 + 0 + \mathsf{weight}((q_1, +1, q_2)) = 3 \geq 0$,
- $1 + \sum_{j \in [3]} (\mathsf{weight}(f_j') + \mathsf{weight}(e_j)) = 3 + \mathsf{weight}(f_{(q_2, -1, q_3)}) + \mathsf{weight}((q_3, -1, q_2))$
  $= 3 - 1 - 1 = 1 \geq 0$,
- $1 + \sum_{j \in [4]} \mathsf{weight}(f_j') + \mathsf{weight}(e_j) = 1 + 0 + \mathsf{weight}((q_2, -1, q_3)) = 0 \geq 0$,

$- 1 + \sum_{j \in [5]} \mathsf{weight}(f'_j) + \mathsf{weight}(e_j) = 0 + 0 + \mathsf{weight}((q_3, +1, q_4)) = 1 \geq 0,$

$- 1 + \sum_{j \in [6]} \mathsf{weight}(f'_j) + \mathsf{weight}(e_j) = 1 + 0 + \mathsf{weight}((q_4, -1, q_2)) = 0 \geq 0,$

$- 1 + \sum_{j \in [7]} \mathsf{weight}(f'_j) + \mathsf{weight}(e_j) = 0 + 0 + \mathsf{weight}((q_2, +1, q_5)) = 1 \geq 0.$

The type-2 reachability criteria are dual to the type-1 reachability criteria.

Definition 7 (Type-2 reachability criteria). *Let $n, n' \in \mathbb{N}$. Then a path flow f from q to q' is said to satisfy the type-2 reachability criteria for (n, n') if f^{op} satisfies the type-1 reachability criteria for (n', n) in G^{op}, where $f^{op}((v', -z, v)) = f((v, z, v'))$ for each $(v, z, v') \in E$.*

Example 7. Let $(n, n') = (1, 3)$ and f_3 be the path flow from q_7 to q_{11} such that $f_3((q_7, -1, q_{10})) = 1$, $f_3((q_{10}, +1, q_{10})) = 2$, and $f_3((q_{10}, +1, q_{11})) = 1$. Then f_3 satisfies the type-2 reachability criteria for $(1, 3)$ since f_3^{op} satisfies the type-1 reachability criteria for $(3, 1)$ in G^{op}.

- $G_{f_3^{op}}$ is the graph comprising the edges $(q_{11}, -1, q_{10})$, $(q_{10}, -1, q_{10})$, and $(q_{10}, +1, q_7)$. It contains no positive cycles.
- $\mathsf{weight}(f_3^{op}) = (-1) \times 1 + (-1) \times 2 + (+1) \times 1 = -2 = 1 - 3.$
- f_3^{op} has an edge decomposition $\{(f'_i, v_i, v'_i, e_i)\}_{i \in [3]}$ where $(f'_1, v_1, v'_1, e_1) = (f_\perp, q_{11}, q_{11}, (q_{11}, -1, q_{10}))$, $(f'_2, v_2, v'_2, e_2) = (f_{(q_{10}, -1, q_{10})}, q_{10}, q_{10}, (q_{10}, -1, q_{10}))$, $(f'_3, v_3, v'_3, e_3) = (f_\perp, q_{10}, q_{10}, (q_{10}, +1, q_7))$, moreover,

- $3 + \mathsf{weight}(f'_1) + \mathsf{weight}(e_1) = 2 \geq 0,$
- $3 + \sum_{j \in [2]} (\mathsf{weight}(f'_j) + \mathsf{weight}(e_j)) = 2 - 1 - 1 = 0 \geq 0,$
- $3 + \sum_{j \in [3]} (\mathsf{weight}(f'_j) + \mathsf{weight}(e_j)) = 0 + 0 + 1 = 1 \geq 0.$

It remains to present the type-3 reachability criteria.

Definition 8 (Cycle template). *Let $G = (V', E')$ be a subgraph of G_A, $v \in V'$ and $n \in \mathbb{N}$. A positive v-cycle template w.r.t. n in G is a cycle $\pi = \pi_1 \cdot \pi_2 \cdot \pi_3$ such that there is a vertex $v' \in V'$ satisfying that*

- *π_2 is a positive simple v'-cycle,*
- *if $v = v'$, then $\pi_1 = \pi_3 = \varepsilon$, otherwise, π_1 (resp. π_3) is a simple path from v to v' (resp. from v' to v),*
- *$\mathsf{drop}(\pi_1 \cdot \pi_2) \geq -n$.*

A negative v-cycle template w.r.t. n is a cycle $\pi = \pi_1 \cdot \pi_2 \cdot \pi_3$ such that $\pi^{op} = \pi_3^{op} \cdot \pi_2^{op} \cdot \pi_1^{op}$ is a positive v-cycle template w.r.t. n in G^{op}.

Example 8. The cycle $\pi_1 \cdot \pi_2 \cdot \pi_3$, where $\pi_1 = \pi_3 = \varepsilon$ and $\pi_2 = (q_5, +1, q_5)$, is a positive q_5-cycle template in G_A w.r.t. 1 since $\mathsf{drop}(\pi_1 \cdot \pi_2) = 1 \geq -1$. Moreover, $\pi_4 \cdot \pi_5 \cdot \pi_6$, where $\pi_4 = (q_7, -1, q_8)$, $\pi_5 = (q_8, -1, q_9)(q_9, -1, q_8)$, and $\pi_6 = (q_8, +1, q_7)$, is a negative q_7-cycle template w.r.t. 1 in G_A since $\pi_6^{op} \cdot \pi_5^{op} \cdot \pi_4^{op}$ satisfies that $\mathsf{drop}(\pi_6^{op} \cdot \pi_5^{op}) = -1 \geq -1$, thus is a positive q_7-cycle template w.r.t. 1 in G_A^{op}.

Definition 9 (Type-3 reachability criteria). *Let* $n, n' \in \mathbb{N}$. *Then a path flow* f *from* q *to* q' *is said to satisfy the type-3 reachability criteria for* (n, n') *if the following constraints hold.*

- *there is a positive* q-*cycle template w.r.t.* n *in* $G_\mathcal{A}$,
- weight$(f) = n' - n$,
- *there is a negative* q'-*cycle template w.r.t.* n' *in* $G_\mathcal{A}$.

Example 9. Let f_2 be the path flow from q_5 to q_7 such that $f_2((q_5, -1, q_6)) = f_2((q_6, +1, q_7)) = 1$ and $f_2(e') = 0$ for all the other edges e'. Then f_2 satisfies the type-3 reachability criteria for $(1, 1)$: weight$(f_2) = 0 = 1 - 1$, moreover, $\pi_1 \cdot \pi_2 \cdot \pi_3$ in Example 8 is a positive q_5-cycle template w.r.t. 1 in $G_\mathcal{A}$ and $\pi_4 \cdot \pi_5 \cdot \pi_6$ is a negative q_7-cycle template w.r.t. 1 in $G_\mathcal{A}$.

The following lemma captures reachability in $G_\mathcal{A}$.

Lemma 2 ([18]). *Let* $q, q' \in Q$ *and* $n, n' \in \mathbb{N}$. *Then* (q', n') *is reachable from* (q, n) *in* $G_\mathcal{A}$ *iff there is a path flow* f *from* q *to* q' *which can be split into three path flows* f_1, f_2, f_3 *such that*

- $f = f_1 + f_2 + f_3$,
- *there are* $q_1, q_2 \in Q$ *and* $n'', n''' \in \mathbb{N}$ *satisfying that*

- f_1 *is a path flow from* q *to* q_1 *(note that* f_1 *may be the zero flow* $f_\perp$, *in this case,* $q_1 = q$), *moreover, if* $f_1 \neq f_\perp$, *then* f_1 *satisfies the type-1 reachability criteria for* (n, n''),
- f_2 *is a path flow from* q_1 *to* q_2 *(note that* f_2 *may be the zero flow* $f_\perp$, *in this case,* $q_2 = q_1$), *moreover, if* $f_2 \neq f_\perp$, *then* f_2 *satisfies the type-3 reachability criteria for* (n'', n'''),
- f_3 *is a path flow from* q_2 *to* q' *(note that* f_3 *may be the zero flow* $f_\perp$, *in this case,* $q' = q_2$), *moreover, if* $f_3 \neq f_\perp$, *then* f_3 *satisfies the type-2 reachability criteria for* (n''', n').

Example 10. Let $f = f_1 \cdot f_2 \cdot f_3$ be path flow from q_0 to q_{11}, where f_1 is the path flow from q_0 to q_5 in Example 6, f_2 is a path flow from q_5 to q_7 in Example 9, and f_3 is a path flow from q_7 to q_{11} in Example 7. Then from Example 6, Example 9, and Example 7, we know that f_1 satisfies the type-1 reachability criteria for $(1, 1)$, f_2 satisfies the type-3 reachability criteria for $(1, 1)$, and f_3 satisfies the type-2 reachability criteria for $(1, 3)$. Therefore, according to Lemma 2, $(q_{11}, 3)$ is reachable from $(q_0, 1)$ in $G_\mathcal{A}$.

In the sequel, we show how the constraints in Lemma 2 can be defined by EPA formulae. We use the variables $(x_e)_{e \in E}$ to represent the path flow f in Lemma 2. Moreover, we use the variables $(y_{e,1})_{e \in E}$, $(y_{e,2})_{e \in E}$, $(y_{e,3})_{e \in E}$ to represent the path flows f_1, f_2, and f_3.

Type-1 Reachability Criteria. Our goal is to formalize by an EPA formula $\psi_{q,q_1}^{(\mathrm{T1RC})}$ that the path flow f_1 from q to q_1 represented by $(y_{e,1})_{e \in E}$ satisfies the type-1 reachability criteria. Let the variables x, x_1 represent the counter values of

q, q_1 respectively. From the definition of the type-1 reachability criteria, it is sufficient to show that the absence of positive cycles and the existence of an edge decomposition in G_{f_1} can be encoded in EPA. In the sequel, we illustrate how to encode by an EPA formula the existence of an edge decomposition. The EPA formula $\psi^{(\mathrm{APC})}((y_{e,1})_{e \in E})$ to encode the absence of positive cycles is omitted, due to the page limit.

For each edge e, we introduce integer variables idx_e and sum_e, and the integer variables $(y_{e,e'})_{e' \in E}$. Intuitively, each edge e is associated with an index idx_e indicating the position of the last occurrence of e along the edge decomposition, $(y_{e,e'})_{e' \in E}$ specifies the flow of e' associated with the edge e, i.e., the number of occurrences of e' along the path up to the last occurrence of e. We use sum_e to represent the sum of the weights of all the edges preceding the last occurrence of e in the edge decomposition. Besides, x, x_1 represent the counter value at q and q_1 respectively. Then the existence of an edge decomposition from q to q_1 is encoded by the EPA formula

$$\psi^{\mathrm{EDC}}_{q,q_1}((y_{e,1})_{e \in E}, (idx_e, sum_e)_{e \in E}, (y_{e,e'})_{e,e' \in E}) ::=$$
$$\psi^{(\mathrm{IDX})}_{q,q_1}((y_{e,1})_{e \in E}, (idx_e)_{e \in E}) \wedge \psi^{(\mathrm{EDG})}_{q,q_1}((y_{e,1})_{e \in E}, (idx_e)_{e \in E}, (y_{e,e'})_{e,e' \in E}) \wedge$$
$$\psi^{(\mathrm{NN})}_{q,q_1}((y_{e,1})_{e \in E}, (idx_e, sum_e)_{e \in E}, (y_{e,e'})_{e,e' \in E}),$$

where $\psi^{(\mathrm{IDX})}_{q,q_1}((y_{e,1})_{e \in E}, (idx_e)_{e \in E})$ intuitively specifies that the variables idx_e with $y_{e,1} > 0$ are mutually distinct and represent an order of the edges corresponding to their last occurrences in a path flow from q to q_1. Formally, it specifies that $\{idx_e \mid y_{e,1} > 0\} = [i]$, where i is the number of edges e with $y_{e,1} > 0$. Moreover, $idx_e = i$ for some e with $t(e) = q_1$,

$$\psi^{(\mathrm{IDX})}_{q,q_1} ::= \bigwedge_{e \in E} (y_{e,1} > 0 \rightarrow idx_e > 0 \wedge y_{e,1} = 0 \rightarrow idx_e = 0) \wedge$$
$$\bigvee_{e \in E} (y_{e,1} > 0 \wedge idx_e = 1) \wedge \bigwedge_{e,e' \in E, e \neq e'} ((y_{e,1} > 0 \wedge y_{e',1} > 0) \rightarrow idx_e \neq idx_{e'}) \wedge$$
$$\bigwedge_{e \in E} \left((y_{e,1} > 0 \wedge idx_e > 1) \rightarrow \bigvee_{e' \in E} (y_{e',1} > 0 \wedge idx_{e'} + 1 = idx_e) \right) \wedge$$
$$\bigvee_{e \in E, t(e) = q_1} \left(y_{e,1} > 0 \wedge \bigwedge_{e' \in E} idx_{e'} \leq idx_e \right),$$

and $\psi^{(\mathrm{EDG})}_{q,q_1}((y_{e,1})_{e \in E}, (idx_e)_{e \in E}, (y_{e,e'})_{e,e' \in E})$ specifies the constraints on the occurrences of edges in an edge decomposition,

$$\psi^{(\mathrm{EDG})}_{q,q_1} := \bigwedge_{e \in E} \left((y_{e,1} > 0 \wedge idx_e = 1) \rightarrow \psi^{(\mathrm{PF})}_{q,s(e)}((y_{e,e'})_{e' \in E}) \right) \wedge$$
$$\bigwedge_{e,e' \in E} \left((y_{e',1} > 0 \wedge y_{e,1} > 0 \wedge idx_{e'} + 1 = idx_e) \rightarrow \psi^{(\mathrm{PF})}_{t(e'),s(e)}((y_{e,e''})_{e'' \in E}) \right) \wedge$$
$$\bigwedge_{e,e' \in E} ((y_{e,1} > 0 \wedge y_{e',1} > 0 \wedge idx_e < idx_{e'}) \rightarrow y_{e',e} = 0) \wedge$$
$$\bigwedge_{e \in E} (y_{e,1} > 0 \rightarrow (\textstyle\sum_{e' \in E} y_{e',e}) + 1 = y_{e,1}),$$

(Note that $y_{e',e} = 0$ specifies that e does not occur in the path flow for e'.)

Moreover, $\psi_{q,q_1}^{(NN)}$ specifies that the sum of x and the weights of the path flows and edges in the edge decomposition are non-negative,

$$
\begin{aligned}
\psi_{q,q_1}^{(NN)} ::= \bigwedge_{e \in E} &\left((y_{e,1} > 0 \wedge idx_e = 1) \rightarrow sum_e = \mathsf{weight}(e) + \sum_{e' \in E} \mathsf{weight}(e') \cdot y_{e,e'} \right) \wedge \\
&\bigwedge_{e,e' \in E} \left(\begin{array}{l} (y_{e,1} > 0 \wedge y_{e',1} > 0 \wedge idx_e + 1 = idx_{e'}) \rightarrow \\ sum_e + \mathsf{weight}(e') + \sum_{e'' \in E} \mathsf{weight}(e'') \cdot y_{e',e''} = sum_{e'} \end{array} \right) \wedge \\
&\bigwedge_{e \in E} (y_{e,1} > 0 \rightarrow x + sum_e \geq 0).
\end{aligned}
$$

Then we encode the type-1 reachability criteria by the following EPA formula,

$$
\begin{aligned}
\psi_{G_{\mathcal{A}},q,q_1}^{(T1RC)}(x, x_1, (y_{e,1})_{e \in E}) ::= &\; \psi^{(APC)}((y_{e,1})_{e \in E}) \wedge \\
\exists (idx_e, sum_e)_{e \in E}, (y_{e,e'})_{e,e' \in E}. &\left(\begin{array}{l} \psi_{q,q_1}^{(EDC)}((y_{e,1})_{e \in E}, (idx_e, sum_e)_{e \in E}, (y_{e,e'})_{e,e' \in E}) \wedge \\ \psi_{q,q_1}^{(WGT)}((y_{e,1})_{e \in E}, (idx_e, sum_e)_{e \in E}) \end{array} \right),
\end{aligned}
$$

where $\psi_{q,q_1}^{(WGT)}$ specifies that the sum of x and the weights of all the path flows and edges in the edge decomposition is equal to x_1,

$$
\psi_{q,q_1}^{(WGT)} ::= \bigvee_{e \in E, t(e)=q_1} \left(y_{e,1} > 0 \wedge \bigwedge_{e' \in E} idx_{e'} \leq idx_e \wedge x + sum_e = x_1 \right).
$$

One can observe that the size of $\psi_{G_{\mathcal{A}},q,q_1}^{(T1RC)}$ is polynomial in the size of $\mathcal{A}$.

Type-2 Reachability Criteria. Suppose that $(y_{e,3})_{e \in E}$ represents a path flow f_3 from q_2 to q'. Then Lemma 2 says that f_3 satisfies the type-2 reachability criteria, that is, the flow f_3^{op} in $G_{\mathcal{A}}^{op}$ satisfies the type-1 reachability criteria, which is encoded by the EPA formula $\psi_{G_{\mathcal{A}},q_2,q'}^{(T2RC)}$ defined below. Let x_2, x' represents the counter values of q_2 and q' respectively. Then

$$
\begin{aligned}
\psi_{G_{\mathcal{A}},q_2,q'}^{(T2RC)}(x_2, x', (y_{e,3})_{e \in E}) ::= \exists (y_{e',3}^{op})_{e' \in E^{op}}. \; \varphi_{G_{\mathcal{A}}^{op},q',q_2}^{(T1RC)}(x', x_2, (y_{e',3}^{op})_{e' \in E^{op}}) \wedge \\
\bigwedge_{e=(p,c,p') \in E, e'=(p',-c,p) \in E^{op}} y_{e',3}^{op} = y_{e,3}.
\end{aligned}
$$

Type-3 Reachability Criteria. Our goal is to construct an EPA formula $\psi_{G_{\mathcal{A}},q_1,q_2}^{(T3RC)}$ to characterize the type-3 reachability criteria for a path flow represented by $(y_{e,2})_{e \in E}$ from q_1 to q_2. Let x_1, x_2 represent the counter values of q_1, q_2 respectively. Recall that the type-3 reachability criteria specify that there exist a positive q_1-cycle template and a negative q_2-cycle template, as well as a path flow from q_1 to q_2. Since negative cycle templates are the dual of positive cycle templates and we know how to encode a path flow in EPA, it is sufficient to show that the existence of a positive q_1-cycle template can be specified by an EPA formula $\psi_{G_{\mathcal{A}},q_1}^{(PCT)}$. To this end, we introduce integer variables $idx_{e,1}, idx_{e,2}, idx_{e,3}$ for $e \in E$ to represent the three simple paths (or cycles) π_1, π_2, π_3 in a positive q_1-cycle template. Moreover, we introduce integer variables $sum_{p,1}, drop_{p,1}$ and

$sum_{p,2}, drop_{p,2}$ for $p \in Q$ to describe the computation of the sum of edge weights and the drop in the prefixes of π_1 and π_2 respectively. Then

$$\psi_{G_A,q_1}^{(PCT)}(x_1, (idx_{e,i})_{e \in E, i=1,2,3}, (sum_{p,j}, drop_{p,j})_{p \in Q, j=1,2}) ::=$$
$$\bigvee_{p' \in Q} \begin{pmatrix} \psi_{q_1,p'}^{(SP1)}((idx_{e,1})_{e \in E}, (sum_{p,1}, drop_{p,1})_{p \in Q}) \wedge \\ \psi_{p',p'}^{(SC)}((idx_{e,2})_{e \in E}, (sum_{p,2}, drop_{p,2})_{p \in Q}) \wedge \\ \psi_{p',q_1}^{(SP2)}((idx_{e,3})_{e \in E}) \wedge \\ \psi^{(NN)}(x_1, sum_{p',1}, drop_{p',1}, drop_{p',2}) \end{pmatrix},$$

where $\psi_{q_1,p'}^{(SP1)}$, $\psi_{p',p'}^{(SC)}$, and $\psi_{p',q_1}^{(SP2)}$ specify the existence of three simple paths (or cycles) π_1, π_2, π_3 in a positive q_1-cycle template, as well as the computation of the sum of edge weights and the drop in the prefixes of π_1 and π_2. Concretely,

$$\psi_{q_1,p'}^{(SP1)}((idx_{e,1})_{e \in E}, (sum_{p,1}, drop_{p,1})_{p \in Q}) ::=$$
$$\left(q_1 = p' \wedge \bigwedge_{e \in E} idx_{e,1} = 0 \wedge sum_{p',1} = 0 \wedge drop_{p',1} = 0 \right) \vee$$
$$\begin{pmatrix} q_1 \neq p' \wedge \psi_{q_1,p'}^{(SPIDX)}((idx_{e,1})_{e \in E}) \wedge \\ \bigwedge_{e=(q_1,c,p) \in E} (idx_{e,1} = 1 \rightarrow (sum_{p,1} = c \wedge drop_{p,1} = \min(c,0))) \wedge \\ \bigwedge_{e=(p_1,c,p_2) \in E} idx_{e,1} > 1 \rightarrow \begin{pmatrix} sum_{p_1,1} + c = sum_{p_2,1} \wedge \\ drop_{p_2,1} = \min(drop_{p_1,1}, sum_{p_2,1}) \end{pmatrix} \end{pmatrix},$$

where $\psi_{q_1,p'}^{(SPIDX)}$ specifies how the integer variables $idx_{e,1}$ for $e \in E$ can be constrained to represent a simple path from q_1 to p',

$$\psi_{q_1,p'}^{(SPIDX)}((idx_{e,1})_{e \in E}) ::= \bigwedge_{e \in E} idx_{e,1} \geq 0 \wedge \bigwedge_{e=(p,z,p) \in E} idx_{e,1} = 0 \wedge$$
$$\bigvee_{e \in E, s(e)=q_1} idx_{e,1} = 1 \wedge \bigvee_{e \in E, t(e)=p'} \bigwedge_{e' \in E} idx_{e',1} \leq idx_{e,1} \wedge$$
$$\bigwedge_{e,e' \in E, e \neq e'} ((idx_{e,1} > 0 \wedge idx_{e',1} > 0) \rightarrow idx_{e,1} \neq idx_{e',1}) \wedge$$
$$\bigwedge_{e \in E} (idx_{e,1} > 1 \rightarrow \bigvee_{e' \in E, t(e')=s(e)} idx_{e',1} + 1 = idx_{e,1}) \wedge$$
$$\bigwedge_{e,e' \in E, t(e)=s(e')} ((idx_{e,1} > 0 \wedge idx_{e',1} > 0) \rightarrow idx_{e,1} + 1 = idx_{e',1}).$$

The formula $\psi_{p',p'}^{(SC)}((idx_{e,2})_{e \in E}, (sum_{p,2}, drop_{p,2})_{p \in Q})$ and $\psi_{p',q_1}^{(SP2)}((idx_{e,3})_{e \in E})$ can be defined similarly.

Moreover, we define the formula

$$\psi^{(NN)}(x_1, sum_{p',1}, drop_{p',1}, drop_{p',2}) ::=$$
$$x_1 + drop_{p',1} \geq 0 \wedge x_1 + sum_{p',1} + drop_{p',2} \geq 0.$$

Symmetrically, the existence of a negative q_2-cycle template can be specified by an EPA formula $\psi_{G_A^{op},q_2}^{(PCT)}(x_2, (idx_{e',i})_{e' \in E^{op}, i=4,5,6}, (sum_{p,j}, drop_{p,j})_{p \in Q, j=3,4})$, where the variables $idx_{e',4}, idx_{e',5}, idx_{e',6}$ and $sum_{p,3}, drop_{p,3}, sum_{p,4}, drop_{p,4}$

are similar to the variables $idx_{e,1}, idx_{e,2},\ idx_{e,3}$ and $sum_{p,1},\ drop_{p,1},\ sum_{p,2},\ drop_{p,2}$ respectively. It follows that

$$\psi_{G_{\mathcal{A}},q_1,q_2}^{(T3RC)}(x_1,x_2,(y_{e,2})_{e\in E}) ::= \varphi_{q_1,q_2}^{(PF)}((y_{e,2})_{e\in E}) \wedge x_1 + \sum_{e\in E} \mathsf{weight}(e)\cdot y_{e,2} = x_2 \wedge$$

$$\exists(idx_{e,i})_{e\in E,i\in[6]}(sum_{p,j},drop_{p,j})_{p\in Q,j\in[4]}.$$
$$\left(\begin{array}{l} (\psi_{G_{\mathcal{A}},q_1}^{(PCT)}(x_1,(idx_{e,i})_{e\in E,i=1,2,3},(sum_{p,j},drop_{p,j})_{p\in Q,j=1,2}) \wedge \\ \psi_{G_{\mathcal{A}}^{op},q_2}^{(PCT)}(x_2,(idx_{e,i})_{e\in E,i=4,5,6},(sum_{p,j},drop_{p,j})_{p\in Q,j=3,4})) \end{array} \right).$$

Finally, let x and y denote the initial and final counter values of state q and q' respectively. By combining formulae for the type-1, type-2 and type-3 reachability criteria, the EPA formula $\varphi_{G_{\mathcal{A}},q,q'}^{(RC)}$ is defined as

$$\psi_{G_{\mathcal{A}},q,q'}^{(RC)}(x,y) ::= \exists x_1 x_2 \exists (y_{e,i})_{e\in E,i\in[3]}.\ x_1 \geq 0 \wedge x_2 \geq 0 \wedge \bigwedge_{e\in E,i\in[3]} y_{e,i} \geq 0 \wedge$$

$$\left(\begin{array}{l} (q = q' \wedge x = x_1 \wedge x_1 = x_2 \wedge x_2 = y) \vee \\ \left(x = x_1 \wedge x_1 = x_2 \wedge \bigvee \psi_{G_{\mathcal{A}},q,q'}^{(T2RC)}(x_2,y,(y_{e,3})_{e\in E}) \right) \vee \\ \left(x = x_1 \wedge \psi_{G_{\mathcal{A}},q,q'}^{(T3RC)}(x_1,x_2,(y_{e,2})_{e\in E}) \wedge x_2 = y \right) \vee \\ \bigvee_{q_2\in Q} \left(x = x_1 \wedge \psi_{G_{\mathcal{A}},q,q_2}^{(T3RC)}(x_1,x_2,(y_{e,2})_{e\in E}) \wedge \psi_{G_{\mathcal{A}},q_2,q'}^{(T2RC)}(x_2,y,(y_{e,3})_{e\in E}) \right) \vee \\ \left(\psi_{G_{\mathcal{A}},q,q'}^{(T1RC)}(x,x_1,(y_{e,1})_{e\in E}) \wedge x_1 = x_2 \wedge x_2 = y \right) \vee \\ \bigvee_{q_1\in Q} \left(\psi_{G_{\mathcal{A}},q,q_1}^{(T1RC)}(x,x_1,(y_{e,1})_{e\in E}) \wedge x_1 = x_2 \wedge \psi_{G_{\mathcal{A}},q_1,q'}^{(T2RC)}(x_2,y,(y_{e,3})_{e\in E}) \right) \vee \\ \bigvee_{q_1\in Q} \left(\psi_{G_{\mathcal{A}},q,q_1}^{(T1RC)}(x,x_1,(y_{e,1})_{e\in E}) \wedge \psi_{G_{\mathcal{A}},q_1,q'}^{(T3RC)}(x_1,x_2,(y_{e,2})_{e\in E}) \wedge x_2 = y \right) \vee \\ \bigvee_{q_1,q_2\in Q} \left(\begin{array}{l} \psi_{G_{\mathcal{A}},q,q_1}^{(T1RC)}(x,x_1,(y_{e,1})_{e\in E}) \wedge \psi_{G_{\mathcal{A}},q_1,q_2}^{(T3RC)}(x_1,x_2,(y_{e,2})_{e\in E}) \wedge \\ \psi_{G_{\mathcal{A}},q_2,q'}^{(T2RC)}(x_2,y,(y_{e,3})_{e\in E}) \end{array} \right) \end{array} \right).$$

4 Experiments

We implement in Java the algorithm in the preceding Section and develop a tool OCAREACH[1]. OCAREACH computes, for a given OCA $\mathcal{A}$ and a pair of states q,q', an EPA formula $\varphi_{\mathcal{A},q,q'}(x,y)$ representing $R_{\mathcal{A},q,q'}$. Moreover, it integrates the SMT solver Z3 to eliminate the existential quantifiers in $\varphi_{\mathcal{A},q,q'}(x,y)$ as well as to solve the reachability problem from (q,n) to (q',n') for two additional $n,n' \in \mathbb{N}$, by evaluating $\varphi_{\mathcal{A},q,q'}(x,y)$ on n,n'. The performance of OCAREACH are evaluated on two benchmark suites: MOCA, which is manually constructed, and ROCA, which is randomly generated.

MOCA We created 17 OCA benchmarks manually, of sizes ranging from (2 states, 1 transitions) to (10 states, 11 edges). The OCA instances in MOCA have relatively simple transition graphs so that for each instance $(\mathcal{A},q,q')$ in MOCA, we are able to manually construct an EPA formula $\psi'_{\mathcal{A},q,q'}$ as the

---

[1] Available at https://github.com/SpencerL-Y/OCAReach.

ground truth for the reachability relation, then use the SMT solver Z3 to test the equivalence of $\psi'_{\mathcal{A},q,q'}$ and $\psi_{\mathcal{A},q,q'}$ (the output of OCAREACH), so that the correctness of OCAREACH is validated.

ROCA This benchmark suite consists of randomly generated OCA instances by first determining the number of states n, then randomly generating the transitions, based on a sparsity parameter $\eta \in [0,1]$, with the intention that for each pair of states, there exist edges between them, with the probability η. Moreover, assuming that there exist edges between a given pair of states, then the probabilities of zero-transition, $+1$-transition, and -1-transition, are $1/8$, $7/16$, and $7/16$ respectively. We first fix $\eta = 0.2$, and generate 50 instances for each $n \in \{5, 7, 10\}$. Then we fix $n = 4$ and generate 50 instances for each $\eta = 0.2, 0.4, 0.5$.

All the experiments were performed on a laptop with Intel Core i5-8450 processor and 8 GB main memory.

Experimental Results on MOCA. The results are given in Table 1, where time refers to the time to generate the EPA formula, and size refers to the size of the generated formula. We can see that the running time and the generated formula size are roughly proportional to the number of states and transitions. Moreover, for each MOCA instance, we use Z3 to validate the equivalence of the generated formula and the manually constructed ground truth formula.

Table 1. Experimental results on MOCA

State num.	2	2	2	2	3	3	4	4	4
Tranisition num.	1	2	2	5	2	3	3	3	6
Zero-test num.	0	1	1	0	0	1	1	1	1
Time (s)	0.066	0.062	0.078	0.076	0.066	0.072	0.061	0.079	0.093
Size (kB)	0.302	0.404	0.697	0.302	0.133	0.929	0.348	0.325	2.592
State num.	5	6	6	6	7	8	10	10	
Transition num.	6	6	7	8	9	7	11	11	
Zero-test num.	1	2	2	2	2	2	2	3	
Time (s)	0.087	0.078	0.106	0.091	0.106	0.090	0.116	0.117	
Size (kB)	2.057	2.469	7.457	3.078	6.427	4.807	8.443	7.515	

Experimental Results on ROCA. The results are given in Table 2. We can see that when $\eta = 0.2$, if the number of states n is increased from 5 to 10, then the average number of transitions, the average running time, and the average size of the generated formula grow quickly. Moreover, from the experimental results, we can also see that when the number of states $n = 4$, if the sparsity parameter η is increased from 0.2 to 0.5, then the average number of transitions, the average running time, and the average size of the generated formula also grow quickly. We remark that, in practice, the transition graphs of OCA are generally sparse so our approach is potentially scalable.

Table 2. Experimental results on ROCA

(state num. n, sparsity param. η)	(5, 0.2)	(7, 0.2)	(10, 0.2)	(4, 0.2)	(4, 0.3)	(4, 0.5)
Avg. transition num.	4	10	19	3	5.34	8.4
Avg. time (s)	0.012	16.161	362	0.021	0.492	23.334
Avg. size (kB)	6.29	4,470	37,241	4.823	3.161	235.140

5   Conclusion

In this paper, we have shown that the reachability relation of OCA can be represented by an existential Presburger arithmetic formula which can be computed in polynomial time. This result generalizes the well-known result that an existential Presburger arithmetic formula can be computed in polynomial time to define the Parikh image of the regular language of finite automata. We developed a tool OCAREACH and conducted experiments to evaluate the efficiency of our approach. To the best of our knowledge, OCAREACH provides the first tool support for solving the reachability problem of OCA.

References

1. Abdulla, P.A., Čerāns, K.: Simulation is decidable for one-counter nets. In: Sangiorgi, D., de Simone, R. (eds.) CONCUR 1998. LNCS, vol. 1466, pp. 253–268. Springer, Heidelberg (1998). https://doi.org/10.1007/BFb0055627
2. Bardin, S., Leroux, J., Point, G.: FAST extended release. In: Ball, T., Jones, R.B. (eds.) CAV 2006. LNCS, vol. 4144, pp. 63–66. Springer, Heidelberg (2006). https://doi.org/10.1007/11817963_9
3. Blondin, M., Finkel, A., Göller, S., Haase, C., McKenzie, P.: Reachability in two-dimensional vector addition systems with states is PSPACE-complete. In: 30th Annual ACM/IEEE Symposium on Logic in Computer Science, LICS 2015, Kyoto, Japan, 6–10 July 2015, pp. 32–43. IEEE Computer Society (2015)
4. Böhm, S., Göller, S., Jančar, P.: Bisimilarity of one-counter processes is PSPACE-complete. In: Gastin, P., Laroussinie, F. (eds.) CONCUR 2010. LNCS, vol. 6269, pp. 177–191. Springer, Heidelberg (2010). https://doi.org/10.1007/978-3-642-15375-4_13
5. Böhm, S., Göller, S., Jancar, P.: Equivalence of deterministic one-counter automata is NL-complete. In: Boneh, D., Roughgarden, T., Feigenbaum, J. (eds.) Symposium on Theory of Computing Conference, STOC 2013, Palo Alto, CA, USA, 1–4 June 2013, pp. 131–140. ACM (2013)
6. Borosh, I., Treybig, L.B.: Bounds on positive integral solutions of linear Diophantine equations. Proc. Am. Math. Soc. **55**(2), 299–304 (1976)
7. Bouajjani, A., Bozga, M., Habermehl, P., Iosif, R., Moro, P., Vojnar, T.: Programs with lists are counter automata. In: Ball, T., Jones, R.B. (eds.) CAV 2006. LNCS, vol. 4144, pp. 517–531. Springer, Heidelberg (2006). https://doi.org/10.1007/11817963_47
8. Chitic, C., Rosu, D.: On validation of XML streams using finite state machines. In: Amer-Yahia, S., Gravano, L. (eds.)Proceedings of the 7th International Workshop on the Web and Databases, WebDB 2004, 17–18 June 2004, Maison de la Chimie, Paris, France, Colocated with ACM SIGMOD/PODS 2004, pp. 85–90. ACM (2004)

9. Comon, H., Jurski, Y.: Timed automata and the theory of real numbers. In: Baeten, J.C.M., Mauw, S. (eds.) CONCUR 1999. LNCS, vol. 1664, pp. 242–257. Springer, Heidelberg (1999). https://doi.org/10.1007/3-540-48320-9_18

10. Dang, Z.: Pushdown timed automata: a binary reachability characterization and safety verification. Theor. Comput. Sci. **302**(1–3), 93–121 (2003)

11. Demri, S., Gascon, R.: The effects of bounding syntactic resources on Presburger LTL. In: 14th International Symposium on Temporal Representation and Reasoning, TIME 2007, Alicante, Spain, 28–30 June 2007, pp. 94–104. IEEE Computer Society (2007)

12. Dima, C.: Computing reachability relations in timed automata. In: Proceedings of the 17th IEEE Symposium on Logic in Computer Science, LICS 2002, Copenhagen, Denmark, 22–25 July 2002, p. 177. IEEE Computer Society (2002)

13. Fearnley, J., Jurdzinski, M.: Reachability in two-clock timed automata is PSPACE-complete. Inf. Comput. **243**, 26–36 (2015)

14. Fränzle, M., Quaas, K., Shirmohammadi, M., Worrell, J.: Effective definability of the reachability relation in timedautomata. Inf. Process. Lett. **153**, 105871 (2020)

15. Göller, S., Haase, C., Ouaknine, J., Worrell, J.: Model checking succinct and parametric one-counter automata. In: Abramsky, S., Gavoille, C., Kirchner, C., Meyer auf der Heide, F., Spirakis, P.G. (eds.) ICALP 2010. LNCS, vol. 6199, pp. 575–586. Springer, Heidelberg (2010). https://doi.org/10.1007/978-3-642-14162-1_48

16. Göller, S., Lohrey, M.: Branching-time model checking of one-counter processes and timed automata. SIAM J. Comput. **42**(3), 884–923 (2013)

17. Göller, S., Mayr, R., To, A.W.: On the computational complexity of verifying one-counter processes. In Proceedings of the 24th Annual IEEE Symposium on Logic in Computer Science, LICS 2009, Los Angeles, CA, USA, 11–14 August 2009, pp. 235–244. IEEE Computer Society (2009)

18. Haase, C.: On the complexity of model checking counter automata. Ph.D. thesis (2012)

19. Haase, C.: Subclasses of Presburger arithmetic and the weak EXP hierarchy. In: Proceedings of the Joint Meeting of the 23rd EACSL Annual Conference on Computer Science Logic (CSL) and the 29th Annual ACM/IEEE Symposium on Logic in Computer Science (LICS), CSL-LICS 2014, New York, NY, USA. Association for Computing Machinery (2014)

20. Haase, C., Kreutzer, S., Ouaknine, J., Worrell, J.: Reachability in succinct and parametric one-counter automata. In: Bravetti, M., Zavattaro, G. (eds.) CONCUR 2009. LNCS, vol. 5710, pp. 369–383. Springer, Heidelberg (2009). https://doi.org/10.1007/978-3-642-04081-8_25

21. Haase, C., Ouaknine, J., Worrell, J.: Relating reachability problems in timed and counter automata. Fundam. Inform. **143**(3–4), 317–338 (2016)

22. Hague, M., Lin, A.W.: Model checking recursive programs with numeric data types. In: Gopalakrishnan, G., Qadeer, S. (eds.) CAV 2011. LNCS, vol. 6806, pp. 743–759. Springer, Heidelberg (2011). https://doi.org/10.1007/978-3-642-22110-1_60

23. Ibarra, O.H.: Reversal-bounded multicounter machines and their decision problems. J. ACM **25**(1), 116–133 (1978)

24. Jancar, P., Kucera, A., Moller, F., Sawa, Z.: DP lower bounds for equivalence-checking and model-checking of one-counter automata. Inf. Comput. **188**(1), 1–19 (2004)

25. Kučera, A.: Efficient verification algorithms for one-counter processes. In: Montanari, U., Rolim, J.D.P., Welzl, E. (eds.) ICALP 2000. LNCS, vol. 1853, pp. 317–328. Springer, Heidelberg (2000). https://doi.org/10.1007/3-540-45022-X_28

26. Lafourcade, P., Lugiez, D., Treinen, R.: Intruder deduction for AC-like equational theories with homomorphisms. In: Giesl, J. (ed.) RTA 2005. LNCS, vol. 3467, pp. 308–322. Springer, Heidelberg (2005). https://doi.org/10.1007/978-3-540-32033-3_23
27. Leroux, J., Sutre, G.: Flat counter automata almost everywhere!. In: Peled, D.A., Tsay, Y.-K. (eds.) ATVA 2005. LNCS, vol. 3707, pp. 489–503. Springer, Heidelberg (2005). https://doi.org/10.1007/11562948_36
28. Seidl, H., Schwentick, T., Muscholl, A., Habermehl, P.: Counting in trees for free. In: ICALP, pp. 1136–1149 (2004)
29. Smrčka, A., Vojnar, T.: Verifying parametrised hardware designs via counter automata. In: Yorav, K. (ed.) HVC 2007. LNCS, vol. 4899, pp. 51–68. Springer, Heidelberg (2008). https://doi.org/10.1007/978-3-540-77966-7_8
30. Xu, Z., Chen, T., Wu, Z.: Satisfiability of compositional separation logic with tree predicates and data constraints. In: de Moura, L. (ed.) CADE 2017. LNCS (LNAI), vol. 10395, pp. 509–527. Springer, Cham (2017). https://doi.org/10.1007/978-3-319-63046-5_31

Compiling FL^{res} on Finite Words

Wanwei Liu[✉], Liangze Yin, and Tun Li

College of Computer Science, National University of Defense Technology,
Changsha 410073, China
wwliu@nudt.edu.cn

Abstract. Interpreting temporal logics on finite traces has specific use
in many fields, and it attracts more and more attention in recent years.
Foundation formulas (FL for short) is the core part of PSL, which has
once been an industrial standard of specification language accepted by
IEEE, and has now been adopted in SystemVerilog. We in this paper
present a variant of FL, called FL^{res}, whose semantics is defined w.r.t.
finite words. In comparison to the original FL, the only syntactic restriction is that the "length-matching and" operator cannot appear in the
first argument when doing concatenation. This restriction in syntax
would not change the expressiveness, whereas could gain a much succinct automata based decision procedure. Namely, an FL^{res} formula φ
can be equivalently transformed into a 2-way (or, stuttering) alternating
finite automaton with $\mathcal{O}(|\varphi|)$ states. Subsequently, one can convert it to
a 1-way nondeterministic finite automaton with $2^{\mathcal{O}(|\varphi|)}$ states.

1 Introduction

Temporal logics, acting as the specification part in model checking, in some sense,
are a major feature effecting the algorithms and complexity of verification. As
a consequence, the disputes on relative merits among temporal logics have been
an ever-lasting topic for logicians. Such argument mainly focus on, for example,
expressiveness (regular or not), syntactic succinctness, and so on.

Almost 15 years ago, after a fierce argument in academic and industrial communities, PSL (Property Specification Language) [1,7] has once been accepted
as an industrial standard (IEEE-1850). At that moment, such a logic seemed
to be a 'hotch-potch'—the majority of PSL is a logic on linear structure, called
Foundation Formulas (FL for short), which can be viewed as an extension of
LTL [17] equipped with extended regular expressions (SERE) as auxiliary ingre-
dients; meanwhile, it also involves the branching feature, called *Optional Branching Extension* (OBE, for short), and this part is essentially CTL [6]. In 2010 or
so, PSL has been adopted by the standard of SystemVerilog [10]—the branching part is completely excluded, some notations are altered, and some syntactic
sugars are introduced.

The semantics of FL can be given on both finite and infinite traces. For his-
torical reasons, logicians are mainly concerned about the latter fashion when

---

Supported by NSFC under grant Nos 61872371, 61802415, and U19A2062.

J. Pang and L. Zhang (Eds.): SETTA 2020, LNCS 12153, pp. 108–123, 2020.
https://doi.org/10.1007/978-3-030-62822-2_7

doing model checking, and such a feature has been intensively studied. Nevertheless, particular use of temporal logics can be found when semantics are given on finite models. For example, when we interpreting LTL upon finite words, we gain an important variant, called LTL$_f$, which is very useful in AI domain—for example, the planning problem can be boiled down to the synthesis problem of LTL$_f$ (cf. [8,9]). In addition, to monitor the behaviors of hardware, one usually pays attention to the finite prefixes of temporal logics [11].

Indeed, LTL$_f$ is not expressive enough to describe some properties—as pointed by Wolper [19], the property "p holds at every even moment" cannot be expressed by LTL—that proof also works for the finite version. Nevertheless, such property can be expressed by the FL^{res} formula $p \wedge ((p; true)^+ \mapsto (p; true))$. Indeed, when taking procedural constraints into consideration, LTL$_f$ is not expressive enough in this case when doing planning.

One can, of course, use regular expressions or (nondeterministic) finite automata as specifications, yet they are not so convenient to deal with the case when some constraints should hold simultaneously. For the consideration of flexibility in use, the original definition of FL is rather verbose. If we take an insight into such logic, we may find that the extended part (opposing to LTL) comes from three aspects:

- First, as we have mentioned, FL employs an extended version of regular expression as components in formulas.
- Second, FL involves some new temporal connectives and formula combinators, such as T, $\mapsto$, etc.
- To make the logic more flexible, FL also investigates some helper mechanisms, for example, it distinguishes strong/weak satisfactions of some specific formulas, and it also introduces clocks.

Actually, the first two extensions are essential in succinctness, because, weak/strong satisfaction can be interchangeable via simply applying negation to the dual formulas, whereas clocks can be encoded into the model together with newly introduced propositions.

In this paper, we study how to give an automata-theoretic decision procedure of FL-like logics upon finite models. To this end, we specially tailored a variant of FL which preserves the most distinctive features, but is simple enough in syntax to define. We name this variant FL^{res}. In comparison to the original FL, the only syntactic restriction is that the "length-matching and" operator cannot appear in the former component when doing concatenation. It can be seen that such a small restriction would not distort the essence and expressiveness of the logic[1]. To obtain a transformation from formulas to nondeterministic automata with linear exponent in size, we take two-way alternating automata as the intermediate representation. However, when giving an inductive construction, we encounter

---

[1] Because, SERE and RE are the same in expressiveness. Our logic uses a restricted version of SERE, whereas it subsumes standard RE.

the fact that the "length-matching and" is not distributive to concatenation[2]. To circumvent this difficulty, we impose this constraint to the variant.

We show that, given an FL^{res} φ formula with length n, we can compile it into a nondeterministic finite automaton that has $2^{\mathcal{O}(n)}$ states. To do this, we first transform φ into to a two-way alternating finite automata with $\mathcal{O}(n)$ states. Subsequently, we temporarily convert the two-way alternating automata to one-way nondeterministic automata with quadratically exponential state blow-up. Once again, thanks to the speciality of the logic, we can further sharpen the exponent into $\mathcal{O}(n)$.

Related Work. In [18], Ruah, Fisman and Ben-David presented a conversion from SafetyPSL^{det} to co-universal automata. In [3], Bustan, Fisman and Havlicek provided the transformation from LTL_WR (which is the core of FL) to nondeterministic Büchi automata. Jin *et al.* have provided a construction supporting full SEREs in [11]. They use finite automata with local variables (LAFA) to develop the decision procedure. In [4] and [5], the authors present a symbolic encoding from PSL to nondeterministic Büchi automata. Outputs of these work are automata on infinite words. Note that techniques on automata conversion on infinite words are totally different than on finite words (cf. [15]) Ever since 2014, similar work has been done towards some specific fragments, such as LTL$_f$ [12–14]. In our paper, we show how to extend this to a much richer logic without changing the complexity.

The rest part of this paper is organized as follows. Section 2 briefly introduces FL^{res} and revisits the notion of finite automata. Section 3 shows how to compile an FL^{res} formula into a two-way alternating finite automaton in the linear size. In Sect. 4, we provide a two-phase transformation to further transform the previous two-way alternating automaton into a one-way nondeterministic one with singly exponential state blow-up. We finally summarize the whole paper in Sect. 5.

2   Preliminaries

2.1   The Logic FL^{res}

Let us fix a set AP, called *atomic propositions*. A *letter* is a subset of AP, and a (finite) *word* is a sequence of letters. *Boolean expressions* are formulas built up from propositions belonging to AP and Boolean connectives like $\neg$, $\wedge$, $\vee$ etc. In what follows, we follow the convention using l, w, b, r (possibly with subscripts) to denote an individual letter, word, Boolean expression, restricted SERE, respectively.

Given a word $w = l_0 l_1 \ldots l_{n-1}$, its *length* (denoted $|w|$) is n. The ith letter of w is denoted by w^i and the segment of w starting from its ith letter and ending with its jth (including) letter is denoted by $w^{i..j}$. Moreover, we denote by $w^{i..}$ the suffix of w starting from its ith letter.

---

[2] For example, the language of $\left(a^+\&\&(a^+;b)\right);b^+$ is empty, whereas $(a^+;b^+)\&\&(a^+;b;b^+)$ matches abb.

(Non-empty) *REs* (Regular Expressions) are inductively defined as follows.

– Every Boolean expression b is an RE.
– If r, r_1 and r_2 are REs, then the followings are also REs.
  • $r_1;r_2$ • $r_1\|r_2$ • r^+.

Subsequently, we define *restricted SEREs* (restricted Sequential Extended Regular Expressions) as follows.

– Each RE is a restricted SERE.
– If r_1 and r_2 are restricted SEREs, then both $r_1\|r_2$ and $r_1\&\&r_2$ are restricted SEREs.
– If r_1 is an RE, r_2 is a restricted SERE, then both $r_1;r_2$ and $r_1:r_2$ are restricted SEREs.

Each restricted SERE r induces a class of words, said to be its *language*, denoted by $\mathscr{L}(r)$. Inductively:

– $w \in \mathscr{L}(b)$ iff $|w| = 1$ and w^0 satisfies b (that is, assigning the propositions in w^0 to *true* and other propositions to *false*, then b is evaluated to *true*).
– $w \in \mathscr{L}(r_1;r_2)$ iff $w = w_1w_2$ and $w_1 \in \mathscr{L}(r_1)$, $w_2 \in \mathscr{L}(r_2)$.
– $w \in \mathscr{L}(r_1:r_2)$ iff $w = w_1lw_2$ and $w_1l \in \mathscr{L}(r_1)$, $lw_2 \in \mathscr{L}(r_2)$.
– $w \in \mathscr{L}(r_1\&\&r_2)$ iff $w \in \mathscr{L}(r_1)$ and $w \in \mathscr{L}(r_2)$.
– $w \in \mathscr{L}(r_1\|r_2)$ iff $w \in \mathscr{L}(r_1)$ or $w \in \mathscr{L}(r_2)$.
– $w \in \mathscr{L}(r^+)$ (here r is an RE) iff $w = w_1w_2 \ldots w_m$ for some $m \geq 1$ and each $w_i \in \mathscr{L}(r)$.

FL^{res} formulas are inductively defined as follows, note that the last two items embody the restrictions.

– Every Boolean expression b is an FL^{res} formula.
– If φ is an FL^{res} formula, then $\neg\varphi$ is an FL^{res} formula.
– If φ_1 and φ_2 are FL^{res} formulas then $\varphi_1 \wedge \varphi_2$ is an FL^{res} formula.
– If φ is an FL^{res} formula, then $\mathsf{X}\varphi$ is an FL^{res} formula.
– If φ_1 and φ_2 are FL^{res} formulas, then $\varphi_1 \mathsf{U} \varphi_2$ is an FL^{res} formula.
– If r is an RE and φ an FL^{res} formula, then $r\mathsf{T}\varphi$ is an FL^{res} formula.
– If r_1 is an RE and r_2 is a restricted SERE, then $r_1 \mapsto r_2$ is an FL^{res} formula.

For the semantics of FL^{res} formulas, we focus our concerns on that w.r.t. finite words in this paper. Given an FL^{res} formula φ and a finite word w:

– If $\varphi = b$, then $w \models \varphi$ iff w^0 satisfies b.
– If $\varphi = \neg\varphi'$, then $w \models \varphi$ iff $w \not\models \varphi'$.
– If $\varphi = \varphi_1 \wedge \varphi_2$, then $w \models \varphi$ iff $w \models \varphi_1$ and $w \models \varphi_2$.
– If $\varphi = \mathsf{X}\varphi'$, then $w \models \varphi$ iff $|w| > 1$ and $w^{1\cdots} \models \varphi'$.
– If $\varphi = \varphi_1 \mathsf{U} \varphi_2$, then $w \models \varphi$ iff there is some $k < |w|$, such that $w^{k\cdots} \models \varphi_2$ and for each $0 \leq i < k$, $w^{i\cdots} \models \varphi_1$.
– If $\varphi = r\mathsf{T}\varphi'$, then $w \models \varphi$ iff for every $i < |w|$, $w^{0..i} \in \mathscr{L}(r)$ implies that $w^{i\cdots} \models \varphi'$.

- If $\varphi = r_1 \mapsto r_2$, then $w \models \varphi$ iff for every $i < |w|$, $w^{0..i} \in \mathscr{L}(r_1)$ implies that $w^{i..} \in \mathscr{L}(r_2)$.

Remark 1. Remind that in this paper, we explicitly exclude the empty word (ϵ) from standard regular expressions. In comparison to standard SEREs, the restricted version does not allow the former component to involve "&&" when doing concatenation. This would not change the essence of the expressiveness, for example, for a standard RE r with $\mathscr{L}(r) = \{\epsilon\} \cup \mathscr{L}(r')$, where r' is non-empty, then $r\mathsf{T}\varphi$ can be equivalently written as $\varphi \wedge (r'\mathsf{T}\varphi)$. However, such a minor restriction prevent state explosion in automata construction.

2.2 Two-Way Alternating Finite Automata

In this section, we revisit the notion of *two-way alternating finite automata* (2AFA, for short).

Given a set S, we denote by $\mathcal{B}^+(S)$ the class of *positive formulas* over S, it consists of formulas built up from members in S with $\wedge$ and $\vee$. For each $\theta \in \mathcal{B}^+(S)$, we use $\bar{\theta}$ to denote the *dual* of θ. In detail, $\bar{\theta}$ switches $\wedge$ and $\vee$ appearing in θ.

Given a subset S' of S and $\theta \in \mathcal{B}^+(S)$, we say S' *satisfies* θ if when assigning elements in S' to be *true* and elements in $S \backslash S'$ to be *false* then θ is evaluated to be *true*.

For example, suppose $S = \{s_1, s_2, s_3\}$ and $\theta = (s_1 \wedge s_2) \vee s_3$, then $\bar{\theta} = (s_1 \vee s_2) \wedge s_3$, both $\{s_1, s_3\}$ and $\{s_3\}$ satisfy θ.

A *tree* T is a subset of $\mathbb{N}^*$, which fulfills the "prefix-closed" property: namely, for each $r \in \mathbb{N}^*$ and $c \in \mathbb{N}$, $r \cdot c \in T$ implies $r \in T$ and $r \cdot (c + 1) \in T$ implies $r \cdot c \in T$. Each element in a tree is said to be a *node*, the node ϵ is the *root node*.

Given an arbitrary set S, an *S-labeled tree* is a tuple $\langle T, \rho \rangle$ where T is a tree and $\rho : T \to S$, is the *labeling function*.

A 2AFA is a tuple $\mathcal{A} = \langle \Sigma, Q, \delta, q_0, F \rangle$, where:

- Σ is the *alphabet*.
- Q is a finite set of *states*.
- $\delta : Q \times \Sigma \to \mathcal{B}^+(Q \times \{-1, 0, 1\})$, is the *transition function*.
- $q_0 \in Q$, is the *initial state*.
- $F \subseteq Q$, is the set of *final states*.

Given a word $w \in \Sigma^*$, a *run* of $\mathcal{A}$ over w is a $Q \times \mathbb{N}$-labeled finite tree $\langle T, \rho \rangle$ fulfilling the following requirements.

- $\rho(\epsilon) = (q_0, 0)$.
- For every non-leaf node $r \in T$ with $\rho(r) = (q, k)$, the set $\{(q', \Delta) \mid \exists c \in \mathbb{N},$ s.t. $r \cdot c \in T$ and $\rho(r \cdot c) = (q', k + \Delta)\}$ satisfies $\delta(q, w^k)$.

The run is *accepting* if every leaf node in the tree labeled with some element in $F \times \{|w|\}$.

w is said to be *accepted* by $\mathcal{A}$ if it has an accepting run of $\mathcal{A}$ over it. The class of (finite) words accepted by $\mathcal{A}$ is denoted by $\mathscr{L}(\mathcal{A})$.

Especially, a 2AFA $\langle \Sigma, Q, \delta, q, F \rangle$ is *nondeterministic* if for every $q \in Q$ and $a \in \Sigma$, $\delta(q, a)$ involves no $\wedge$; it is said to be *universal* if for every $q \in Q$ and $a \in \Sigma$, $\delta(q, a)$ involves no $\vee$; it is *deterministic* if it is both nondeterministic and universal.

A 2AFA $\langle \Sigma, Q, \delta, q, F \rangle$ is said to be *one-way* if for every $q \in Q$ and $a \in \Sigma$, $\delta(q, a) \in \mathcal{B}^+(Q \times \{1\})$; is said to be *stuttering* if for every $q \in Q$ and $a \in \Sigma$, $\delta(q, a) \in \mathcal{B}^+(Q \times \{0, 1\})$.

From now on, we use four-letter acronyms to describe the type of automata. The first two letters are selected from $\{2, \epsilon, 1\}$ and $\{A, N, U, D\}$, respectively, they describe the transition structure of the automata. The last two letters are fixed to be 'F' and 'A', since we always use the *finite* acceptance condition automata. For example, we write 1NFA for the abbreviation of one-way nondeterministic finite automata and ϵAFA for stuttering alternating finite automata.

As usual, for a 1NFA $\langle \Sigma, Q, \delta, q_0, F \rangle$, we also write the transition function δ into the form of $Q \times \Sigma \to 2^Q$.

Suppose the 2AFA $\mathcal{A} = \langle \Sigma, Q, \delta, q_0, F \rangle$, we use $\overline{\mathcal{A}}$ to denote its *dual automaton*, which is the 2AFA $\langle \Sigma, Q, \overline{\delta}, q_0, Q \backslash F \rangle$, where $\overline{\delta}(q, a) = \overline{\delta(q, a)}$ for every $q \in Q$ and $a \in \Sigma$.

Theorem 1. *[16] Let Σ be the alphabet of $\mathcal{A}$, then $\mathcal{L}(\overline{\mathcal{A}}) = \Sigma^* \backslash \mathcal{L}(\mathcal{A})$.*

Remark 2. The proof of the above theorem is given w.r.t. alternating automata on infinite trees. However, it is easy to be adapted to the special case of 2AFAs.

3   From FL^{res} to 2AFA

We now start to introduce the automata decision procedure of FL^{res} formulas. We in this section first show how to convert an FL^{res} formula into a 2AFA, and then give the conversion from 2AFA to 1NFA in the next section.

First of all, for each restricted SERE r, we construct a 2AFA $\mathcal{A}_r$, such that $\mathcal{L}(\mathcal{A}_r) = \mathcal{L}(r)$. This construction is inductively given by the structure of r.

1. For a Boolean expression b, the automaton $\mathcal{A}_b$ is $\langle 2^{AP}, \{q_0, q_1, q_2\}, \delta, q_0, \{q_1\} \rangle$, where $\delta(q_1, l) = \delta(q_2, l) = (q_2, 1)$ for every $l \subseteq AP$,

$$\delta(q_0, l) = \begin{cases} (q_1, 1), & \text{if } l \text{ satisfies } b \\ (q_2, 1), & \text{otherwise} \end{cases}.$$

2. Given an RE r_1 and a restricted SERE r_2, suppose $\mathcal{A}_{r_i} = \langle 2^{AP}, Q_i, \delta_i, q_{0i}, F_i \rangle$ $(i = 1, 2)$, then $\mathcal{A}_{r_1; r_2} = \langle 2^{AP}, Q_1 \cup Q_2, \delta, q_{01}, F_2 \rangle$ and $\mathcal{A}_{r_1 : r_2} = \langle 2^{AP}, Q_1 \cup Q_2, \delta', q_{01}, F_2 \rangle$, where[3]

$$\delta(q, l) = \begin{cases} \delta_1(q, l), & \text{if } q \in Q_1 \backslash F_1 \\ \delta_1(q, l) \vee (q_{02}, 0), & \text{if } q \in F_1 \\ \delta_2(q, l), & \text{if } q \in Q_2 \end{cases}$$

---

[3]   We assume $Q_1 \cap Q_2 = \emptyset$ in the sequel. Otherwise, just need a systematic state renaming.

and

$$\delta'(q,l) = \begin{cases} \delta_1(q,l), & \text{if } q \in Q_1 \backslash F_1 \\ \delta_1(q,l) \vee (q_{02}, -1), & \text{if } q \in F_1 \\ \delta_2(q,l), & \text{if } q \in Q_2 \end{cases}.$$

3. Suppose r_1 and r_2 are two restricted SEREs, and $\mathcal{A}_{r_i} = \langle 2^{AP}, Q_i, \delta_i, q_{0i}, F_i \rangle$ $(i = 1, 2)$. Then $\mathcal{A}_{r_1 \| r_2} = \langle 2^{AP}, Q_1 \cup Q_2 \cup \{q_0\}, \delta, q_0, F_1 \cup F_2 \rangle$ and $\mathcal{A}_{r_1 \&\& r_2} = \langle 2^{AP}, Q_1 \cup Q_2 \cup \{q_0\}, \delta', q_0, F_1 \cup F_2 \rangle$, where $q_0 \notin Q_1 \cup Q_2$ and for each $l \subseteq AP$,

$$\delta(q,l) = \begin{cases} \delta_1(q,l), & \text{if } q \in Q_1 \\ \delta_2(q,l), & \text{if } q \in Q_2 \\ (q_{01}, 0) \vee (q_{02}, 0), & \text{if } q = q_0 \end{cases}$$

and

$$\delta'(q,l) = \begin{cases} \delta_1(q,l), & \text{if } q \in Q_1 \\ \delta_2(q,l), & \text{if } q \in Q_2 \\ (q_{01}, 0) \wedge (q_{02}, 0), & \text{if } q = q_0 \end{cases}.$$

4. Suppose r is an RE and $\mathcal{A}_r = \langle 2^{AP}, Q, \delta, q_0, F \rangle$, then $\mathcal{A}_{r+} = \langle 2^{AP}, Q, \delta', q_0, F \rangle$, where for each $l \subseteq AP$,

$$\delta'(q,l) = \begin{cases} \delta(q,l), & \text{if } q \notin F \\ \delta(q,l) \vee (q_0, 0), & \text{if } q \in F \end{cases}.$$

The correctness of the above construction can be inductively proved according to definition. Since restricted SEREs could never generate the word ϵ, we can safely use the "backward" transitions in constructing two-way automata.

Subsequently, we give the procedure to convert an FL^{res} formula φ to a 2AFA $\mathcal{A}_\varphi$ with $\mathcal{O}(|\varphi|)$ states. This is also an inductive construction based on the formula structure.

1. The base case is $\varphi = b$. Then, we just let $\mathcal{A}_\varphi = \langle 2^{AP}, \{q_0, q_1, q_2\}, \delta, q_0, \{q_1\} \rangle$, where for every $l \subseteq AP$, $\delta(q_1, l) = (q_1, 1)$, $\delta(q_2, l) = (q_2, 1)$ and

$$\delta(q_0, l) = \begin{cases} (q_1, 1), & \text{if } l \text{ satisfies } b \\ (q_2, 1), & \text{otherwise} \end{cases}.$$

Clearly, $w \models \varphi$ if and only if $w \in \mathscr{L}(\mathcal{A}_\varphi)$ in this case.
2. If $\varphi = \neg\varphi'$, then just let $\mathcal{A}_\varphi = \overline{\mathcal{A}_{\varphi'}}$. From induction hypothesis and Theorem 1, we have $w \models \varphi$ iff $w \not\models \varphi'$ iff $w \notin \mathscr{L}(\mathcal{A}_{\varphi'})$ iff $w \in \mathscr{L}(\mathcal{A}_\varphi)$.
3. If $\varphi = \varphi_1 \wedge \varphi_2$, and suppose $\mathcal{A}_{\varphi_i} = \langle 2^{AP}, Q_i, \delta_i, q_{0i}, F_i \rangle$ $(i = 1, 2)$, then let $A = \langle 2^{AP}, Q_1 \cup Q_2 \cup \{q_0\}, \delta, q_0, F_1 \cup F_2 \rangle$, where $q_0 \notin Q_1 \cup Q_2$, $Q_1 \cap Q_2 = \emptyset$ and for each $l \subseteq AP$,

$$\delta(q,l) = \begin{cases} \delta_1(q,l), & \text{if } q \in Q_1 \\ \delta_2(q,l), & \text{if } q \in Q_2 \\ (q_{01}, 0) \wedge (q_{02}, 0), & \text{if } q = q_0 \end{cases}.$$

It is straightforward to check that $\mathscr{L}(\mathcal{A}_\varphi) = \mathscr{L}(\mathcal{A}_{\varphi_1}) \cap \mathscr{L}(\mathcal{A}_{\varphi_2})$. By induction hypothesis, $w \in \mathscr{L}(\mathcal{A}_\varphi)$ iff $w \in \mathscr{L}(\mathcal{A}_{\varphi_1})$ and $w \in \mathscr{L}(\mathcal{A}_{\varphi_2})$ iff $w \models \varphi_1$ and $w \models \varphi_2$ iff $w \models \varphi$.

4. If $\varphi = \mathsf{X}\varphi'$ and suppose $\mathcal{A}_{\varphi'} = \langle 2^{AP}, Q, \delta', q_0', F \rangle$, then $\mathcal{A}_{\varphi} = \langle 2^{AP}, Q \cup \{q_0\}, \delta, q_0, F \rangle$, where $q_0 \notin Q$ and for each $l \subseteq AP$,

$$\delta(q, l) = \begin{cases} \delta'(q, l), & \text{if } q \neq q_0 \\ (q_0', 1), & \text{if } q = q_0 \end{cases}.$$

It is clear that $w \in \mathscr{L}(\mathcal{A}_{\varphi})$ iff $w^{1\cdots} \in \mathscr{L}(\mathcal{A}_{\varphi'})$ iff $w^{1\cdots} \models \varphi'$ iff $w \models \varphi$.

5. If $\varphi = \varphi_1 \cup \varphi_2$ and suppose that $\mathcal{A}_{\varphi_i} = \langle 2^{AP}, Q_i, \delta_i, q_{0i}, F_i \rangle$ $(i = 1, 2)$, then let $\mathcal{A}_{\varphi} = \langle 2^{AP}, Q_1 \cup Q_2 \cup \{q_0\}, \delta, F_1 \cup F_2 \rangle$, where $q_0 \notin Q_1 \cup Q_2$ and for each $l \subseteq AP$,

$$\delta(q, l) = \begin{cases} \delta_1(q, l), & \text{if } q \in Q_1 \\ \delta_2(q, l), & \text{if } q \in Q_2 \\ (q_{02}, 0) \vee ((q_{01}, 0) \wedge (q_0, 1)), & \text{if } q = q_0 \end{cases}.$$

Clearly, a word $w \in \mathscr{L}(\mathcal{A}_{\varphi})$ iff either $w \in \mathscr{L}(\mathcal{A}_{\varphi_2})$ or $w \in \mathscr{L}(\mathcal{A}_{\varphi_1})$ and $w^{1\cdots} \in \mathscr{L}(\mathcal{A}_{\varphi})$. By induction hypothesis, that is equivalent to say $w \in \mathscr{L}(\mathcal{A}_{\varphi})$ iff either $w^{0\cdots} \models \varphi_2$ or $w^{0\cdots} \models \varphi_1$. Repeat this discussion, since w is finite word, we can eventually infer that $w \in \mathscr{L}(\mathcal{A}_{\varphi})$ iff $w^{i\cdots} \models \varphi_2$ for some i and $w^{j\cdots} \models \varphi_1$ for all $j < i$. Thus, $w \in \mathscr{L}(\mathcal{A}_{\varphi})$ iff $w \models \varphi_1 \cup \varphi_2$.

6. The last two cases are almost identical. If $\varphi = r\mathsf{T}\varphi'$ (resp. $\varphi = r \mapsto r'$), assume $\mathcal{A}_r = \langle 2^{AP}, Q_r, \delta_r, q_{0_r}, F_r \rangle$, $\mathcal{A}_{\varphi'} = \langle 2^{AP}, Q_{\varphi'}, \delta_{\varphi'}, q_{0_{\varphi'}}, F_{\varphi'} \rangle$ (resp. $\mathcal{A}_{r'} = \langle 2^{AP}, Q_{r'}, \delta_{r'}, q_{0_{r'}}, F_{r'} \rangle$). Then, consider the automaton $\mathcal{C}_{\varphi} = \langle 2^{AP}, Q_r \cup Q_{\varphi'}, \delta, q_{0_r}, Q_{\varphi'} \backslash F_{\varphi'} \rangle$ (resp. $\mathcal{C}_{\varphi} = \langle 2^{AP}, Q_r \cup Q_{r'}, \delta', q_{0_r}, Q_{r'} \backslash F_{r'} \rangle$), where for each $l \subseteq AP$,

$$\delta(q, l) = \begin{cases} \delta_r(q, l), & \text{if } q \in Q_r \backslash F_r \\ \delta_r(q, l) \vee (q_{0_{\varphi'}}, -1), & \text{if } q \in F_r \\ \delta_{\varphi'}(q, l), & \text{if } q \in Q_{\varphi'} \end{cases}$$

(resp.

$$\delta(q, l) = \begin{cases} \delta_r(q, l), & \text{if } q \in Q_r \backslash F_r \\ \delta_r(q, l) \vee (q_{0_{r'}}, -1), & \text{if } q \in F_r \\ \delta_{r'}(q, l), & \text{if } q \in Q_{r'} \end{cases}$$

)

Since r is an RE, it is clear that a word w is accepted by $\mathcal{C}_{\varphi}$ iff there is some $k < |w|$ such that $w^{0..k} \in \mathscr{L}(r)$ and $w^{k\cdots} \notin \mathscr{L}(\mathcal{A}_{\varphi'})$ (resp. $w^{k\cdots} \notin \mathscr{L}(r')$). Therefore, $w \in \mathscr{L}(\mathcal{C}_{\varphi})$ iff $w \not\models \varphi$. Consequently, let $\mathcal{A}_{\varphi} = \overline{\mathcal{C}_{\varphi}}$, then for any $w \in (2^{AP})^*$, $w \in \mathscr{L}(\mathcal{A}_{\varphi})$ iff $w \models \varphi$.

Therefore, for the logic FL^{res}, we have the following theorem.

Theorem 2. *Given an FL^{res} formula φ, there is a 2AFA $\mathcal{A}_{\varphi}$ with $\mathcal{O}(|\varphi|)$ states, such that for each $w \in (2^{AP})^*$, $w \in \mathscr{L}(\mathcal{A}_{\varphi})$ if and only if $w \models \varphi$.*

4   From 2AFA to 1NFA

Much work has been done for converting two-way automata to one-way automata.

For example, Birget [2] has shown that a 2AFA can be transformed to a 1AFA with quadratic blow-up. It is well known that an n-state 1AFA can be reduced to an equivalent 1NFA with 2^n states. Thus, one can convert a 2AFA to a 1NFA with $2^{\mathcal{O}(n^2)}$ states.

Nevertheless, based on the speciality of FL^{res}, we in this paper give a two-step construction: We first provide a conversion with $2^{\mathcal{O}(n^2)}$ state blow-up. Subsequently, via observing the restriction of the formulas' form and the naïve construction, we show how to sharpen the state set of the resulting automaton with size $2^{\mathcal{O}(n)}$.

4.1   A Naïve Construction

We now consider a direct conversion from 2AFA to 1NFA, this approach also causes $2^{\mathcal{O}(n^2)}$ state blow-up, and it is used in translating ϵAFA to 1NFA, which is discussed in the next section.

Given a set S, a *staged graph* over S is a labeled graph $\mathcal{G} = \langle V, E, \lambda \rangle$, where:

- V is a finite set of *vertices*.
- $\lambda : V \to S \times \mathbb{N}$, is the *labeling function* fulfilling that $v_1 \neq v_2$ implies $\lambda(v_1) \neq \lambda(v_2)$.
- $E \subseteq V \times V$ is the set of *edges*. Moreover, given two vertices v and v' with $\lambda(v) = (s, k)$ and $\lambda(v') = (s', k')$, then $\langle v, v' \rangle \in E$ only if $k - k' \in \{-1, 0, 1\}$.

We say a vertex v is a *k-vertex* if $\lambda(v) \in S \times \{k\}$. We say an edge $\langle v, v' \rangle$ is a *k-edge* if v is a k-vertex, moreover,

- $\langle v, v' \rangle$ is *forward* if v' is a $(k+1)$-vertex;
- $\langle v, v' \rangle$ is *stuttering* if v' is a k-vertex;
- $\langle v, v' \rangle$ is *backward* if v' is a $(k-1)$-vertex.

Given a staged graph $\mathcal{G} = \langle V, E, \lambda \rangle$, we define its *degree* $\deg(\mathcal{G}) = \max\{k \mid \exists v, v' \in V, (v, v') \in E, \lambda(v) \in V \times \{k\}\}$.

A *path* of $\mathcal{G}$ is a finite or infinite vertex sequence $v_1 v_2 \ldots$ where each $\langle v_i, v_{i+1} \rangle \in E$.

Given a staged graph $\mathcal{G} = \langle V, E, \lambda \rangle$ over S, its *k-th stage*, denoted by $\mathcal{G}[k]$, is the sub staged graph $\langle V_{k-1} \cup V_k \cup V_{k+1}, E_k, \lambda_k \rangle$, where $V_i = \{v \mid \lambda(v) \in S \times \{i\}\}$, $E_i = \{(v, v') \in E \mid \lambda(v) \in S \times \{i\}\}$ and λ_i is the restriction of λ on $V_{i-1} \cup V_i \cup V_{i+1}$.

Given a 2AFA $\mathcal{A} = \langle \Sigma, Q, \delta, q_0, F \rangle$ a word $w \in \Sigma^*$, and a staged graph $\mathcal{G} = \langle V, E, \lambda \rangle$ over Q, we say $\mathcal{G}$ is an *acceptance witness* of w w.r.t $\mathcal{A}$ if:

(A) $\deg(\mathcal{G}) = |w| - 1$, and there is a unique vertex $v_0 \in V$ such that $\lambda(v) = (q_0, 0)$.

(B) For each $v \in V$ with $\lambda(v) = (q, k)$, the set $\{(q', -1) \mid \exists v' \in V$ s.t. $(v, v') \in E$ and $\lambda(v') = (q', k-1)\} \cup \{(q', 0) \mid \exists v' \in V$ s.t. $(v, v') \in E$ and $\lambda(v') = (q', k)\} \cup \{(q', 1) \mid \exists v' \in V$ s.t. $(v, v') \in E$ and $\lambda(v') = (q', k+1)\}$ satisfies $\delta(q, w^k)$.

(C) There is at least one $|w|$-vertex; and for each $|w|$-vertex v, we have $\lambda(v) \in F \times \{|w|\}$.

(D) There is no infinite path in $\mathcal{G}$, and every maximal path ends with a $|w|$-vertex.

(E) Each vertex is initially reachable, namely, for each $v \in V$, there is a path $v_0 v_1 \ldots v_k = v$ involved in $\mathcal{G}$.

Lemma 1. *Given a 2AFA $\mathcal{A} = \langle \Sigma, Q, \delta, q_0, F \rangle$ and a word $w \in \Sigma^*$, $w \in \mathscr{L}(\mathcal{A})$ if and only if there is an acceptance witness of w with respect to $\mathcal{A}$.*

Proof. We say a run $\langle T, \rho \rangle$ is *memoryless* provided that for every $x, x' \in T$, $\rho(x) = \rho(x')$ implies: if $\exists x \cdot c \in T$, then $\exists x' \cdot c' \in T$, such that $\rho(x' \cdot c') = \rho(x \cdot c)$.

Clearly, $\mathcal{A}$ has an accepting run over w if and only if $\mathcal{A}$ has a memoryless accepting run over w. Indeed, if $\rho(x) = \rho(y)$, we may replace the subtree rooted at y by the subtree rooted at x.

If $w \in \mathscr{L}(\mathcal{A})$ and (T, ρ) is a (memoryless) accepting run of $\mathcal{A}$ over w, then we create the staged graph as follows:

- For each state q and integer $0 \leq i \leq |w|$, we create a vertex v and give its label to (q, i).
- We add an edge to the graph from the vertex labeled (q, i) to the vertex labeled (q', i') iff there is some $x \in T$ with $\rho(c) = (q, i)$ and some $x \cdot c \in T$ with $\rho(x \cdot c) = (q', i)$.
- Set the vertex labeled with $(q_0, 0)$ as the initial vertex, and then remove all the vertices those are not initially reachable.

It can be directly checked if this staged graph fulfills constraints (A)–(C) of the accepting witness. Notice that the run tree is memoryless, thus each path in the staged graph uniquely corresponds to a path in the tree. Because the tree is finite, there's no infinite path in the graph. Moreover, since each leaf of T must be labeled by a tuple $(q_f, |w|)$ for some final state q_f of $\mathcal{A}$, hence each maximal path must end with a $|w|$-vertex. Therefore, this stage graph is an accepting witness of w w.r.t. $\mathcal{A}$.

Conversely, let $\langle V, E, \lambda \rangle$ be an accepting witness of w w.r.t. $\mathcal{A}$, then we may construct an accepting run $\langle T, \rho \rangle$ of $\mathcal{A}$ over w by the following manner.

- Create a root vertex ϵ, and let $\rho(\epsilon) = (q_0, 0)$, where q_0 is the initial state of $\mathcal{A}$. Since $\langle V, E, \lambda \rangle$ is an accepting witness, there is some $v_0 \in V$ with $\lambda(v_0) = (q_0, 0)$.
- Inductively, for an already-created node $x \in T$, assume that $\rho(x) = (q, i)$ and let $v \in V$ be the vertex fulfilling $\lambda(v) = (q, i)$. Then, for each $(v, v_c) \in E$ $(c = 0, 1, \ldots)$, we create a child $x \cdot c$ of x, and set $\rho(x \cdot c) = \lambda(v_c)$.

Since no infinite path in the graph, the labeled tree must be finite. From the third and the fourth constraints, we have that what labeled at each leaf node of T must belong to $F \times |w|$ (where F is $\mathcal{A}$'s final state set). Hence (T, ρ) is an accepting run of $\mathcal{A}$ over w. According to the definition, $w \in \mathscr{L}(\mathcal{A})$. $\qquad \square$

Given a staged graph $\mathcal{G} = \langle V, E, \lambda \rangle$ over Q, for each $0 \le i \le \deg(\mathcal{G})$, we can encode $\mathcal{G}[i]$ with a tuple (E_B, E_S, E_F), where each of E_B, E_S and E_F belongs to $2^{Q \times Q}$. i.e,

- $(q, q') \in E_B$ iff there is an edge $(v, v') \in E$ such that $\lambda(v) = (q, i)$ and $\lambda(v') = (q', i-1)$;
- $(q, q') \in E_S$ iff there is an edge $(v, v') \in E$ such that $\lambda(v) = (q, i)$ and $\lambda(v') = (q', i)$;
- $(q, q') \in E_F$ iff there is an edge $(v, v') \in E$ such that $\lambda(v) = (q, i)$ and $\lambda(v') = (q', i+1)$;

Subsequently, the staged graph $\mathcal{G}$ can be encoded with a word W over the alphabet $(2^{Q \times Q})^3$, where $|W| = \deg(\mathcal{G}) + 1$ and each W^i is the encoding of $\mathcal{G}[i]$. With this, we can represent a staged graph with a finite alphabet and without losing of any information.

The conversion from 2AFA to 1NFA is based on the above encoding. Given a 2AFA $\mathcal{A}$, we first construct a 1NFA $\widehat{\mathcal{N}}$ with alphabet $\Sigma \times (2^{Q \times Q})^3$, such that $(l_0, N_0) \ldots (l_m, N_m)$ is accepted by $\widehat{\mathcal{N}}$ iff $N_0 \ldots N_m$ is an encode of the acceptance witness of $l_0 \ldots l_m$ w.r.t. $\mathcal{A}$.

To fulfill this, the states must provide sufficient information to check the aforementioned constraints. Constraints (A)–(C) can be immediately checked. However, to prevent the generation of infinite path, we have to guarantee there is no loops in the staged graph—since the graph is finite, an infinite path exists iff a loop exists. To do this, we need to remember all the tuples (q, q') such that some vertex labeled with (q, i) can reach the vertex labeled with (q', i) via a path involved in the previous stages. Thus, we must also memorize the forward edges in the previous stage. Notably, some i-vertices can only be reached from the initial vertex via an $(i+1)$-vertex. To check the last constraint, we employ an additional component, which memorizes such vertices in the present stage. These vertices must be connected with the vertices in the next stage via some backward edges.

Suppose $\mathcal{A} = \langle \Sigma, Q, \delta, q_0, F \rangle$, then the 1NFA $\widehat{\mathcal{N}} = \langle \widehat{\Sigma}, \widehat{Q}, \widehat{\delta}, \widehat{q_0}, \widehat{F} \rangle$, where:

1. $\widehat{\Sigma} = \Sigma \times (2^{Q \times Q})^3$.
2. $\widehat{Q}$ consists a distinct state $\widehat{q_0}$ and all the tuples of (P, O, E, R), where:
   - $P \subseteq Q$, which represents the states labeled in the current stage.
   - $O \subseteq P$, which memorizes the states (corresponding to vertices) can only be reached via some backward edges in the next stage.
   - $E \subseteq Q \times Q$ and $\{q \mid \exists q', (q, q') \in E\} \subseteq P$, this component memorizes the forward edges in the current stage.
   - $R \subseteq P \times P$, and for each $q \in Q$, $(q, q) \notin R$. Assuming the current stage is the i-th stage, then $(q, q') \in R$ stands for that there is a path involved in the previous stages which starts from the vertex labeled with (q, i) ends to the vertex labeled with (q', i).
3. Given a letter $a = \langle l, (E_B, E_S, E_F) \rangle$, the state $(P', O', E', R') \in \widehat{Q}$ belongs to $\widehat{\delta}(\widehat{q_0}, a)$ only if:

- $q_0 \in P'$.
- $E_B = \emptyset$, $E_F \neq \emptyset$;
- $(q_1, q_2) \in E_S$ implies $q_1 \in P'$ and $q_2 \in P'$; and $(q_1, q_2) \in E_F$ implies $q_1 \in P'$.
- $E' = E_F$.
- R' fulfills: (1). $E_S \subseteq R'$; (2). $(q_1, q_2) \in R'$ and $(q_2, q_3) \in R'$ implies $(q_1, q_3) \in R'$.
- $O' = P' \backslash H'$, where H' is the minimal set of states fulfilling: 1) $q_0 \in H'$; 2) $q_1 \in H'$ and $(q_1, q_2) \in E_S$ implies $q_2 \in H'$.
- For every $q \in P'$, the set $\{(q', 0) \mid (q, q') \in E_S\} \cup \{(q'', 1) \mid (q, q'') \in E_F\}$ satisfies $\delta(q, l)$.

For a state $(P, O, E, R) \in \widehat{Q}$ and the letter $a = \langle l, (E_B, E_S, E_F) \rangle \in \widehat{\Sigma}$, the state $(P', O', E', R') \in \widehat{Q}$ is in $\widehat{\delta}((P, O, E, R), a)$ only if:
- $E_F \neq \emptyset$ and for each $q \in O$, there is a q' such that $(q', q) \in E_B$.
- For each $(q, q') \in E$ implies $q \in P$ and $q' \in P'$.
- $(q_1, q_2) \in E_S$ implies $q_1 \in P'$ and $q_2 \in P'$; $(q_1, q_2) \in E_F$ implies $q_1 \in P'$; $(q_1, q_2) \in E_B$ implies $q_1 \in P'$ and $q_2 \in P$.
- $E' = E_F$.
- R' is the minimal set fulfills: (1). $E_S \subseteq R'$; (2). $(q_1, q_2) \in E_B$, $(q_2, q_3) \in R$, $(q_3, q_4) \in E$ implies $(q_1, q_4) \in R'$; (3). $(q_1, q_2) \in R'$ and $(q_2, q_3) \in R'$ implies $(q_1, q_3) \in R'$. (4). for every $q \in Q$, $(q, q) \notin R'$.
- $O' = P' \backslash H'$. Where H' is the minimal set fulfilling: (1). $q_1 \in P \backslash O$ and $(q_1, q_2) \in E$ implies $q_2 \in H'$; (2). $q_1 \in H'$ and $(q_1, q_2) \in R'$ implies $q_2 \in H'$.
- For every $q \in P'$, the set $\{(q', -1) \mid (q, q') \in E_B\} \cup \{(q''0) \mid (q, q'') \in E_S\} \cup \{(q''', 1) \mid (q, q''') \in E_F\}$ satisfies $\delta(q, l)$.

4. $(P, O, E, R) \in \widehat{F}$ only if $O = \emptyset$ and $E \neq \emptyset$, $(q, q') \in E$ implies $q' \in F$.

Given a 1NFA $\mathcal{A}_1 = \langle \Sigma_1 \times \Sigma_2, Q, \delta_1, q_0, F \rangle$, we say that the 1NFA $\mathcal{A}_2 = \langle \Sigma_1, Q, \delta_2, q_0, F \rangle$ is the *projection* of $\mathcal{A}_1$ on Σ_1 (denoted by $\mathcal{A}_2 = \mathcal{A}_1|_{\Sigma_1}$) if: for each $q \in Q$ and $a \in \Sigma_1$, $q' \in \delta_2(q, a)$ iff $\exists b \in \Sigma_2$, such that $q' \in \delta_1(q, (a, b))$.

Lemma 2. *Given a 1NFA $\mathcal{A}_1 = \langle \Sigma_1 \times \Sigma_2, Q, \delta_1, q_0, F \rangle$, and let the 1NFA $\mathcal{A}_2 = \mathcal{A}_1|_{\Sigma_1}$. Then $l_0 \ldots l_m \in \mathcal{L}(\mathcal{A}_2)$ if and only if there is a word $l'_1 \ldots l'_m \in (\Sigma_2)^*$ such that $(l_0, l'_0) \ldots (l_m, l'_m) \in \mathcal{L}(\mathcal{A}_1)$.*

Proof. Since $\mathcal{A}_1$ and $\mathcal{A}_2$ are 1NFAs, a run of $\mathcal{A}_i$ ($i = 1,2$) over a word w can be viewed as a state sequence $q_0 q_1 \ldots q_{|w|}$, where $q_{|w|} \in F$ and each $q_{k+1} \in \delta_i(q_k, w^k)$ (when $i = 1$, $w^k \in \Sigma_1 \times \Sigma_2$; when $i = 2$, $w^k \in \Sigma_1$).

Given a word $w \in (\Sigma_1)^*$ and let it be $l_0 \ldots l_m$. If $w \in \mathcal{L}(\mathcal{A}_2)$, then there is a sequence $q_0 q_1 \ldots q_{m+1} \in Q^*$, where $q_{m+1} \in F$ and each $q_{k+1} \in \delta_2(q_k, l_k)$. Since $\mathcal{A}_2 = \mathcal{A}_1|_{\Sigma_1}$, for each $0 \leq k \leq m$, there is a l'_k such that $q_{k+1} \in \delta_1(q_k, (l_k, l'_k))$. Therefore, the word $(l_0, l'_0) \ldots (l_m, l'_m) \in \mathcal{L}(\mathcal{A}_1)$.

Conversely, suppose that $l'_0 \ldots l'_m \in (\Sigma_2)^*$ such that $(l_0, l'_0) \ldots (l_m, l'_m) \in \mathcal{L}(\mathcal{A}_1)$. Let the corresponding accepting run be $p_0 \ldots p_m$, where each $p_{k+1} \in \delta_1(p_k, (l_k, l'_k))$. Since $\mathcal{A}_2 = \mathcal{A}_1|_{\Sigma_1}$, we have each $p_{k+1} \in \delta_1(p_k, l_k)$. Therefore, $p_0 \ldots p_m$ is an accepting run of $\mathcal{A}_2$ over w. Hence $w \in \mathcal{L}(\mathcal{A}_2)$. $\square$

Now, let $\mathcal{N} = \widehat{\mathcal{N}}|_\Sigma$, then given a word $w = w^0 \ldots w^{m-1}$, we have: $w \in \mathscr{L}(\mathcal{A})$ iff there is an accepting witness of $\mathcal{A}$ over w iff there is some $W = (w^0, a^0) \ldots (w^{m-1}, a^{m-1}) \in \mathscr{L}(\widehat{\mathcal{N}})$ (where each $a^i \in (2^{Q \times Q})^3$) iff $w \in \mathscr{L}(\mathcal{N})$. Thus, we have the following theorem.

Theorem 3. *Given an n-state 2AFA $\mathcal{A}$, there is a 1NFA $\mathcal{N}$ with $2^{\mathcal{O}(n^2)}$ states such that $\mathscr{L}(\mathcal{A}) = \mathscr{L}(\mathcal{N})$.*

4.2   Sharpen the Exponent of State Space Size

In the previous section, we give a transformation from 2AFAs and then to 1NFAs, which causes a quadratically exponential state blow-up. Indeed, for the FL^{res} formulas, it is possible to transform them into 1NFAs with $2^{\mathcal{O}(n)}$ state blow-up, if we further take the speciality of such formulas into consideration.

In the previous construction, only in the following two cases we need "backward" transitions:

- When constructing automata for the restricted SEREs being of the form $r_1: r_2$.
- When constructing automata for the FL^{res} formulas being of the form $r\mathsf{T}\varphi$ or $r \mapsto r'$.

The optimization is based on the following observation:

- When constructing automata for restricted SEREs, if the input is an RE, then what we get must be an ϵNFA.
- In FL^{res}, for the restricted SERE $r_1: r_2$, we require that r_1 must be an RE; for the formula $r\mathsf{T}\varphi$ or $r \mapsto r'$, we also require that r is an RE.

On the other hand, an ϵNFA can be translated to a 1NFA with the same state set: Given an ϵNFA $\langle \Sigma, Q, \delta, q_0, F \rangle$, we define the function $\mathcal{E}_\delta : Q \times \Sigma \to 2^Q$. $\mathcal{E}_\delta(q, a)$ is the minimal subset of Q fulfilling:

- if $\{(q', 0)\}$ satisfies $\delta(q, a)$ then $q' \in \mathcal{E}_\delta(q, a)$.
- if $q' \in \mathcal{E}_\delta(q, a)$ and $\{(q'', 0)\}$ satisfies $\delta(q', a)$ then $q' \in \mathcal{E}_\delta(q, a)$.

Subsequently, we let $\mathcal{F}_\delta(q, a) = \{q' \mid (q', 1) \text{ satisfies } \delta(q, a)\}$. Then, consider the 1NFA $\langle \Sigma, Q, \delta', q_0, F \rangle$, where

$$\delta'(q, a) = \bigvee_{q' \in \mathcal{F}_\delta(q,a)} ((q', 1) \vee \bigvee_{q'' \in \mathcal{E}_\delta(q',a)} (q'', 1)),$$

it accepts precisely the same language of the given ϵNFA.

Therefore, for each RE r, we may construct a 1NFA with $\mathcal{O}(|r|)$ states, which recognizes the same language.

We now adapt the existing construction and show that:

- For each restricted SERE r, there is an ϵAFA $\mathcal{A}_r$, such that $\mathscr{L}(r) = \mathscr{L}(\mathcal{A}_r)$. It suffices to modify the construction of the restricted SEREs being of the form $r_1 : r_2$ as follows:

  Given the restricted SERE $r_1 : r_2$, suppose that the 1NFA for r_1 is $\mathcal{A}_{r_1} = \langle 2^{AP}, Q_1, \delta_1, q_{01}, F_1 \rangle$ and the ϵAFA for the restricted SERE r_2 is $\mathcal{A}_{r_2} = \langle 2^{AP}, Q_2, \delta_2, q_{02}, F_2 \rangle$. Then let $\mathcal{A}_{r_1 : r_2} = \langle 2^{AP}, Q_1 \cup Q_2, \delta, q_{01}, F_2 \rangle$, where for each $l \subseteq AP$,

$$
\delta(q, l) = \begin{cases} \delta_2(q, l), & \text{if } q \in Q_2 \\ \delta_1(q, l) \vee \delta_2(q_0, l), & \text{if } \exists q_f \in Q_1 \text{ such that} \{(q_f, 1)\} \text{ satisfies } \delta_1(q, l) \\ \delta_1(q, l), & \text{otherwise} \end{cases}
$$

- For each FL^{res} formula φ, there is an ϵAFA $\mathcal{A}_\varphi$, such that $w \models \varphi$ iff $w \in \mathscr{L}(\mathcal{A}_\varphi)$.

  It suffices to modify the automata construction for the FL^{res} formulas being of the form $r \mathsf{T} \varphi$ or $r \mapsto r'$ as follows.

  If $\varphi = r \mathsf{T} \varphi'$ (resp. $\varphi = r \mapsto r'$), assume the 1NFA $\mathcal{A}_r = \langle 2^{AP}, Q_r, \delta_r, q_{0_r}, F_r \rangle$, the ϵAFA $\mathcal{A}_{\varphi'} = \langle 2^{AP}, Q_{\varphi'}, \delta_{\varphi'}, q_{0_{\varphi'}}, F_{\varphi'} \rangle$ (resp. $\mathcal{A}_{r'} = \langle 2^{AP}, Q_{r'}, \delta_{r'}, q_{0_{r'}}, F_{r'} \rangle$). Then, we first construct the automaton $\mathcal{C}_\varphi = \langle 2^{AP}, Q_r \cup Q_{\varphi'}, \delta, q_{0_r}, Q_{\varphi'} \backslash F_{\varphi'} \rangle$ (resp. $\mathcal{C}_\varphi = \langle 2^{AP}, Q_r \cup Q_{r'}, \delta', q_{0_r}, Q_{r'} \backslash F_{r'} \rangle$), where for each $l \subseteq AP$,

$$
\delta(q, l) = \begin{cases} \overline{\delta_{\varphi'}(q, l)}, & \text{if } q \in Q_{\varphi'} \\ \delta_r(q, l) \vee \delta_{\varphi'}(q_{0_{\varphi'}}, l), & q \in Q_r \text{ and } \exists q_f \in F_r \text{ such that } q_f \in \delta_r(q, l) \\ \delta_r(q, l), & \text{otherwise} \end{cases}
$$

(resp.

$$
\delta(q, l) = \begin{cases} \overline{\delta_{r'}(q, l)}, & \text{if } q \in Q_{r'} \\ \delta_r(q, l) \vee \delta_{r'}(q_{0_{r'}}, l), & q \in Q_r \text{ and } \exists q_f \in F_r \text{ such that } q_f \in \delta_r(q, l) \\ \delta_r(q, l), & \text{otherwise} \end{cases}
$$

)

Let $\mathcal{A}_\varphi = \overline{\mathcal{C}_\varphi}$, then $\mathcal{A}_\varphi$ is an ϵAFA and it is easy to check that for each $w \in (AP)^*$, $w \models \varphi$ iff $w \in \mathscr{L}(\mathcal{A}_\varphi)$.

As a consequence, we have the following theorem.

Theorem 4. *Given an FL^{res} formula φ, there is an ϵAFA $\mathcal{A}_\varphi$ with $\mathcal{O}(|\varphi|)$ states such that for every $w \in (AP)^*$, $w \models \varphi$ if and only if $w \in \mathscr{L}(\mathcal{A}_\varphi)$.*

Converting an ϵAFA to a 1NFA is never a hard task. Because that the accepting witness of an ϵAFA must have the additional constraint:

(F) There is no backward edge

besides the other five constraints mention in Page 9.

Now, the encoding of $\mathcal{G}[i]$ just requires a letter in $(2^{Q \times Q})^2$, which memorizes the set of i-stuttering edges and i-forward edges. Moreover, for an accepting witness of an ϵAFA, if an infinite path exists, its infinite suffix must be involved among vertices of the same level. This can be locally checked. Hence, what we must memorize is the set of states in the present level.

Then, given an ϵAFA $\mathcal{A} = \langle \Sigma, Q, \delta, q_0, F \rangle$, we construct the 1DFA $\widehat{\mathcal{N}} = \langle \widehat{\Sigma}, 2^Q \cup \{q_{err}\}, \widehat{\delta}, \{q_0\}, \widehat{F} \rangle$ where:

1. $\widehat{\Sigma} = \Sigma \times (2^{Q \times Q})^2$.
2. Given a set $Q' \subseteq Q$ and $a = (l, (E_S, E_F)) \in \widehat{\Sigma}$, if:
   - $(q_1, q_2) \in E_S$ implies $q_1, q_2 \in Q'$, and $(q_1, q_2) \in E_F$ implies $q_1 \in Q'$;
   - for each $q \in Q'$, the set $\{(q', 0) \mid (q, q') \in E_S\} \cup \{(q'', 1) \mid (q, q'') \in E_F\}$ satisfies $\delta(q, l)$;
   - for every state sequence $q_1, \ldots, q_m$ such that $(q_i, q_{i+1}) \in E_s$, it must be $q_1 \neq q_m$,
   then we let $\widehat{\delta}(Q', a) = \{q'' \mid \exists q' \in Q. (q', q'') \in E_F\}$. Otherwise, let $\widehat{\delta}(Q', a) = q_{err}$. In addition, for each $a \in \widehat{\Sigma}$, we let $\widehat{\delta}(q_{err}, a) = q_{err}$.
3. $\widehat{F} = \{Q' \mid Q' \subseteq F\}$.

According to the construction, it is not difficult to check that $(l_0, N_0) \ldots (l_m, N_m)$ is accepted by $\widehat{\mathcal{N}}$ iff $N_0, \ldots, N_m$ is an encoding of an accepting witness of $l_0 \ldots l_m$ w.r.t. $\mathcal{A}$. Let $\mathcal{N} = \widehat{\mathcal{N}}|_\Sigma$, then we have $\mathscr{L}(\mathcal{A}) = \mathscr{L}(\mathcal{N})$, because:

- On one hand, if $w = l_0, l_1, \ldots, l_m \in \Sigma^* \in \mathscr{L}(\mathcal{A})$, then there is an accepting run $\langle T, \rho \rangle$ of $\mathcal{A}$ over w. Since $\mathcal{A}$ is an ϵAFA, the run can be encoded via a sequence $N_0, N_1, \ldots, N_m \in (2^{Q \times Q})^*$. Therefore, $(l_0, N_0), (l_1, N_1), \ldots, (l_m, N_m) \in \mathscr{L}(\widehat{\mathcal{N}})$. According to Lemma 2, we have $w \in \mathscr{L}(\widehat{\mathcal{N}}|_\Sigma) = \mathscr{L}(\mathcal{N})$.
- For the other way round, if $w = l_0, l_1, \ldots, l_m \in \mathscr{L}(\mathcal{N})$, again from Lemma 2, there exists a sequence $N_0, N_1, \ldots, N_m$ making $(l_0, N_0), (l_1, N_1), \ldots, (l_m, N_m) \in \mathscr{L}(\widehat{\mathcal{N}})$. From the construction of $\widehat{\mathcal{N}}$, we know that $N_0, N_1, \ldots, N_m$ is just an encoding of some accepting witness of $\mathcal{A}$ on w, hence $w \in \mathscr{L}(\mathcal{A})$.

As the consequence, we have the following theorem.

Theorem 5. *Given a FL^{res} formula φ, there is a 1NFA $\mathcal{A}_\varphi$ with $2^{\mathcal{O}(|\varphi|)}$ states, such that for each $w \in (AP)^*$, $w \models \varphi$ if and only if $w \in \mathscr{L}(\mathcal{A}_\varphi)$.*

5   Concluding Remarks

In this paper, we present the temporal logic FL^{res}, which is a special fragment of PSL and its semantics is defined on finite words. In comparison to LTL_WR and SafetyPSL^{det}, this fragment has less syntactical constraints, and hence gains more flexibility.

We then show how to compile an FL^{res} formula φ into a 1NFA with $2^{\mathcal{O}(|\varphi|)}$ states. The main observation is that we can first transform it into a 2AFA, and then a special optimization can be conducted upon the previous step.

As an attempt, we investigate the process of compiling an industrial used specification language towards finite models, we hope that our work could be useful in some specific domain (say, AI), like some other recent related work, such as for LTL$_f$.

References

1. Accellera: Accellera property languages reference manual, June 2004. http://www.eda.org/vfv/docs/PSL-v1.1.pdf
2. Birget, J.C.: State-complexity of finite-state devices, state compressibility and incompressibility. Math. Syst. Theory **26**(3), 237–269 (1993)
3. Bustan, D., Fisman, D., Havlicek, J.: Automata construction for PSL. Technical Report MCS05-04, IBM Haifa Research Lab, May 2005
4. Cimatti, A., Roveri, M., Semprini, S., Tonetta, S.: From PSL to NBA: a modular symbolic encoding. In: FMCAD 2006 (2006)
5. Cimatti, A., Roveri, M., Tonetta, S.: Symbolic compilation of PSL. IEEE Trans. Comput. Aided Des. Integr. Circ. Syst. **27**(10), 1737–1750 (2008)
6. Clarke, E.M., Emerson, E.A.: Design and synthesis of synchronization skeletons using branching time temporal logic. In: Kozen, D. (ed.) Logic of Programs 1981. LNCS, vol. 131, pp. 52–71. Springer, Heidelberg (1982). https://doi.org/10.1007/BFb0025774
7. Eisner, C., Fisman, D.: A Practical Introduction to PSL. Springer, New York (2006). https://doi.org/10.1007/978-0-387-36123-9
8. De Giacomo, G., Vardi, M.: Linear temporal logic and linear dynamic logic on finite traces. In: IJCAI 2013, pp. 2000–2007. AAAI Press (2013)
9. De Giacomo, G., Vardi, M.: Synthesis for LTL and IDL on finite traces. In: IJCAI 2015, pp. 1558–1564. AAAI Press (2015)
10. IEEE Computer Society and IEEE Standards Association Corporate Advisory Group: IEEE standard for SystemVerilog – unified hardware design, specification, and verification language, December 2017
11. Jin, N., Shen, C.: Dynamic verifying the properties of the simple subset of PSL. In: 1st IEEE Symposium of Theoretical Aspects on Software Engineering, pp. 173–182. IEEE Society (2007)
12. Li, J., Rozier, K.Y., Pu, G., Zhang, Y., Vardi, M.Y.: SAT-based explicit LTL$_f$ satisfiability checking. CoRR, abs/1811.03176 (2018)
13. Li, J., Zhang, L., Pu, G., Vardi, M.Y., He, J.: LTL$_f$ satisfiability checking. In: ECAI 2014, volume 263 of Frontiers in Artificial Intelligence and Applications, pp. 513–518. IOS Press (2014)
14. Li, J., Zhu, S., Pu, G., Zhang, L., Vardi, M.Y.: SAT-based explicit LTL reasoning and its application to satisfiability checking. Formal Methods Syst. Des. **54**(2), 164–190 (2019)
15. Löding, C.: Optimal bounds for transformations of Ω-automata. In: Rangan, C.P., Raman, V., Ramanujam, R. (eds.) FSTTCS 1999. LNCS, vol. 1738, pp. 97–109. Springer, Heidelberg (1999). https://doi.org/10.1007/3-540-46691-6_8
16. Muller, D.E., Schupp, P.E.: Alternating automata on infinite trees. Theoret. Comput. Sci. **54**, 267–276 (1987)
17. Pnueli, A.: The temporal logic of programs. In: Proceedings of 18th IEEE Symposium on Foundation of Computer Science (FOCS 1977), pp. 46–57. IEEE Computer Society (1977)
18. Ruah, S., Fisman, D., Ben-David, S.: Automata construction for on-the-fly model checking PSL safety simple subset. Technical Report H0234, IBM Haifa Research Lab, April 2005
19. Wolper, P.: Temporal logic can be more expressive. Inf. Control **56**(1–2), 72–99 (1983)

Symbolic Model Checking with Sentential Decision Diagrams

Lieuwe Vinkhuijzen$^{(\boxtimes)}$ and Alfons Laarman

Leiden University, Leiden, The Netherlands
{l.t.vinkhuijzen,a.w.laarman}@liacs.leidenuniv.nl
https://www.universiteitleiden.nl/en/staffmembers/lieuwe-vinkhuijzen
http://alfons.laarman.com/

Abstract. We demonstrate the viability of symbolic model checking using Sentential Decision Diagrams (SDD), in lieu of the more common Binary Decision Diagram (BDD). The SDD data structure can be up to exponentially more succinct than BDDs, using a generalized notion of variable order called a variable tree ("vtree"). We also contribute to the practice of SDDs, giving a novel heuristic for constructing a vtree that minimizes SDD size in the context of model checking, and identifying which SDD operations form a performance bottleneck.

Experiments on 707 benchmarks, written in various specification languages, show that SDD often use an order of magnitude less memory than BDDs, at the expense of a smaller slowdown in runtime performance.

1 Introduction

Model checking is an automated way for verifying whether a system satisfies its specification [1]. Binary Decision Diagrams [2] (Binary DDs or BDDs) first revolutionized symbolic model checking [3]. But the representation may explode in size on certain instances [4,5]. Later SAT and SMT based techniques, such as BMC [5] and IC3 [6], have been shown to scale even better.

DDs have the unique capability to manipulate (Boolean) functions. Due to this property, they can be used to encode a system in a bottom-up fashion [7]. In model checking, for example, this can be exploited to 'learn' transition relations on-the-fly [8], to soundly [9] implement the semantics of the underlying system. This fundamental difference from SAT also makes DDs valuable in various other applications [10–12].

To improve the performance of DDs, various more concise versions have been proposed [13–19]. One such data structure is the Sentential Decision Diagram (SDD)[20], recently proposed by Darwiche. SDDs subsume BDDs in the sense that every BDD is an SDD, and SDDs support the same functionality for function manipulation. Specifically, SDDs support the operations of conjunction, disjunction, negation operations, and existential quantification, making them suitable for the role of data structure in symbolic model checking. Since every BDD is an SDD, they need not use more memory than BDDs, and if an SDD's *variable*

© Springer Nature Switzerland AG 2020
J. Pang and L. Zhang (Eds.): SETTA 2020, LNCS 12153, pp. 124–142, 2020.
https://doi.org/10.1007/978-3-030-62822-2_8

tree (vtree) is chosen well, then an SDD has the potential to use exponentially less memory than a BDD [21]. While SDDs have already shown potential for CAD applications [22], they have not yet been tried for model checking. And because of the relevance of DDs in many other applications, an evaluation of the performance of SDDs is also of interest in its own right.

The biggest obstacle to overcome, therefore, is to find a good vtree for the SDD. A vtree is to an SDD as a variable order is to a BDD. In BDD-based symbolic model checking, the BDD's variable order determines the size of the BDD in memory, and the choice of variable order may determine whether or not the verifier runs out of memory.

We propose in Sect. 3 three heuristics for constructing vtrees. First, we propose that the vtree is constructed in two phases. In phase 1, we build an abstract variable tree which minimizes the distance between dependent variables in the system. In phase 2, the leaves that represent integer variables are "folded out", and are replaced by "augmented right-linear" vtrees on 32 variables. These heuristics *statically* construct a vtree, before model checking, so that the vtree is preserved throughout the analysis.

We implemented our approach in the language-independent model checker model checker LTSmin [8][1], using the SDD package provided by the Automated Reasoning Group at UCLA [23]. To evaluate the method, we test the performance of SDDs on 707 benchmarks from a diverse set of inputs languages: DVE [24] (293), Petri nets [25] (357), Promela [26] (57). We test several configurations, corresponding to using all heuristics above, or only a subset, with and without dynamic vtree search (i.e., modifying the vtree during model checking). These languages represent very different domains. By obtaining good results across all domains, we gain confidence that the advantage of SDDs over BDDs is robust.

Experiments show that SDDs often use an order of magnitude less memory than BDDs on the same problem, primarily on the more difficult instances. Among instances that were solved by both SDDs and BDDs, 75% were solved with a smaller SDD, and among those instances, the SDD was on average 7.9 times smaller than the BDD. On the other hand, the SDD approach is up to an order of magnitude slower than the BDD; 82% of the instances were solved faster with BDDs, with an average speedup of 2.7. We investigate the causes of this slowdown in SDDs, but also demonstrate with larger benchmarks, that memory/time trade-off is worthwhile as we can solve larger instances with SDDs. Our analysis shows that the set intersection and union operations in SDDs are relatively fast, whereas existential quantification can be a performance bottleneck. This is despite the recent discovery that set intersection and union have exponential worst-case behaviour in theory [7].

---

[1] Our implementation's source code is available at https://doi.org/10.5281/zenodo.3940936.

2   Background

2.1   Sentential Decision Diagrams

A Sentential Decision Diagram (SDD), recently proposed by Darwiche [20], is a
data structure which stores a set $K \subseteq \{0,1\}^n$ of same-length bit vectors. In our
context, a bit vector represents a state of a system, and variables are represented
using multiple bits. Like Binary Decision Diagrams (BDDs) [15], SDDs are a
canonical representation for each set and allow, e.g., union and intersection,
with other sets. Following is a succinct exposition of the data structure.

Suppose we wish to store the set $K \subseteq \{0,1\}^n$ of length n bit vectors. If $n = 1$,
then K is one of four base cases, $K \in \{\emptyset, \{0\}, \{1\}, \{0,1\}\}$. Otherwise, if $n \geq 2$,
then we decompose K into a union of simpler sets, as follows. Choose an integer
$1 \leq a < n$. Split each string into two parts: the first a bits and the last $n - a$
bits, called the prefix and the postfix.

For a string $p \in \{0,1\}^a$, let $Post(p) \subseteq \{0,1\}^{n-a}$ be the set of postfixes
$s \in \{0,1\}^{n-a}$ with which p can end. More precisely:

$$Post(p) = \{s \in \{0,1\}^{n-a} \mid ps \in K\} \tag{1}$$

where ps is the concatenation of p with s.

Next, define an equivalence relation on the set $\{0,1\}^a$ where $p_1 \sim p_2$ when
$Post(p_1) = Post(p_2)$. Suppose that this equivalence relation partitions the set
$\{0,1\}^a$ into the ℓ sets $P_1, \ldots, P_\ell$. Let $\overline{p_1} \in P_1, \ldots, \overline{p_\ell} \in P_\ell$ be arbitrary represen-
tatives from the respective sets. Then we can represent K as

$$K = \bigcup_{i=1}^{\ell} P_i \times Post(\overline{p_i}) \tag{2}$$

The sets P_i, P_j are disjoint for $i \neq j$, because these sets form a partition of
$\{0,1\}^a$, so the Cartesian products $P_i \times Post(\overline{p_i}), P_j \times Post(\overline{p_j})$ are also disjoint
for $i \neq j$. Hence we have decomposed K into a disjoint union of smaller sets.

To build an SDD for K, recursively decompose the sets $P_1, \ldots, P_\ell$ and
$Post(\overline{p_1}), \ldots, Post(\overline{p_\ell})$, until the base case is reached, where the bit vectors
have length 1. To this end, choose two integers $1 \leq a_1 < a$ and $a \leq a_2 < n$
and decompose the sets P_i with respect to a_1 and decompose the sets $Post(\overline{p_i})$
with respect to a_2. In the literature, the sets P_i are called the *primes*, the sets
$Post(\overline{p_i})$ the *subs*, and the sets $P_i \times Post(\overline{p_i})$ are called the *elements* of K.

Example 1. Figure 1 shows an SDD for a set of length-6 bitstrings, normalized
to the vtree on the right. A rectangle represents a set. A box within a rectangle
represents an element of that set, with its prime on the left and its sub on
the right. The box represents the Cartesian product of its prime and sub. In
particular, the SDD nodes' labels indicate which vtree node they are normalized
to. A $\top$ represents $\{0,1\}$, and $\bot$ represents the empty set.

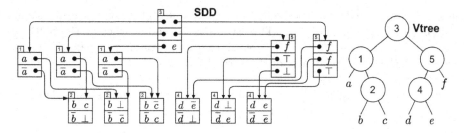

Fig. 1. An SDD and the vtree it is normalised to. Rectangles are SDD nodes, labelled with the vtree node they are normalized to.

Variable Trees. In the construction of the SDD, the choice of the integer a determines how the top level of the SDD decomposes into tuples. The left and right partitions are then further decomposed, recursively, resulting in a full binary tree, called a *variable tree*, or "vtree" for short. This binary tree is full in the sense that each node is either a leaf, labelled with a single variable, or else it is an internal node with two children (internal nodes do not correspond to variables). An SDD's variable tree, then, determines how the smaller sets decompose and therefore completely determines the SDD. SDDs are called a *canonical representation* for this reason. Consequently, searching for a small SDD reduces to searching for a good vtree.

A left-to-right traversal of a vtree induces a variable order. When we say that an algorithm for vtree optimization preserves the variable order, we mean that the algorithm produces a new vtree with the same induced variable order. A *right-linear* vtree is one in which every internal node's left child is a leaf. BDDs are precisely those SDDs with a right-linear vtree, hence SDDs generalize BDDs.

Example 2. Figure 2 shows an SDD normalised to a right-linear vtree for the same set K as in Example 1. The label in a round node indicates the vtree

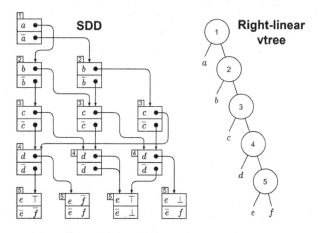

Fig. 2. An SDD normalized to a right-linear vrtee.

node it is normalised to. Although the vtrees are different, they induce the same variable order $A < B < C < D$. This SDD has six nodes, whereas the SDD in Fig. 1 has seven nodes. We see, therefore, that the variable tree can affect the size of the SDD, independently of the variable order.

Formal semantics An SDD node t formally represents a set of strings denoted by $\langle t \rangle$, as follows. The node may be of one of two types:

1. t is a terminal node labelled with a set $A \in \{\emptyset, \{0\}, \{1\}, \{0, 1\}\}$, in which case $\langle t \rangle = A$.
2. t is a decomposition node, and $t = \{(p_1, s_1), \ldots, (p_\ell, s_\ell)\}$, where p_i and s_i are other SDD nodes. Then $\langle t \rangle = \bigcup_{i=1}^{\ell} \langle p_i \rangle \times \langle s_i \rangle$

Queries and Transformations. Because SDDs are a canonical representation, equivalence of two SDDs can be checked in constant time, provided that they obey the same variable tree. SDDs support polynomial-time model counting and model enumeration. Whether SDDs support polynomial-time conjunction and disjunction was an open question which was recently answered in the negative, unfortunately, by Van den Broeck and Darwiche [7]². However, they find empirically that this worst-case behaviour rarely manifests in practice.

2.2   Model Checking and Reachability

Model checkers verify whether the behavior of a system M conforms to a specification φ. To support reactive systems, the property φ is expressed in a temporal logic, such as, LTL [27], CTL [28] or the modal μ-calculus [29]. The formal check involves deciding semantic entailment, i.e., $M \models \varphi$, and can be implemented as a fixpoint computation on the semantic interpretation of the system [1], typically a transition system (Kripke structure). Since the fixpoint computations reduce to reachability, we only need to focus on solving reachability to evaluate and compare the performance of various decision diagrams in model checking.

The reachability procedure is a repeated image computation with the symbolic transition relation R until a *fixpoint* is reached. Starting from $A := S_0$, we compute $A_{i+1} := A_i \cup R(A_i)$, until this computation converges, i.e., an iteration adds no more states. In each iteration, the set A_i contains a set of system states.

---

² More precisely, they show that exponential blowups may occur when disjoining two SDDs if the output SDD must obey the same vtree, but it remains an open question whether the blowup is unavoidable when the vtree is allowed to change.

In symbolic model checking, we store the set A_i using a decision diagram, e.g., an SDD. In order to encode the relation R, the vtree will contain, for every variable $x \in X$, a "primed copy" $x' \in X'$. The SDD encoding the transition relation will contain one satisfying assignment for each transition $(s,t) \in R$ (and no more). We therefore denote this SDD as $R(X,X')$; and similarly the SDDs representing sets as $A(X)$. For reachability with SDDs, we need to compute the image function of the transition relation. Equation 3 shows how the image is computed using elementary manipulation operations on SDDs (conjunction, existential quantification and variable renaming). The conjunction constrains the relation to the transitions starting in A; the existential quantification yields the target states only and the renaming relabels target states in X instead of X' variables.

$$\text{Image}(R, A) \triangleq (\exists X : R(X, X') \wedge A(X))[X' := X] \tag{3}$$

In our context, we have the specification of the system we wish to model check. Consequently, we know in advance which variables and actions exist, (e.g., in a Petri net the variables are the places and the actions are the transitions), and therefore we know which read/write dependencies exist between actions and variables[3]. We use this information to design heuristics for SDDs. The integers in our systems are at most 16-bit, so each integer is represented by 16 primed and unprimed variables in the relation (for details, see Sect. 5).

3   Vtree Heuristics

We propose three heuristics for constructing vtrees based on the read/write dependencies in the system being verified. Section 3.1 proposes that the vtree is constructed in two phases, and Sect. 3.2 and 3.3 propose heuristics to be used in the two respective phases. Since the vtree structure can influence SDD size independent of the variable order, as shown in the previous section, we assume a good variable order and give heuristics which construct a vtree which preserves that variable order. The input to our vtree construction is therefore a good variable order, provided by existing heuristics [31], along with the known read/write dependencies between those variables, derived from the input that we wish to model check. We then construct the vtree using the heuristics explained below, preserving the variable order. The resulting vtree is then preserved throughout the reachability procedure, or, if dynamic vtree search is enabled, serves as the initial vtree.

---

[3] While for some specification languages this information has to be estimated using static analysis, there are ways to support dynamic read/write dependencies [30], but for the sake of simplicity, we do not consider them here.

Our application requires that we store relations rather than states, so our vtrees will contain two copies of each variable, as explained in Sect. 2.2.

3.1 Two-Phase Vtree Construction

Any vtree heuristic will have to deal with the fact that the system's variables are integers, whereas an SDD (or a BDD) encodes each bit as an individual variable, so that an integer is represented by multiple variables. Therefore, our first heuristic is that we propose that a vtree be constructed in two phases.

In the first phase, one builds a small vtree called an "abstract variable tree", containing all of the system's variables as leaves. In the second phase, we "fold out" the leaves corresponding to variables that represent more than one bit, i.e., whose domain is larger than $\{0, 1\}$. Folding out a leaf means replacing it by a larger vtree on several variables. For example, a leaf representing a 32-bit integer variable will be folded out into a vtree on 64 variables (namely 32 state variables and 32 primed copies). Figure 3 illustrates this process. In this example, a system with four 4-bit integer variables, p, x, y, z, may lead, during phase 1, to the abstract variable tree in the top of the picture. In phase 2, the leaves may be folded out into, in this case, vtrees on 8 bits, producing either the bottom left or right vtree.

Note that this never produces a right-linear vtree, even if both the abstract variable tree and the integer's vtree are right-linear.

3.2 Abstract Variable Tree Heuristic

To design the abstract variable tree, we adopt the intuition that, if a system reads variable x in order to determine the value to write to variable y, then, all other things equal, it would be better if the distance in the vtree between x and y was small.

To capture this intuition, we define a penalty function $p(T)$ (Eq. 4) on a vtree T, which we call the *minimum distance* penalty. We then try to minimize the value of this penalty function by applying local changes to the vtree. The penalty function will simply be the sum, over all read-write dependencies in the system, of the distance between the read and write variable in the vtree. By distance in the vtree, denoted d_T, we mean simply the length of the unique path in the abstract variable tree from the leaf labelled with variable x to the leaf labelled with variable y. Here A is the set of a system's actions, R_a is the set of variables read by action a, and W_a is the set of variables written to by action a.

$$p(T) = \sum_{a \in A} \sum_{(r,w) \in R_a \times W_a} d_T(r, w) \qquad (4)$$

This heuristic is inspired by various variable ordering heuristics, such as Cuthill-Mckee [32] and the bandwidth and wavefront reduction algorithms [31], all of which try to minimize the distances between dependent variables.

3.3   Folding Out Vtrees for Large Variable Domains

We consider two options for folding out an abstract variable. First, such a variable may be folded out into a right-linear vtree, i.e., to a BDD. Figure 3 (left) shows this approach. Second, we introduce the "augmented right-linear vtree", which is a right-linear vtree except that each pair of corresponding state and prime bit is put under a shared least common ancestor. The idea is that a state and primed bit are more closely correlated to one another than to other bits. Figure 3 (right) shows this approach.

Note that in both options, the resulting vtree is not a right-linear vtree.

4   Related Work

Many algorithms exist for static variable ordering for BDDs, e.g., the Cuthill-McKee algorithm [32], Sloan [33] and MINCE [34]; see [35] for a survey. These algorithms exploit event-locality: the observation that most events involve only very few of a system's variables. By using an order in which variables appear next to each other when they appear together in many events, the size of a BDD can decrease relative to variable orders which do not take this into account. Finding an optimal order is NP-Hard [36], so these algorithms heuristically minimize certain distance metrics [37].

We are not aware of any work which attempts to statically construct vtrees. Works in this direction are Darwiche [20] and Oztok and Darwiche [38], which show that a CNF formula with bounded treewidth, or CV-width, respectively, can be compiled into a polynomial-size SDD if a vtree is known which reflects the tree decomposition of the formula. Unfortunately, finding the tree decomposition is NP-Hard [39], and indeed even hard to approximate [40], although this can be done in linear time when the treewidth is bounded [41].

Choi and Darwiche [22] introduce *dynamic vtree search*, that is, they modify the vtree in between SDD operations, aiming to reduce the SDD size. This is useful even when space is not a bottleneck, because, all other things equal, algorithms run faster on small SDDs than on large ones. When dynamic vtree search is enabled in our experiments, we use the implementation of Choi and Darwiche.

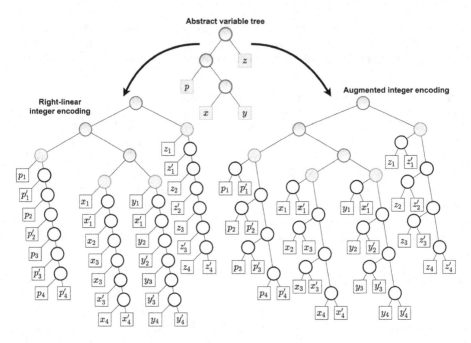

Fig. 3. An abstract variable tree (top) with four 4-bit integers can be folded out in two ways: To a vtree with right-linear integer encoding (left) or with augmented integer encoding (right).

5 Experiments

We evaluate our methods on 707 benchmarks, consisting of 293 DVE models, 357 Petri Net models and 57 Promela models. The benchmarks are provided[4] by Meijer and van den Pol [31], who collected them from the BEEM database [42] and the 2015 Petri Net Model Checking Competition [43], selecting those problems that can be handled by the static variable ordering algorithms. To utilize these different specification languages, we extended[5] the LTSmin model checker [8] with an SDD package [23]. The language-independent interface of LTSmin [8] represents all variables as 16-bit integers. Both the BDD and the SDD packages benchmarked here utilize the same interface. As explained in the introduction, we are interested in evaluating the performance of SDDs with respect to BDDs, to study the feasibility of SDDs for model checking and identify bottlenecks in SDD implementations.

To implement the abstract variable tree heuristic described in Sect. 3.2, we perform a vtree search before executing the reachability procedure in the model checker. We greedily perform local modifications on the vtree until either (i) no possible modification improves the value of the penalty function p (Eq. 4),

---

[4] The benchmarks are available at https://github.com/utwente-fmt/BW-NFM2016.

[5] Again, the implementation is available at https://doi.org/10.5281/zenodo.3940936.

or (ii) our budget of n local modifications is exhausted, where n is the number of program variables, or (iii) 30 s have elapsed. The local modifications are restricted to *vtree rotations*, which is an operation which inverts the roles of parent and child for a particular pair of adjacent internal vtree nodes. This operation preserves the induced variable order.

We experiment with two BDD configurations and four SDD configurations, listed in Table 1. Each configuration is tested on all 707 benchmarks, with a timeout of 10 min (600 s) per benchmark. Experiments are done on a Linux machine with two 2.10 GHz Intel Xeon CPU E5-2620 v4 CPUs, which each have 20 MB cache and 16 cores, with 90 GB of main memory. The BDDs are implemented using the Sylvan multicore BDD package (version 1.4.0) [44]. The SDDs are implemented using the SDD package (version 2.0) [23]. Before vtree construction, we apply the Cuthill-Mckee (BCM) [32] variable reordering heuristic provided by LTSmin [31]. The input to our vtree construction is the variable order found by BCM, along with the known read/write dependencies between those variables. We perform a small case study of six problems from the DVE set with a timeout of 3 h instead of 10 min.

Table 1 lists the parameter settings used for benchmarks. The first row denotes the BDD configuration against which we compare our method. The SDD configurations are such that, in each next row, we "turn on" one more vtree heuristic. The BCM in the variable order column refers to the Cuthill-Mckee ordering heuristic [32], which is performed once, before vtree construction and model checking. The column "Augmented int" records whether integer leaves in the abstract variable tree are folded out to a right-linear or an augmented right-linear representation. The "vtree heuristic" denotes whether the abstract variable tree was right-linear ("No") or was constructed using the minimum distance penalty ("Min. distance"). The row BDD refers to the single-threaded implementation, whereas the row BDD(32) uses the multi-threaded (32-core) implementation [44], which we include only for reference as SDDs [23] are still single-threaded.

Dynamic vtree search [22] is the SDD analog of dynamic variable reordering, that is, it modifies the vtree during execution, aiming to reduce the size of the SDD. The column "Dynamic vtree search" records whether vtree search was enabled during reachability analysis. In that case, at most half the time is spent on vtree search.

The memory usage is computed as follows. A BDD node takes up 24 bytes. An SDD node takes up 72 bytes, plus 8 bytes per element (an SDD node has at least two elements). That this measure is fair for SDDs was verified by Darwiche in personal communication. We take this approach instead of relying on the memory usage as reported by the operating system, which is not indicative of the size of the SDD/BDD due to the use of hash tables. For each benchmark, we will report the peak memory consumption, that is, the amount of memory in use when the BDD/SDD was at its largest during the reachability procedure.

Table 1. The parameter settings used in the experiments.

Configuration name	Variable order	Two-phase construction	Augmented int	vtree heuristic	Dynamic vtree search
BDD	BCM	(N/A)	(N/A)	(N/A)	No
BDD(32)	BCM	(N/A)	(N/A)	(N/A)	No
SDD(r)	BCM	Yes	No	No	No
SDD(r,a)	BCM	Yes	Yes	No	No
SDD(d,a)	BCM	Yes	Yes	Min. distance	No
SDD(d,a) + s	BCM	Yes	Yes	Min. distance	Yes

5.1 Results

Figure 4 and 5 show the results of the experiments. In each plot, a blue "×" represents a DVE instance, a green "△" a Petri net instance, and a red "+" a Promela instance. Instances on the black diagonal line are solved using an equal amount of time or memory by both approaches, instances on a gray diagonal line are solved by one method with an order of magnitude advantage over the other. All graphs are formatted such that benchmarks that were solved better by the more advanced configuration appear as a point below the diagonal line; otherwise, if the less advanced configuration performed better, then it appears above the diagonal line. The horizontal and vertical lines of instances near the top left of the figures, represent instances where one or both methods exceeded the timeout limit.

Figure 4 (top) shows that the simplest SDD configuration, SDD(r), tends to outperform BDDs in terms of memory, especially on more difficult instances, but not in terms of time, often taking an order of magnitude longer. As a result of the 600 s timeout, BDDs manage to solve many instances that SDDs fail to solve. The middle row shows that using augmented integer vtrees is not perceptibly better than using right-linear vtrees. The bottom row shows that using our minimum distance heuristic improves both running time and diagram size. Finally, Fig. 5 (top) shows that adding dynamic vtree search yields even smaller diagrams, and on difficult instances, tends to be slightly faster.

Figure 5 (bottom) compares SDD(d,a) + s to BDDs. It shows that memory usage is often an order of magnitude lower than that of BDDs on the same benchmark. The effect is even more pronounced than in Fig. 4 (top). Unfortunately, this configuration often uses more time than BDDs do.

We see that two of our heuristics improve the performance of SDDs, at least as far as memory is concerned, namely, (i) using two-phase vtree construction instead of a BDD (Fig. 4, top) and (ii) using the minimum abstract variable tree distance heuristic (Fig. 4, bottom).

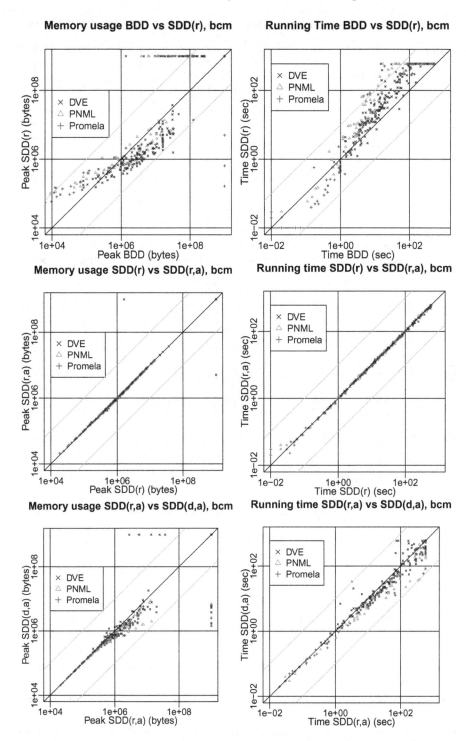

Fig. 4. Memory (left) and time (right) consumption comparisons of various SDD configurations. (Color figure online)

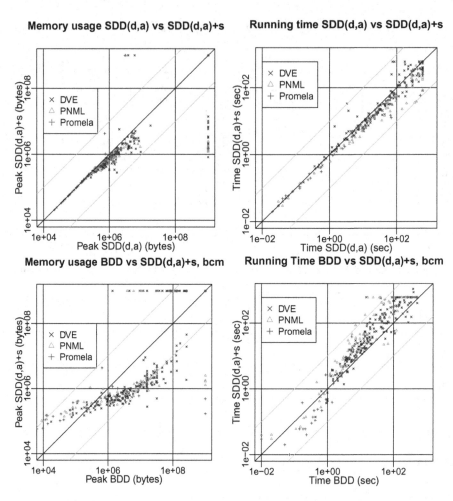

Fig. 5. Memory (left) and time (right) consumption comparisons (continued). (Color figure online)

Table 2 and Table 3 show the relative speedup and memory improvements of all pairs of methods. A cell indicates the ratio by which the column method outperformed the row method, restricted to those benchmarks on which it outperformed the row method. For example, Table 2, shows that, on the 264 benchmarks that both SDD(r) and BDD solved, SDD(r) uses less memory than BDD on 172 benchmarks, and on those benchmarks, uses 3.1 times less memory on average, whereas on the remaining 92 instances, BDD used 5.5 times less memory than SDD(r).

From the tables we see that no method dominates another, even in just one metric. However, we do see that SDD(d,a)+s often uses much less memory than BDD (namely on 75% of benchmarks that both methods solved), and then on average by a factor 7.9. Strikingly, Fig. 5 reveals that this advantage becomes progressively larger as the instances become more difficult. We also see that each heuristic helps a little bit, with the exception of augmented integer vtrees. That is, in the sequence BDD, SDD(r), SDD(d,a), SDD(d,a)+s, each next configuration, compared with the previous, is better on more instances than it is worse (There is one exception: SDD(d,a)+s is often smaller but slower than SDD(d,a)).

Table 2. Average ratio of memory usage on instances that the column method solved using less memory than the row method. Numbers in brackets indicate the number of benchmark instances on which the column method outperformed the row method. We leave out BDD(32), since its memory use is equal to BDD.

Memory	BDD	SDD(r)	SDD(r,a)	SDD(d,a)	SDD(d,a)+s
BDD	1	3.1 (172)	3.1 (173)	4.4 (193)	7.9 (220)
SDD(r)	5.5 (92)	1	1.02 (138)	1.5 (186)	2.3 (216)
SDD(r,a)	5.7 (91)	1.01 (128)	1	1.5 (182)	2.3 (218)
SDD(d,a)	6.2 (82)	1.1 (75)	1.1 (79)	1	1.6 (212)
SDD(d,a) + s	6.9 (72)	1.2 (48)	1.1 (46)	1.1 (62)	1

Table 3. Average ratio of time used on instances that the column method solved using less time than the row method. Numbers in brackets indicate the number of benchmark instances on which the column method outperformed the row method.

Time	BDD	BDD(32)	SDD(r)	SDD(r,a)	SDD(d,a)	SDD(d,a)+s
BDD	1	6.1 (321)	2.2 (45)	1.9 (46)	1.9 (54)	2.1 (51)
BDD(32)	1.2 (11)	1	2.4 (21)	2.1 (21)	2.1 (22)	2.1 (23)
SDD(r)	3.8 (219)	17.2 (243)	1	1.04 (121)	1.8 (187)	2.1 (144)
SDD(r,a)	3.7 (218)	17.0 (243)	1.1 (145)	1	1.7 (189)	2.1 (149)
SDD(d,a)	2.8 (221)	13.2 (253)	1.6 (74)	1.5 (72)	1	2.0 (78)
SDD(d,a) + s	2.7 (240)	13.3 (269)	1.4 (120)	1.3 (115)	1.4 (196)	1

The results of the case study with a timeout of 3 h are shown in Table 4, and are included in Fig. 5 (bottom left). In this problem set, SDDs consumed 31 times less memory on average.

5.2 SDD Runtime Profiles

Figure 6 breaks up the time spent on the most difficult instances into the three SDD operations (Existential quantification, intersection and union of sets), and the glue code which connects LTSmin to the SDD package (LTSmin's Partitioned Next-State Interface (PINS), is described in [8]). For a few instances (pouring, lup, and peg_solitaire) the glue code takes the most runtime. We verified

Table 4. Time and peak memory consumption (kB) on six large problems. Times are in seconds.

Metric	Name	synapse.7	telephony.4	szymansky.5	sched_world.3	sokoban.1	telephony.7
Space	SDD(d,a) + s	6804	20893	24587	45694	1838	19453
	BDD	88905	131214	165836	259544	261113	262210
Time	SDD(d,a) + s	836	1078	4918	1789	858	2295
	BDD	73	19	42	41	28	36

that in these cases the input system contains few locality (the PINS dependency matrix is dense), which is not what LTSmin was designed for, so we will not discuss these instances further.

In the SDD packages, we see that the main bottleneck is existential quantification and vtree search, whereas intersection and especially union take less time. The vtree search pays off, because in this setting the model checking procedure performed best as we discussed in the previous section. It comes as no surprise that existential quantification is a bottleneck, because quantification for multiple variables is NP-Hard and all variables are bit-blasted in LTSmin. It is, in some sense, good news: There is a lot performance to be gained by eliminating this bottleneck, and there is good hope that this is possible, because NP-Hard problems can often be made tractable in many easy instances by developing good

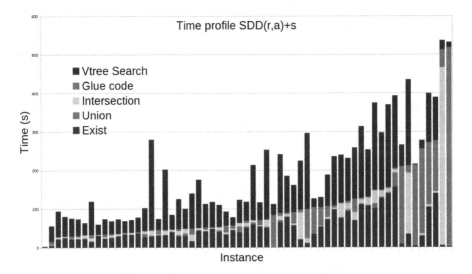

Fig. 6. The time profile of SDD configuration SDD(d,a)+s, split among the three primary SDD set operations of Intersection, Union and Existential quantification, and the glue code which connects LTSmin to SDD. Shown are the DVE and PNML instances that were solved in more than 100 s. The instances are sorted by the time taken by the SDD operations, plus glue code.

heuristics. The SDD package currently employs no special heuristics to perform existential quantification.

We were unable identify unique characteristics in terms of their number of variables or their number of actions for the outlier instances in which set intersection is the bottleneck (e.g., `elevator2.3`).

6   Conclusion and Future Work

Sentential Decision Diagrams are a viable alternative to Binary Decision Diagrams for use in symbolic model checking. The size in memory of an SDD is determined by its vtree, and choosing this vtree was the foremost challenge when implementing SDD-based model checking. This challenge was satisfactorily met with novel heuristics. Our experiments show that the novel heuristics yield SDDs that are often an order of magnitude smaller than BDDs on the same problem, and this advantage becomes larger on more difficult instances. These results are robust to the difficulty of the instance, as the performance of BDDs on our benchmark set spans five orders of magnitude, from 10kB of memory to 300MB of memory. That SDDs are slower contrasts with findings of Choi and Darwiche [22]. We suggest three avenues for research in the near future.

1. Combine variable order heuristics with vtree structure heuristics
2. Use more advanced data structures than SDD
3. Eliminate the speed bottlenecks in SDDs; specifically, develop (heuristics for) faster existential quantification algorithms.

For Item 2, the Zero-Suppressed Sentential Decision Diagram [17], and the Tagged Sentential Decision Diagram [14,18], look like promising next steps, because both do well when representing sparse sets, which is the case in the current application. Using Uncompressed Sentential Decision Diagrams looks promising in theory, but recent work suggests that much still needs to be done before they can be considered a tractable data structure [7].

Acknowledgements. This work is part of the research programme VENI with project number 639.021.649, which is financed by the Netherlands Organisation for Scientific Research (NWO).

References

1. Baier, C., Katoen, J.-P.: Principles of Model Checking. The MIT Press, Cambridge (2008)
2. Bryant, R.E.: Graph-based algorithms for Boolean function manipulation. IEEE Trans. Comput. **35**(8), 677–691 (1986)
3. McMillan, K.L.: Symbolic model checking: an approach to the state explosion problem. Ph.d. thesis. UMI No. GAX92-24209 (1992)
4. Darwiche, A., Marquis, P.: A knowledge compilation map. J. Artif. Intell. Res. **17**, 229–264 (2002)

5. Biere, A., Cimatti, A., Clarke, E., Zhu, Y.: Symbolic model checking without BDDs. In: Cleaveland, W.R. (ed.) TACAS 1999. LNCS, vol. 1579, pp. 193–207. Springer, Heidelberg (1999). https://doi.org/10.1007/3-540-49059-0_14
6. Bradley, A.R.: SAT-based model checking without unrolling. In: Jhala, R., Schmidt, D. (eds.) VMCAI 2011. LNCS, vol. 6538, pp. 70–87. Springer, Heidelberg (2011). https://doi.org/10.1007/978-3-642-18275-4_7
7. Van den Broeck, G., Darwiche, A.: On the role of canonicity in knowledge compilation. In: Twenty-Ninth AAAI Conference on Artificial Intelligence (2015)
8. Kant, G., Laarman, A., Meijer, J., van de Pol, J., Blom, S., van Dijk, T.: LTSmin: high-performance language-independent model checking. In: Baier, C., Tinelli, C. (eds.) TACAS 2015. LNCS, vol. 9035, pp. 692–707. Springer, Heidelberg (2015). https://doi.org/10.1007/978-3-662-46681-0_61
9. Livshits, B., et al.: In defense of soundiness: a manifesto. Commun. ACM **58**(2), 44–46 (2015)
10. Requeno, J.I., Colom, J.M.: Compact representation of biological sequences using set decision diagrams. In: Rocha, M., Luscombe, N., Fdez-Riverola, F., Rodríguez, J., (eds.) 6th International Conference on Practical Applications of Computational Biology & Bioinformatics, vol. 154, pp. 231–239. Springer, Berlin, Heidelberg (2012). https://doi.org/10.1007/978-3-642-28839-5_27
11. Bergman, D., Cire, A.A., van Hoeve, W.-J., Hooker, J.N.: Discrete optimization with decision diagrams. INFORMS J. Comput. **28**(1), 47–66 (2016)
12. Niemann, P., Zulehner, A., Drechsler, R., Wille, R.: Overcoming the trade-off between accuracy and compactness in decision diagrams for quantum computation. IEEE Trans. Comput. Aid. Des. Integr. Circuits Syst. (2020)
13. Minato, S.: Zero-suppressed BDDs for set manipulation in combinatorial problems. In: 30th ACM/IEEE Design Automation Conference, pp. 272–277. IEEE (1993)
14. van Dijk, T., Wille, R., Meolic, R.: Tagged BDDs: combining reduction rules from different decision diagram types. In: Proceedings of the 17th Conference on Formal Methods in Computer-Aided Design, pp. 108–115. FMCAD Inc. (2017)
15. Bryant, R.E.: Chain reduction for binary and zero-suppressed decision diagrams. In: Beyer, D., Huisman, M. (eds.) TACAS 2018. LNCS, vol. 10805, pp. 81–98. Springer, Cham (2018). https://doi.org/10.1007/978-3-319-89960-2_5
16. Babar, J., Jiang, C., Ciardo, G., Miner, A.: Binary decision diagrams with edge-specified reductions. In: Vojnar, T., Zhang, L. (eds.) TACAS 2019. LNCS, vol. 11428, pp. 303–318. Springer, Cham (2019). https://doi.org/10.1007/978-3-030-17465-1_17
17. Nishino, M., Yasuda, N., Minato, S., Nagata, M.: Zero-suppressed sentential decision diagrams. In: Thirtieth AAAI Conference on Artificial Intelligence (2016)
18. Fang, L., Fang, B., Wan, H., Zheng, Z., Chang, L., Yu, Q.: Tagged sentential decision diagrams: combining standard and zero-suppressed compression and trimming rules (2019)
19. Nakamura, K., Denzumi, S., Nishino, M.: Variable shift SDD: a more succinct sentential decision diagram. In: Faro, S., Cantone, D., (eds.) 18th International Symposium on Experimental Algorithms (SEA 2020), volume 160 of Leibniz International Proceedings in Informatics (LIPIcs), pp. 22:1–22:13, Dagstuhl, Germany. Schloss Dagstuhl-Leibniz-Zentrum für Informatik (2020)
20. Darwiche, A.: SDD: a new canonical representation of propositional knowledge bases. In: Proceedings of the Twenty-Second International Joint Conference on Artificial Intelligence-Volume, vol. 2, pp. 819–826. AAAI Press (2011)
21. Bova, S.: SDDs are exponentially more succinct than OBDDs. In: Thirtieth AAAI Conference on Artificial Intelligence (2016)

22. Choi, A., Darwiche, A.: Dynamic minimization of sentential decision diagrams. In: Twenty-Seventh AAAI Conference on Artificial Intelligence (2013)
23. UCLA Automated Reasoning Group. The SDD package (2018). http://reasoning. cs.ucla.edu/sdd/
24. Baranová, Z., Barnat, J., Kejstová, K., Kučera, T., Lauko, H., Mrázek, J., Ročkai, P., Štill, V.: Model Checking of C and C++ with DIVINE 4. In: D'Souza, D., Narayan Kumar, K. (eds.) ATVA 2017. LNCS, vol. 10482, pp. 201–207. Springer, Cham (2017). https://doi.org/10.1007/978-3-319-68167-2_14
25. Kordon, F., et al.: MCC'2017 – the seventh model checking contest. In: Koutny, M., Kristensen, L.M., Penczek, W. (eds.) Transactions on Petri Nets and Other Models of Concurrency XIII. LNCS, vol. 11090, pp. 181–209. Springer, Heidelberg (2018). https://doi.org/10.1007/978-3-662-58381-4_9
26. Holzmann, G.J.: The model checker SPIN. IEEE TSE **23**, 279–295 (1997)
27. Pnueli, A.L The temporal logic of programs. In: 18th Annual Symposium on Foundations of Computer Science (SFCS 1977), pp. 46–57. IEEE (1977)
28. Clarke, E.M., Emerson, E.A.: Design and synthesis of synchronization skeletons using branching time temporal logic. In: Kozen, D. (ed.) Logic of Programs 1981. LNCS, vol. 131, pp. 52–71. Springer, Heidelberg (1982). https://doi.org/10.1007/BFb0025774
29. Kozen, D.: Results on the propositional μ-calculus. Theor. Comput. Sci. **27**(3), 333–354 (1983)
30. Meijer, J., Kant, G., Blom, S., van de Pol, J.: Read, write and copy dependencies for symbolic model checking. In: Yahav, E. (ed.) HVC 2014. LNCS, vol. 8855, pp. 204–219. Springer, Cham (2014). https://doi.org/10.1007/978-3-319-13338-6_16
31. Meijer, J., van de Pol, J.: Bandwidth and wavefront reduction for static variable ordering in symbolic reachability analysis. In: Rayadurgam, S., Tkachuk, O. (eds.) NFM 2016. LNCS, vol. 9690, pp. 255–271. Springer, Cham (2016). https://doi.org/10.1007/978-3-319-40648-0_20
32. Cuthill, E., McKee, J.: Reducing the bandwidth of sparse symmetric matrices. In: Proceedings of the 1969 24th National Conference, pp. 157–172. ACM (1969)
33. Sloan, S.W.: A fortran program for profile and wavefront reduction. Int. J. Numer. Meth. Eng. **28**(11), 2651–2679 (1989)
34. Aloul, F., Markov, I., Sakallah, K.: Mince: a static global variable-ordering for sat and BDD. In: International Workshop on Logic and Synthesis, pp. 1167–1172 (2001)
35. Rice, M., Kulhari, S.: A survey of static variable ordering heuristics for efficient BDD/MDD construction. University of California, Technical report (2008)
36. Bollig, B., Wegener, I.: Improving the variable ordering of OBDDs is NP-complete. IEEE Trans. Comput. **45**(9), 993–1002 (1996)
37. Siminiceanu, R.I., Ciardo, G.: New metrics for static variable ordering in decision diagrams. In: Hermanns, H., Palsberg, J. (eds.) TACAS 2006. LNCS, vol. 3920, pp. 90–104. Springer, Heidelberg (2006). https://doi.org/10.1007/11691372_6
38. Oztok, U., Darwiche, A.: CV-width: a new complexity parameter for CNFs. In: ECAI, pp. 675–680 (2014)
39. Arnborg, S., Corneil, D.G., Proskurowski, A.: Complexity of finding embeddings in AK-tree. SIAM J. Algebraic Discrete Methods **8**(2), 277–284 (1987)
40. Yu, W., Austrin, P., Pitassi, T., Liu, D.: Inapproximability of treewidth and related problems. J. Artif. Intell. Res. **49**, 569–600 (2014)
41. Bodlaender, H.L.: A linear-time algorithm for finding tree-decompositions of small treewidth. SIAM J. Comput. **25**(6), 1305–1317 (1996)

42. Pelánek, R.: BEEM: benchmarks for explicit model checkers. In: Bošnački, D., Edelkamp, S. (eds.) SPIN 2007. LNCS, vol. 4595, pp. 263–267. Springer, Heidelberg (2007). https://doi.org/10.1007/978-3-540-73370-6_17
43. Kordon, F., et al.: MCC'2015 – the fifth model checking contest. In: Koutny, M., Desel, J., Kleijn, J. (eds.) Transactions on Petri Nets and Other Models of Concurrency XI. LNCS, vol. 9930, pp. 262–273. Springer, Heidelberg (2016). https://doi.org/10.1007/978-3-662-53401-4_12
44. van Dijk, T., van de Pol, J.: Sylvan: multi-core decision diagrams. In: Baier, C., Tinelli, C. (eds.) TACAS 2015. LNCS, vol. 9035, pp. 677–691. Springer, Heidelberg (2015). https://doi.org/10.1007/978-3-662-46681-0_60

Probably Approximately Correct Interpolants Generation

Bai Xue[1,2(✉)] and Naijun Zhan[1,2]

[1] State Key Laboratory of Computer Science, Institute of Software, CAS,
Beijing, China
{xuebai,znj}@ios.ac.cn
[2] University of Chinese Academy of Sciences, Beijing, China

Abstract. In this paper we propose a linear programming based method to generate interpolants for two Boolean formulas in the framework of probably approximately correct (PAC) learning. The computed interpolant is termed as a PAC interpolant with respect to a violation level $\epsilon \in (0,1)$ and confidence level $\beta \in (0,1)$: with at least $1 - \beta$ confidence, the probability that the PAC interpolant is a true interpolant is larger than $1 - \epsilon$. Unlike classical interpolants which are used to justify that two formulas are inconsistent, the PAC interpolant is proposed for providing a formal characterization of how inconsistent two given formulas are. This characterization is very important, especially for situations that the two formulas cannot be proven to be inconsistent. The PAC interpolant is computed by solving a scenario optimization problem, which can be regarded as a statistically sound formal method in the sense that it provides formal correct guarantees expressed using violation probabilities and confidences. The scenario optimization problem is reduced to a linear program in our framework, which is constructed by a family of independent and identically distributed samples of variables in the given two Boolean formulas. In this way we can synthesize interpolants for formulas that existing methods are not capable of dealing with. Three examples demonstrate the merits of our approach.

1 Introduction

Given two Boolean formulas ϕ and ψ, a classical Craig interpolant is a Boolean formula h in terms of only common symbols and variables of ϕ and ψ that over-approximates ϕ and remains inconsistent with ψ [7], implying that the two formulas ϕ and ψ are inconsistent. Interpolation-based techniques have been drawing both practical and theoretic attention in recent years. From a practical perspective, interpolant has been broadly applied to a variety of research areas, especially for formal verification, e.g., theorem proving [21,26], model-checking

---

This work has been supported through grants by NSFC under grant No. 61836005, 61625206, the CAS Pioneer Hundred Talents Program under grant No. Y8YC235015, and the MoE, Singapore, Tier-2 grant #MOE2019-T2-2-040.

J. Pang and L. Zhang (Eds.): SETTA 2020, LNCS 12153, pp. 143–159, 2020.
https://doi.org/10.1007/978-3-030-62822-2_9

[23] and predicate abstraction [16,18,24]. Because of their inherently modular and local reasoning interpolant-based techniques can substantially increase the scalability of formal techniques.

In existing literature there are various efficient algorithms for automatically synthesizing interpolants for various theories, e.g., decidable fragments of first-order logic, linear arithmetic, array logic, equality logic with uninterpreted functions (EUF), etc., and their combinations [6,18–20,24,25,27,28,35]. In contrast, interpolant generation for non-linear theory and its combination with the afore-mentioned theories is still in infancy, although nonlinear inequalities are ubiquitous in software involving sophisticated number theoretic functions as well as hybrid systems [36,37]. Many existing methods to synthesizing interpolants for non-linear theory are applicable to polynomial formulas, e.g., [8,11,12]. These methods encode the interpolant generation problem for two Boolean formulas as a semi-definite programming problem, which falls within the convex optimization framework and can be solved efficiently via interior-point methods in polynomial time. Although they are "polynomially" solvable, semidefinite programs with dimension above 10,000 have been extremely hard to solve in practice [1]. Recently, a method built on top of the SMT solver iSAT [10] was proposed to generate interpolants in the presence of non-linear constraints in [22]. [28] regarded interpolants as classifiers in supervised machine learning and used support vector machines (SVMs) in classification techniques and counterexample-guided techniques for linear interpolations generation. [5] extended the idea in [28] by using kernel trick to non-linear interpolant generation and by exploiting symbolic computation to guarantee the convergence, soundness and completeness of the approach. This method is promising since it can deal with superficially non-linear formulas and SVMs are routinely used in large scale data processing. However, the search for counterexamples is nontrivial generally, particularly, it cannot guarantee the convergence in case the two considered formulas are unbounded. [13,14] presented an approach to extract interpolants for non-linear formulas, which possibly contain transcendental functions and differential equations, from proofs of unsatisfiability generated by δ-decision procedure based on interval constraint propagation (ICP) [2]. Unfortunately, all of these approaches for nonlinear formulas suffer from so-called "curse of dimensionality" and thus cannot be applied to formulas with high-dimensional variables. Besides, if an interpolant is not found, these methods cannot give a characterization of how inconsistent the two formulas of interest are.

In this paper we attempt to motivate the integration of formal methods with machine learning [30], and propose a linear programming based method to generate reliable interpolants in the sense of featuring a rigorously quantified confidence for two Boolean formulas. Our method falls within the framework of PAC learning [17,33] and the generated interpolant provides a formal characterization of how inconsistent the two Boolean formulas of interest are. Given a violation level $\epsilon \in (0,1)$ and a confidence level $\beta \in (0,1)$, the objective is to compute PAC interpolants with respect to ϵ and β: With at least $1 - \beta$ confidence, the probability that a PAC interpolant is a true interpolant is larger than $1 - \epsilon$. Such interpolant in our method is computed based on scenario optimization [3], which encodes as a linear programming problem. In this scenario optimization framework, we first extract a set of independent and identically distributed samples of variables in the two Boolean formulas. A sufficient lower bound on the number of extracted samples can be computed from the specified violation level ϵ and confidence level β. After generating samples, we then construct a linear program for computing a PAC interpolant with respect to ϵ and β. Several examples demonstrate the performance of our approach.

In this paper we make use of capabilities of machine learning to assess large data sets to enable interpolant synthesis for large-scale formulas. The advantages of our method are summarized below.

1. The PAC interpolant is able to provide a characterization of how inconsistent two formulas are. This characterization is very important, especially when classical interpolants cannot be obtained to decide whether the two formulas are inconsistent.
2. The scale of the constructed linear program does not directly depend on the dimension of the variables in the considered formulas. It only depends on ϵ, β and the number of unknown parameters in a pre-specified interpolant template. Moreover, linear programming problems with hundreds of thousands or even millions of variables are routinely solved [15] in polynomial time via interior-point methods. Thus, it can deal with formulas with variables of arbitrarily high-dimension.

This remainder of this paper is structured as follows. In Sect. 2 we formalize the concept of PAC interpolants. Section 3 elucidates our PAC interpolant generation method that is based on scenario optimization. After evaluating our method on several examples in Sect. 4, we conclude this paper in Sect. 5.

2 Preliminaries

In this section, we first give a brief introduction on some notions used throughout this paper and then describe the PAC interpolant generation problem of interest.

2.1 Interpolants

Craig showed that given two formulas ϕ and ψ in a first-order theory $\mathcal{T}$ such that $\phi \models \psi$, there always exists an *interpolant* I over the common symbols and variables of ϕ and ψ such that $\phi \models I, I \models \psi$. In the verification literature, this terminology has been abused following [24], where a reverse interpolant I over the common variables of ϕ and ψ is defined by

Definition 1 (Interpolant). *Given two formulas ϕ and ψ in a theory $\mathcal{T}$, a formula I is an* interpolant *of ϕ and ψ if (1) $\phi \models I$, (2) $I \wedge \psi \models \bot$ and (3) I only contains those symbols and non-logical variables that are common to both ϕ and ψ.*

From Definition 1, we conclude that if there exists an interpolant I for formulas ϕ and ψ, the two formulas ϕ and ψ are inconsistent, i.e., $\phi \wedge \psi \models \bot$. This is especially useful in the safety verification scenario [31]. For instance, if $\{(x, y) \in \mathbb{R}^2 \mid \phi(x, y)\}$ denotes the set of unsafe states and $\{(x, y) \in \mathbb{R}^2 \mid \psi(x, y)\}$ denotes the set of reachable states of a system of interest, we can conclude that the system is safe if we can find an interpolant I for the two formulas ϕ and ψ.

The interpolant synthesis problem is described in Definition 2.

Definition 2. *Let $\phi(\boldsymbol{x})$ and $\psi(\boldsymbol{x})$ be two formulas defined as follows,*

$$\phi(\boldsymbol{x}) : \vee_{i=1}^{l} \phi_i(\boldsymbol{x}) \ with$$
$$\phi_1(\boldsymbol{x}) : f_{1,1}(\boldsymbol{x}) \rhd 0 \wedge \cdots \wedge f_{1,m_1}(\boldsymbol{x}) \rhd 0,$$
$$\cdots$$
$$\phi_l(\boldsymbol{x}) : f_{l,1}(\boldsymbol{x}) \rhd 0 \wedge \cdots \wedge f_{l,m_l}(\boldsymbol{x}) \rhd 0$$

and

$$\psi(\boldsymbol{x}) : \vee_{i=1}^{k} \psi_i(\boldsymbol{x}) \ with$$
$$\psi_1(\boldsymbol{x}) : g_{1,1}(\boldsymbol{x}) \rhd 0 \wedge \cdots \wedge g_{1,n_1}(\boldsymbol{x}) \rhd 0,$$
$$\cdots$$
$$\psi_k(\boldsymbol{x}) : g_{k,1}(\boldsymbol{x}) \rhd 0 \wedge \cdots \wedge g_{k,n_k}(\boldsymbol{x}) \rhd 0,$$

where $\boldsymbol{x} \in \mathbb{R}^r$ are variable vectors, $r \in \mathbb{N}$, $\rhd \in \{<, \leq, >, \geq\}$, $f_{i,j}s$ are nonlinear functions from $\mathbb{R}^r$ to $\mathbb{R}$, $i = 1, \ldots, l$, $j = 1, \ldots, m_i$, and $g_{i,j}s$ are nonlinear functions from $\mathbb{R}^r$ to $\mathbb{R}$, $i = 1, \ldots, k$, $j = 1, \ldots, n_i$. Suppose both $\{\boldsymbol{x} \mid \phi(\boldsymbol{x})\}$ and $\{\boldsymbol{x} \mid \psi(\boldsymbol{x})\}$ are bounded subsets in $\mathbb{R}^r$. Find a real-valued function $h(\boldsymbol{x}) : \mathbb{R}^r \to \mathbb{R}$ such that $h(\boldsymbol{x}) > 0$ is an interpolant for ϕ and ψ, i.e.

$$\begin{aligned} h(\boldsymbol{x}) &> 0, \forall \boldsymbol{x} \in \mathcal{F}_1 \\ h(\boldsymbol{x}) &\leq 0, \forall \boldsymbol{x} \in \mathcal{F}_2, \end{aligned} \quad (1)$$

where $\mathcal{F}_1 = \{\boldsymbol{x} \mid \phi(\boldsymbol{x})\}$ and $\mathcal{F}_2 = \{\boldsymbol{x} \mid \psi(\boldsymbol{x})\}$.

Direct computations of interpolants for nonlinear formulas ϕ and ψ are nontrivial. In this paper we attempt to use finite randomization to learn interpolants. The learned interpolants are called PAC interpolants, whose concept is presented in Subsect. 2.2.

2.2 PAC Interpolants

This subsection introduces PAC interpolants.

Suppose that A_i and B_j are respectively endowed with a σ-algebra $\mathcal{D}_{A_i}$ and $\mathcal{D}_{B_j}$, and that probabilities Pr_{A_i} and Pr_{B_j} are respectively assigned over $\mathcal{D}_{A_i}$ and $\mathcal{D}_{B_j}$, where

$$A_i = \{\boldsymbol{x} \mid \phi_i(\boldsymbol{x})\}$$

and

$$B_j = \{\boldsymbol{x} \mid \psi_j(\boldsymbol{x})\},$$

$i = 1, \ldots, l, \ j = 1, \ldots, k$. Throughout this paper, we assume uniform distributions over both spaces A_i and B_j.

Suppose now that

$$\Delta = A_1 \times \ldots \times A_l \times B_1 \times \ldots \times B_k \qquad (2)$$

is endowed with a $\sigma-$algebra $\mathcal{D}$. Obviously, $\cup_{i=1}^{l} A_i = \mathcal{F}_1$ and $\cup_{j=1}^{k} B_j = \mathcal{F}_2$. According to the product measure theorem, there exists a probability measure Pr over $\mathcal{D}$ such that

$$\mathrm{Pr} = \mathrm{Pr}_{A_1} \times \cdots \times \mathrm{Pr}_{A_l} \times \mathrm{Pr}_{B_1} \times \cdots \mathrm{Pr}_{B_k}. \qquad (3)$$

Clearly, a uniform distribution is assigned on the space Δ.

Definition 3. *A real-valued function* $h(\boldsymbol{x}) : \mathbb{R}^r \to \mathbb{R}$ *is a* PAC *interpolant with respect to* $\epsilon \in (0,1)$ *and* $\beta \in (0,1)$ *for formulas* ϕ *and* ψ*, where* ϕ *and* ψ *are formulas in Definition 2, if with probability no smaller than* $1 - \beta$,

$$\mathrm{Pr}(\{\boldsymbol{w} \in \Delta \, | h(\boldsymbol{x}_{A_i}) > 0, h(\boldsymbol{x}_{B_j}) \leq 0, i = 1, \ldots, l, j = 1, \ldots, k\}) \geq 1 - \epsilon, \qquad (4)$$

where

$$\boldsymbol{w} = (\boldsymbol{x}_{A_1}, \ldots, \boldsymbol{x}_{A_l}, \boldsymbol{x}_{B_1}, \ldots, \boldsymbol{x}_{B_k}) \in \Delta,$$

$\boldsymbol{x}_{A_i} \in A_i$ *and* $\boldsymbol{x}_{B_j} \in B_j$, $i = 1, \ldots, l$, $j = 1, \ldots, k$. *We then say that the function* $h(\boldsymbol{x})$ *is* $\mathtt{CI}(\epsilon, \beta)$.

The probability β in Definition 3, which is related to Pr, refers to the confidence associated to the randomized solution algorithm. According to Definition 3, with at least $1 - \beta$ confidence, the probability Pr that $\mathtt{CI}(\epsilon, \beta)$ satisfies the conditions (1) is $1 - \epsilon$. That is, with at least $1 - \beta$ confidence, the probability Pr that $\mathtt{CI}(\epsilon, \beta)$ indeed is a true interpolant for formulas ϕ and ψ is $1 - \epsilon$.

Remark 1. It is worth pointing out here that $\mathtt{CI}(\epsilon, \beta)$ may not satisfy the conditions (1) even if $\epsilon = 0$ and $\beta = 0$. Therefore, $\mathtt{CI}(0,0)$ may not be the a true interpolant.

We further give an explanation of PAC interpolants below.

In some situations it is not sufficient to know whether the formulas ψ and ϕ are inconsistent or not. It is also important to know how inconsistent the two formulas are, by quantifying the amount of states such that the formulas are inconsistent. This characterization is not only useful when existing traditional methods cannot decide whether $\mathcal{F}_1$ intersects $\mathcal{F}_2$ or the two formulas ϕ and ψ are inconsistent, but also useful when the two formulas ϕ and ψ are not inconsistent. The PAC interpolants can help achieve such characterization.

Corollary 1. *If* $h(\boldsymbol{x})$ *is* $\mathtt{CI}(\epsilon, \beta)$ *for formulas* ψ *and* ϕ*, where* ψ *and* ϕ *are formulas in Definition 2, then with confidence no smaller than* $1 - \beta$,

$$\begin{aligned} \mathrm{Pr}_{A_i}(\{\boldsymbol{x} \in A_i \mid h(\boldsymbol{x}) > 0\}) &\geq 1 - \epsilon \ and \\ \mathrm{Pr}_{B_j}(\{\boldsymbol{x} \in B_j \mid h(\boldsymbol{x}) \leq 0\}) &\geq 1 - \epsilon \end{aligned} \qquad (5)$$

for $i \in \{1, \ldots, l\}$ *and* $j \in \{1, \ldots, k\}$.

Proof. Let $\Delta_i = \{w \in \Delta \mid h(x_{A_i}) > 0\}$ and $\tilde{\Delta} = \{w \in \Delta \mid h(x_{A_i}) > 0, h(x_{B_j}) \le 0, i = 1, \ldots, l, j = 1, \ldots, k\}$, where w is as in Definition 3. Obviously, $\tilde{\Delta} \subseteq \Delta_i$. According to (3),

$$\Pr(\Delta_i) = \Pr_{A_i}(\{x \in A_i \mid h(x) > 0\})$$

holds. Also, since $\tilde{\Delta} \subseteq \Delta_i$ for $i = 1, \ldots, l$ and (4), we have that with confidence no smaller than $1 - \beta$,

$$\Pr_{A_i}(\{x \in A_i \mid h(x) > 0\}) \ge 1 - \epsilon.$$

Similarly, we have that with confidence no smaller than $1 - \beta$,

$$\Pr_{B_j}(\{x \in B_j \mid h(x) \le 0\}) \ge 1 - \epsilon.$$

$\square$

Corollary 1 tells that if a PAC interpolant $\text{CI}(\epsilon, \beta)$ is obtained for formulas ϕ and ψ, then with confidence at least $1 - \beta$, the probability measure of states in $C_{i,j} = A_i \cap B_j$ satisfies

$$\Pr_{A_i}(C_{i,j}) \le \min\{1, \epsilon + \frac{\epsilon\lambda(B_j)}{\lambda(A_i)}\}, \tag{6}$$

where $\lambda(A_i)$ and $\lambda(B_j)$ respectively represent the Lebesgue measure of the sets A_i and B_j, $i = 1, \ldots, l$, $j = 1, \ldots, k$. The states in $C_{i,j}$ are the ones such that the two formulas ϕ_i and ψ_j are consistent.

(6) is obtained as follows: Since $C_{i,j} = \{x \in C_{i,j} \mid h(x) > 0\} \cup \{x \in C_{i,j} \mid h(x) \le 0\}$. According to (5), we have that

$$\begin{aligned}
&\Pr_{A_i}(\{x \in C_{i,j} \mid h(x) \le 0\}) \\
&\le \Pr_{A_i}(\{x \in A_i \mid h(x) \le 0\}) \le \epsilon
\end{aligned} \tag{7}$$

and

$$\begin{aligned}
&\Pr_{A_i}(\{x \in C_{i,j} \mid h(x) > 0\}) \\
&= \Pr_{B_j}(\{x \in C_{i,j} \mid h(x) > 0\}) \cdot P \\
&\le \frac{\epsilon\lambda(B_j)}{\lambda(A_i)},
\end{aligned} \tag{8}$$

where $P = \frac{\Pr_{A_i}(\{x \in C_{i,j} \mid h(x) > 0\})}{\Pr_{B_j}(\{x \in C_{i,j} \mid h(x) > 0\})}$. Combining (7) and (8), we have (6).

Consequently, the probability measure of the states x in $\{x \mid \phi_i(x)\}$ such that $\phi_i(x) \wedge \psi_j(x) \models \bot$ is larger than or equal to

$$1 - \min\{1, \epsilon + \frac{\epsilon\lambda(B_j)}{\lambda(A_i)}\},$$

with confidence at least $1 - \beta$, $i = 1, \ldots, l$, $j = 1, \ldots, k$. Consequently, the probability measure of the states x in $\{x \mid \phi_i(x)\}$ such that $\phi_i(x) \wedge \psi(x) \models \bot$ is larger than or equal to

$$\max\{0, 1 - \sum_{j=1}^{k}(\epsilon + \frac{\epsilon\lambda(B_j)}{\lambda(A_i)})\},$$

with confidence at least $1 - \beta$, $i = 1, \ldots, l$.

We also have the similar conclusion for ψ_j, $j = 1, \ldots, k$. That is, the probability measure of states in $\{x \mid \psi_j(x)\}$ such that $\psi_j(x) \wedge \phi(x) \models \perp$ is larger than or equal to

$$\max\{0, 1 - \sum_{i=1}^{l}(\epsilon + \frac{\epsilon\lambda(A_i)}{\lambda(B_j)})\},$$

with confidence at least $1 - \beta$.

Let's take (6) as an instance to give a further explanation of PAC interpolants in the safety verification scenario [32]. Let A_i be a set of possibly reachable states of a system of interest and $\mathcal{F}_2$ be a set of unsafe states. Thus, the probability of reaching the unsafe region $\mathcal{F}_2$ is less than or equal to

$$\min\{1, \sum_{j=1}^{k}(\epsilon + \frac{\epsilon\lambda(B_j)}{\lambda(A_i)})\},$$

with at least $1 - \beta$ confidence. If β is extremely small (smaller than 10^{-10}), then we have a priori practical certainty that the unsafe probability does not exceed

$$\min\{1, \sum_{j=1}^{k}(\epsilon + \frac{\epsilon\lambda(B_j)}{\lambda(A_i)})\}.$$

Further, if ϵ is below a threshold as well, it is reasonable to believe that the system is practically safe in real applications.

Especially, if a computed $\mathtt{CI}(\epsilon, \beta)$ is verified to satisfy (1) based on existing methods such as SMT solving and semi-definite programming, the computed $\mathtt{CI}(\epsilon, \beta)$ is a true interpolant and thus the formulas ϕ and ψ are inconsistent.

3   PAC Interpolants Generation

In this section we present our method for generating PAC interpolants. The method is based on the scenario optimization yielding a linear program to be solved.

3.1   Scenario Optimization

The scenario optimization is an intuitive and effective way to deal with robust optimization problems based on finite randomization of the constraints [3]. Concretely, consider the following robust optimization problem:

$$\min_{\gamma \in \Gamma \subseteq \mathbb{R}^m} c^T \gamma$$
$$\text{such that } f_\delta(\gamma) \leq 0, \forall \delta \in \tilde{\Delta}, \tag{9}$$

where Γ is a convex and closed set, and $f_\delta(\gamma)$ are convex functions over the decision variable γ for every δ in a closed set $\tilde{\Delta} \subseteq \mathbb{R}^r$.

Definition 4 (Scenario Optimization). *Extract N independent and identically distributed samples* $(\delta^{(i)})_{i=1}^N$ *from* $\tilde{\Delta}$ *according to probability* P *and solve the convex program* (10):

$$\min_{\gamma \in \Gamma \subseteq \mathbb{R}^m} c^T \gamma$$
$$s.\ t.\ \wedge_{i=1}^N f_{\delta^{(i)}}(\gamma) \le 0. \tag{10}$$

(10) *is a relaxation of* (9) *and the process of solving* (10) *to obtain an approximate solution to* (9) *is called* scenario optimization *of* (9). *Correspondingly, its optimal solution* γ^* *is called* scenario solution *to* (10).

Theorem 1 shows that the solution γ_N^* to (10) satisfies all constraints in (9) except a fraction.

Theorem 1. *[4] Choose a violation level $\epsilon \in (0,1)$ and a confidence level $\beta \in (0,1)$. If (10) is feasible and attains a unique optimal solution, and*

$$N \ge \frac{2}{\epsilon}(\ln \frac{1}{\beta} + m), \tag{11}$$

where m is the number of optimization variables λ, then with confidence at least $1 - \beta$, γ_N^* satisfies all constraints in $\tilde{\Delta}$ but at most a fraction of probability measure ϵ, i.e., P$(\{\delta \mid f_\delta(\gamma_N^*) > 0\}) \le \epsilon$.

In Theorem 1, $1 - \beta$ is the N−fold probability P^N in $\tilde{\Delta}^N = \tilde{\Delta} \times \cdots \times \tilde{\Delta}$, which is the set to which the extracted sample $(\delta^{(1)}, \ldots, \delta^{(N)})$ belongs. A unique optimal solution can be selected from the Tie-break rule if multiple optimal solutions occur for (10), Theorem 1 still holds if the uniqueness of optimal solutions to (10) in Theorem 1 is removed [3]. The minimum number of samples depends logarithmically on β^{-1}, we can choose a high confidence without increasing the required samples too much. Moreover, we observe from Theorem 1 that the number N of required samples does not depend on the dimension of the universally quantified variables δ. This facilitates application of the scenario optimization approach to systems with high-dimensional variables δ. Recently, scenario optimization was used to compute probably approximately safe inputs for a given black-box system such that the system's final outputs fall within a safe range in [33], perform safety verification of hybrid systems in [32] and black-box continuous time dynamical systems in [34].

3.2 PAC Interpolant Generation

In this subsection we elucidate our linear programming based approach for computing the PAC interpolants.

We first select an interpolant template $h(c_1, \ldots, c_{l'}, \boldsymbol{x})$ such that $h(c_1, \ldots, c_{l'}, \boldsymbol{x})$ is for every $\boldsymbol{x} \in \mathbb{R}^n$ a linear function in $c_1, \ldots, c_{l'}$, where $(c_i)_{i=1,\ldots,l'}$ are unknown parameters. For instance, for a two-dimensional state variable $\boldsymbol{x} = (x_1, x_2)^\top$, $w(c_1, c_2, \boldsymbol{x}) = c_1 x_1 + c_2 x_2^2$ is a linear function in c_1 and c_2, and $w(c_1, c_2, \boldsymbol{x}) = c_1 e^{x_1 x_2} + c_2 \ln(x_2)$ is also a linear function over c_1 and c_2. How to select a best interpolant template is not the focus of this paper. Generally, we would use an interpolant template of the polynomial form over $\boldsymbol{x}$. If a given template fails to generate a PAC interpolant, a polynomial template with higher degree would be recommended.

In the following we show how to use scenario optimization from Definition 4 to solve (1) and obtain an approximate solution $(c_j)_{j=1,\ldots,l'}$ such that with confidence at least $1 - \beta$, the probability that $h(c_1, \ldots, c_{l'}, \boldsymbol{x})$ satisfies (1) is larger than or equal to $1 - \epsilon$. That is, $h(c_1, \ldots, c_{l'}, \boldsymbol{x})$ is $\mathtt{CI}(\epsilon, \beta)$.

According to Definition 4, we extract N independent and identically distributed samples

$$\{(\boldsymbol{x}_{A_1,i}, \ldots, \boldsymbol{x}_{A_l,i}, \boldsymbol{x}_{B_1,i}, \ldots, \boldsymbol{x}_{B_k,i}) \in \Delta\}_{i=1}^N$$

from the product space Δ in (2) according to the probability distribution $\mathtt{Pr}$, where $\boldsymbol{x}_{A_j,i} \in A_j = \{\boldsymbol{x} \mid \phi_j(\boldsymbol{x})\}$ for $j = 1, \ldots, l$ and $\boldsymbol{x}_{B_j,i} \in B_j = \{\boldsymbol{x} \mid \psi_j(\boldsymbol{x})\}$ for $j = 1, \ldots, k$, we obtain a linear program (12) over $(c_i)_{i=1,\ldots,l'}$ and γ,

$$\min_{c_i, i=1,\ldots,l',\gamma} -\gamma$$

such that for each $i = 1, \ldots, N$:

$$-h(c_1, \ldots, c_{l'}, \boldsymbol{x}_{A_1,i}) + \gamma + \varepsilon \le 0,$$

$$\ldots$$

$$-h(c_1, \ldots, c_{l'}, \boldsymbol{x}_{A_l,i}) + \gamma + \varepsilon \le 0 \qquad (12)$$

$$h(c_1, \ldots, c_{l'}, \boldsymbol{x}_{B_1,i}) + \gamma \le 0,$$

$$\ldots$$

$$h(c_1, \ldots, c_{l'}, \boldsymbol{x}_{B_k,i}) + \gamma \le 0,$$

$$-U_c \le c_j \le U_c, j = 1, \ldots, l',$$

$$0 \le \gamma \le U_\gamma,$$

where ε is a given positive value, positive values U_c and U_γ are respectively pre-specified upper bounds for $|c_j|$, $j = 1, \ldots, l'$, and γ. (12) can determine the thickest slab separating the two family of samples $(\boldsymbol{x}_{A_j,i})_{j=1,\ldots,l}^{i=1,\ldots,N}$ and $(\boldsymbol{x}_{B_j,i})_{j=1,\ldots,k}^{i=1,\ldots,N}$, where 2γ represents the thickness of the slab. ε is to ensure the positivity of $h(c_1, \ldots, c_{l'}, \boldsymbol{x})$ over $\boldsymbol{x}_{A_j,i}$, $j = 1, \ldots, l$, $i = 1, \ldots, N$.

If $N \ge \frac{2}{\epsilon}(\ln \frac{1}{\beta} + l' + 1)$ and (12) has feasible solutions, we conclude that the function $h(c_1^*, \ldots, c_{l'}^*, \boldsymbol{x})$ is $\mathtt{CI}(\epsilon, \beta)$, where $(c_i^*)_{i=1,\ldots,l'}$ is an optimal solution to (12).

Theorem 2. *Suppose that (12) is feasible with $N \ge \frac{2}{\epsilon}(\ln \frac{1}{\beta} + l' + 1)$ and $(c_i^*)_{i=1,\ldots,l'}$ is an optimal solution to (12), then the function $h(c_1^*, \ldots, c_{l'}^*, \boldsymbol{x})$ is $\mathtt{CI}(\epsilon, \beta)$.*

Proof. We reformulate (12) equivalently as the following linear program over $c_1, \ldots, c_{l'}$ and γ,

$$\min_{c_i, i=1, \ldots, l', \gamma} \gamma$$

such that for each $i = 1, \ldots, N$:

$$- h'_{A_1, i}(c_1, \ldots, c_{l'}, \boldsymbol{w}_i) + \gamma + \varepsilon \leq 0,$$

$$\ldots$$

$$- h'_{A_l, i}(c_1, \ldots, c_{l'}, \boldsymbol{w}_i) + \gamma + \varepsilon \leq 0,$$

$$h'_{B_1, i}(c_1, \ldots, c_{l'}, \boldsymbol{w}_i) + \gamma \leq 0, \tag{13}$$

$$\ldots$$

$$h'_{B_k, i}(c_1, \ldots, c_{l'}, \boldsymbol{w}_i) + \gamma \leq 0,$$

$$- U_c \leq c_j \leq U_c, j = 1, \ldots, l',$$

$$0 \leq \gamma \leq U_\gamma,$$

where $h'_{A_j, i}(c_1, \ldots, c_{l'}, \boldsymbol{w}_i) = h(c_1, \ldots, c_{l'}, \boldsymbol{x}_{A_j, i})$ for $j = 1, \ldots, l$, $h'_{B_j, i}(c_1, \ldots, c_{l'}, \boldsymbol{w}_i) = h(c_1, \ldots, c_{l'}, \boldsymbol{x}_{B_j, i})$ for $j = 1, \ldots, k$, and

$$\boldsymbol{w}_i = (\boldsymbol{x}_{A_1, i}, \ldots, \boldsymbol{x}_{A_l, i}, \boldsymbol{x}_{B_1, i}, \ldots, \boldsymbol{x}_{B_k, i}).$$

The number of decision variables in (13) is $l'+1$, i.e., $c_1, \ldots, c_{l'}$ and γ.

Optimal solutions to (12) are optimal ones to (13), and vice versa. If the optimal solution $(c_1^*, \ldots, c_{l'}^*, \gamma^*)$ to (13) is unique, the function $h(c_1^*, \ldots, c_{l'}^*, \boldsymbol{x})$ is $\mathtt{CI}(\epsilon, \beta)$ according to Theorem 1 and Definition 3. If the linear optimization (13) has multiple optimal solutions then we can take one of optimal solution and set $c_i := c_i^*$ in (13) to obtain a new linear program optimizing over the only variable γ. Obviously, γ^* is still the optimal solution to the resulting new linear optimization problem and its solution is unique. Therefore, by Theorem 1, the function $h(c_1^*, \ldots, c_{l'}^*, \boldsymbol{x})$ is $\mathtt{CI}(\epsilon, \beta)$. $\square$

Our approach for synthesizing PAC interpolants is formally summarized in Algorithm 1.

4   Experiments

In this section we evaluate Algorithm 1 on three examples. Parameters that determine the performance of Algorithm 1 are presented in Fig. 1. All computations were performed on an i7-7500U 2.70 GHz CPU with 32 GB RAM running Windows 10.

Example 1. To enhance the understanding of Algorithm 1, we consider a simple example as follows:

$$\phi(x, y) : (f_1(x, y) \geq 0 \wedge f_2(x, y) \geq 0),$$
$$\psi(x, y) : (g_1(x, y) \geq 0 \wedge g_2(x, y) \geq 0),$$

Algorithm 1. PAC Interpolant Generation

Input: formulas ϕ and ψ; ε in (12); upper bounds U_c and U_γ in (12); violation level $\epsilon \in (0,1)$ and confidence value $\beta \in (0,1)$.

Output: If a $\texttt{CI}(\epsilon, \beta)$ is computed, return "YES" and a $\texttt{CI}(\epsilon, \beta)$; Otherwise, return "UNKNOWN".

1. Select an interpolant template $h(c_1, \ldots, c_{l'}, \boldsymbol{x})$;
2. Compute the number N of samples with respect to ϵ and β according to (11);
3. Extract independent and uniformly distributed N samples from the product space Δ in (2) based on a rejection sampling algorithm [29];
4. **if** an optimal solution $(c_j^*)_{j=1,\ldots,l'}$ is computed via solving (12) **then**
   Return "YES" and $\texttt{CI}(\epsilon, \beta) = h(c_1^*, \ldots, c_{l'}^*, \boldsymbol{x})$;
5. **else**
   Return "UNKNOWN";
6. **end if**

Benchmarks	d_ϕ	d_ψ	Alg.1						
			ϵ	β	N	m	ε	U	T
Ex.1	2	2	0.01	0.01	2322	7	0.1	10	350.76
Ex.2	2	2	0.001	0.001	27816	7	0.1	10	383.69
Ex.3	100	100	0.01	10^{-12}	25927	102	0.1	10	563.91

Fig. 1. *Parameters and performance of our method on the listed examples. $\mathbf{d}_\phi$ and $\mathbf{d}_\psi$: dimensions of variables in formulas ϕ and ψ respectively; ϵ: violation level; β: confidence level; N: the number of extracted samples; m: the number of unknown variables in (12); ε: ε in (12); U: the upper bound for both U_c and U_γ in (12); T: the computation time for computing $\texttt{CI}(\epsilon, \beta)$.*

where $f_1(x, y) = 4 - x^2 - y^2$, $f_2(x, y) = y - x^2$, $g_1(x, y) = 4 - x^2 - y^2$ and $g_2(x, y) = x^2 - y - 0.5$.

The interpolant template is assumed as $c_1 + c_2 x + c_3 y + c_4 x^2 + c_5 xy + c_6 y^2$, where $c_1, \ldots, c_6$ are the unknown parameters. Thus, the number of optimization variables in (12) is 7. Let $\epsilon = 0.01$ and $\beta = 0.01$. According to Theorem 1, we obtain that the number N of samples is at least 2322.

We take 2322 independent and identically distributed samples

$$\{(x_{A_1,k}, y_{A_1,k}, x_{B_1,k}, y_{B_1,k})\}_{k=1}^{2322}$$

from the product space $A_1 \times B_1$ according to the uniform distribution, where

$$(x_{A_1,k}, y_{A_1,k}) \in A_1 = \{(x, y) \mid f_1(x, y) \geq 0, f_2(x, y) \geq 0\}$$

and

$$(x_{B_1,k}, y_{B_1,k}) \in B_1 = \{(x, y) \mid g_1(x, y) \geq 0, g_2(x, y) \geq 0\}$$

with $k = 1, \ldots, N$. This results in the following linear program over $c_1, \ldots, c_6, \gamma$:

$$\min_{c_1,\ldots,c_6,\gamma} \gamma$$

such that for each $k = 1, \ldots, 2322$:

$$- h(x_{A_1,k}, y_{A_1,k}) + \gamma + \varepsilon \leq 0,$$
$$h(x_{B_1,k}, y_{B_1,k}) + \gamma \leq 0,$$
$$- 10 \leq c_i \leq 10, i = 1, \ldots, 6,$$
$$0 \leq \gamma \leq 10,$$

(14)

where $\varepsilon = 0.1$. These extracted samples are shown in Fig. 2.

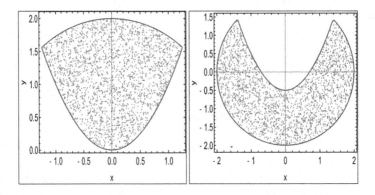

Fig. 2. An illustration of extracted samples. Red curves in the left and right figures are respectively the boundary of $\{(x, y) \mid \phi(x, y)\}$ and $\{(x, y) \mid \psi(x, y)\}$. Gray points in the left and right figures are respectively the extracted samples from $\{(x, y) \mid \phi(x, y)\}$ and $\{(x, y) \mid \psi(x, y)\}$.

Via solving (14), we obtain a $\mathtt{CI}(0.01, 0.01)$:

$$h(x, y) = 2.51547516736 + 0.0165156178714x + 9.99999999665y$$
$$- 9.95141962642x^2 + 0.0513084342584y^2 - 0.00560477791004xy.$$

(15)

That is, with at least 99% confidence, the probability that $h(x, y) > 0$ is an interpolant for $\phi(x, y)$ and $\psi(x, y)$ is larger than or equal to 0.99. The plots of $\{(x, y) \mid \psi(x, y)\}$, $\{(x, y) \mid \phi(x, y)\}$ and $\{(x, y) \mid h(x, y) > 0\}$ are presented in Fig. 3.

Actually, a check using the REDUCE Computer Algebra System [9] proves that $h(x, y)$ in (15) is a true (not just probably approximately correct) interpolant satisfying

$$h(x.y) > 0, \forall(x, y) \in \{(x, y) \mid \phi(x, y)\},$$
$$h(x, y) \leq 0, \forall(x, y) \in \{(x, y) \mid \psi(x, y)\}.$$

(16)

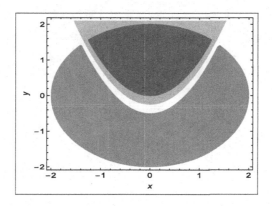

Fig. 3. An illustration of CI(0.01, 0.01) for Example 1. Red, green and gray regions are respectively the set $\{(x, y) \mid \phi(x, y)\}$, $\{(x, y) \mid \psi(x, y)\}$ and $\{(x, y) \mid h(x, y) > 0\}$ (Color figure online).

Example 2. In order to demonstrate the applicability of our method to formulas beyond polynomial ones, we consider nonlinear formulas:

$$\phi(x, y) : f_1(x, y) \leq 0 \wedge f_2(x, y) \leq 0$$
$$\psi(x, y) : (g_{1,1}(x, y) \leq 0 \wedge g_{1,2}(x, y) \geq 0) \vee (g_{2,1}(x, y) \leq 0 \wedge g_{2,2}(x, y) \leq 0)$$

where $f_1(x, y) = y^2 + x^2 - 4$, $f_2(x, y) = y^8 - 2y^4x^2 + 6y^4 + y^2 + \sin(x)^4 - 5x^2 + 5$, $g_{1,1}(x, y) = y^2 + x^2 - 4$, $g_{1,2}(x, y) = y^2 - x^2 - 1$, $g_{2,1}(x, y) = y^2 + x^2 - 4$ and $g_{2,2}(x, y) = 2y^2 - 2yx^2 - 2y + x^4 + 3x^2 - 3$.

Via solving (14), we obtain a CI(0.001, 0.001):

$$\begin{aligned} h(x, y) &= -9.99999999941 + 0.0280147362282x \\ &- 0.312255569319y + 10x^2 - 0.0107265793759xy - 6.16535622183y^2. \end{aligned} \tag{17}$$

That is, with at least 99.9% confidence, the probability that $h(x, y) > 0$ is an interpolant for ϕ and ψ is larger than or equal to 0.999.

Since the formula ϕ is non-polynomial, we use the satisfiability checker iSAT3 [10] to check that $h(x, y)$ in (17) is a true (not just probably approximately correct) interpolant.

The plots of $\{(x, y) \mid \psi(x, y)\}$, $\{(x, y) \mid \phi(x, y)\}$ and $\{(x, y) \mid h(x, y) > 0\}$ are presented in Fig. 4.

Example 3. To demonstrate the applicability of our approach to formulas with high-dimensional variables, we consider a scalable example with variables of high dimension of 100.

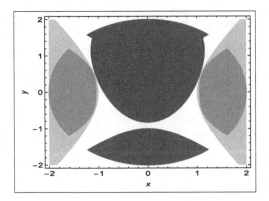

Fig. 4. An illustration of $\text{CI}(0.001, 0.001)$ for Example 2. Red, green and gray regions are respectively the set $\{(x,y) \mid \psi(x,y)\}$, $\{(x,y) \mid \phi(x,y)\}$ and $\{(x,y) \mid h(x,y) > 0\}$. (Color figure online)

$$\phi(\boldsymbol{x}):$$
$$\wedge_{i=1}^{100} [x_i \leq 0 \wedge x_i + 0.5 \geq 0].$$
$$\psi(\boldsymbol{x}):$$
$$\wedge_{i=1}^{100} [-x_i - 0.9 \leq 0 \wedge x_i + 0.4 \leq 0]$$
$$\wedge \sum_{i=1}^{100} x_i - e^{x_{10}} + \cos(x_{50}) \sin(x_{50}) + 0.9 \leq 0.$$

The interpolant template is $c_0 + \sum_{i=1}^{100} c_i x_i$. Algorithm 1 returns a $\text{CI}(0.01, 10^{-12})$. The satisfiability checker iSAT3 [10] fails to check whether the computed $\text{CI}(0.01, 10^{-12})$ is a true interpolant. However, according to (6), we have that the probability of states in $\{\boldsymbol{x} \mid \phi(\boldsymbol{x})\}$ such that such that $\phi(\boldsymbol{x}) \wedge \psi(\boldsymbol{x}) \models \perp$ is larger than $\max\{0, 1 - (0.01 + 0.01\frac{0.5^{100}}{0.5^{100}})\} \geq 0.98$, with confidence at least $1 - 10^{-12}$.

The dimensionality of this example demonstrates that our approach opens up a promising prospect for interpolant synthesis of formulas with high-dimensional variables by selecting appropriate ϵ, β and interpolant templates.

5   Conclusion

In this paper we investigated the generation of interpolants for two Boolean formulas in the framework of PAC learning, attempting to fight against the "curse of dimensionality" suffered by traditional formal methods. A new concept, called PAC Craig interpolants, was introduced to characterize the relationship between two formulas using violation levels and confidence levels. Based on scenario approaches, we could construct a linear programming formulation of the instantiation problem for an interpolant template and compute a PAC interpolant.

Using the computed PAC interpolant, we could characterize how inconsistent the two given formulas are. Besides, one important consequence of our approach is that in contrast to traditional methods for computing interpolants, our method scales well to the high-dimensional formulas. Three examples demonstrated the performance of our approach.

In our future work we would extend our method to safety verification of hybrid systems, as well as the generation of PAC interpolants for Boolean formulas with uncommon variables.

References

1. Andersen, M., Dahl, J., Liu, Z., Vandenberghe, L.: Interior-point methods for large-scale cone programming. In: Optimization for Machine Learning, pp. 55–83 (2011)
2. Benhamou, F., Granvilliers, L.: Continuous and interval constraints. In: Handbook of Constraint Programming. Foundations of Artificial Intelligence, vol. 2, pp. 571–603 (2006)
3. Calafiore, G.C., Campi, M.C.: The scenario approach to robust control design. IEEE Trans. Autom. Control **51**(5), 742–753 (2006)
4. Campi, M.C., Garatti, S., Prandini, M.: The scenario approach for systems and control design. Ann. Rev. Control **33**(2), 149–157 (2009)
5. Chen, M., Wang, J., An, J., Zhan, B., Kapur, D., Zhan, N.: NIL: learning nonlinear interpolants. In: Fontaine, P. (ed.) CADE 2019. LNCS (LNAI), vol. 11716, pp. 178–196. Springer, Cham (2019). https://doi.org/10.1007/978-3-030-29436-6_11
6. Cimatti, A., Griggio, A., Sebastiani, R.: Efficient interpolant generation in satisfiability modulo theories. In: Ramakrishnan, C.R., Rehof, J. (eds.) TACAS 2008. LNCS, vol. 4963, pp. 397–412. Springer, Heidelberg (2008). https://doi.org/10.1007/978-3-540-78800-3_30
7. Craig, W.: Linear reasoning. A new form of the Herbrand-Gentzen theorem. J. Symb. Logic **22**(3), 250–268 (1957)
8. Dai, L., Xia, B., Zhan, N.: Generating non-linear interpolants by semidefinite programming. In: Sharygina, N., Veith, H. (eds.) CAV 2013. LNCS, vol. 8044, pp. 364–380. Springer, Heidelberg (2013). https://doi.org/10.1007/978-3-642-39799-8_25
9. Fitch, J.: Solving algebraic problems with REDUCE. J. Symb. Comput. **1**(2), 211–227 (1985)
10. Fränzle, M., Herde, C., Teige, T., Ratschan, S., Schubert, T.: Efficient solving of large non-linear arithmetic constraint systems with complex Boolean structure. J. Satisf. Boolean Model. Comput. **1**, 209–236 (2007)
11. Gan, T., Dai, L., Xia, B., Zhan, N., Kapur, D., Chen, M.: Interpolation synthesis for quadratic polynomial inequalities and combination with EUF. In: IJCAR 2016, pp. 195–212 (2016)
12. Gan, T., Xia, B., Xue, B., Zhan, N., Dai, L.: Nonlinear Craig interpolant generation. In: Lahiri, S.K., Wang, C. (eds.) CAV 2020. LNCS, vol. 12224, pp. 415–438. Springer, Cham (2020). https://doi.org/10.1007/978-3-030-53288-8_20
13. Gao, S., Kong, S., Clarke, E.M.: Proof generation from delta-decisions. In: SYNASC 2014, pp. 156–163 (2014)
14. Gao, S., Zufferey, D.: Interpolants in nonlinear theories over the reals. In: Chechik, M., Raskin, J.-F. (eds.) TACAS 2016. LNCS, vol. 9636, pp. 625–641. Springer, Heidelberg (2016). https://doi.org/10.1007/978-3-662-49674-9_41

15. Gearhart, J.L., Adair, K.L., Detry, R.J., Durfee, J.D., Jones, K.A., Martin, N.: Comparison of open-source linear programming solvers. Technical report SAND2013-8847 (2013)
16. Graf, S., Saidi, H.: Construction of abstract state graphs with PVS. In: Grumberg, O. (ed.) CAV 1997. LNCS, vol. 1254, pp. 72–83. Springer, Heidelberg (1997). https://doi.org/10.1007/3-540-63166-6_10
17. Haussler, D.: Probably approximately correct learning. University of California, Santa Cruz, Computer Research Laboratory (1990)
18. Henzinger, T., Jhala, R., Majumdar, R., McMillan, K.: Abstractions from proofs. In POPL **2004**, 232–244 (2004)
19. Kapur, D., Majumdar, R., Zarba, C.: Interpolation for data structures. In: FSE 2006, pp. 105–116 (2006)
20. Kovács, L., Voronkov, A.: Interpolation and symbol elimination. In: Schmidt, R.A. (ed.) CADE 2009. LNCS (LNAI), vol. 5663, pp. 199–213. Springer, Heidelberg (2009). https://doi.org/10.1007/978-3-642-02959-2_17
21. Krajíček, J.: Interpolation theorems, lower bounds for proof systems, and independence results for bounded arithmetic. J. Symb. Logic **62**(2), 457–486 (1997)
22. Kupferschmid, S., Becker, B.: Craig interpolation in the presence of non-linear constraints. In: Fahrenberg, U., Tripakis, S. (eds.) FORMATS 2011. LNCS, vol. 6919, pp. 240–255. Springer, Heidelberg (2011). https://doi.org/10.1007/978-3-642-24310-3_17
23. McMillan, K.L.: Interpolation and SAT-based model checking. In: Hunt, W.A., Somenzi, F. (eds.) CAV 2003. LNCS, vol. 2725, pp. 1–13. Springer, Heidelberg (2003). https://doi.org/10.1007/978-3-540-45069-6_1
24. McMillan, K.: An interpolating theorem prover. Theor. Comput. Sci. **345**(1), 101–121 (2005)
25. McMillan, K.L.: Quantified invariant generation using an interpolating saturation prover. In: Ramakrishnan, C.R., Rehof, J. (eds.) TACAS 2008. LNCS, vol. 4963, pp. 413–427. Springer, Heidelberg (2008). https://doi.org/10.1007/978-3-540-78800-3_31
26. Pudlák, P.: Lower bounds for resolution and cutting plane proofs and monotone computations. J. Symb. Logic **62**(3), 981–998 (1997)
27. Rybalchenko, A., Sofronie-Stokkermans, V.: Constraint solving for interpolation. J. Symb. Comput. **45**(11), 1212–1233 (2010)
28. Sharma, R., Nori, A.V., Aiken, A.: Interpolants as classifiers. In: Madhusudan, P., Seshia, S.A. (eds.) CAV 2012. LNCS, vol. 7358, pp. 71–87. Springer, Heidelberg (2012). https://doi.org/10.1007/978-3-642-31424-7_11
29. Steyvers, M.: Computational statistics with MATLAB (2011)
30. Törnblom, J., Nadjm-Tehrani, S.: Formal verification of random forests in safety-critical applications. In: Artho, C., Ölveczky, P.C. (eds.) FTSCS 2018. CCIS, vol. 1008, pp. 55–71. Springer, Cham (2019). https://doi.org/10.1007/978-3-030-12988-0_4
31. Xue, B., Easwaran, A., Cho, N.-J., Fränzle, M.: Reach-avoid verification for non-linear systems based on boundary analysis. IEEE Trans. Autom. Control **62**(7), 3518–3523 (2016)
32. Xue, B., Fränzle, M., Zhao, H., Zhan, N., Easwaran, A.: Probably approximate safety verification of hybrid dynamical systems. In: Ait-Ameur, Y., Qin, S. (eds.) ICFEM 2019. LNCS, vol. 11852, pp. 236–252. Springer, Cham (2019). https://doi.org/10.1007/978-3-030-32409-4_15
33. Xue, B., Liu, Y., Ma, L., Zhang, X., Sun, M., Xie, X.: Safe inputs approximation for black-box systems. In: ICECCS 2019, pp. 180–189. IEEE (2019)

34. Xue, B., Zhang, M., Easwaran, A., Li, Q.: PAC model checking of black-box continuous-time dynamical systems. IEEE Trans. Comput.-Aided Des. Integr. Circuits Syst. (IEEE TCAD) (2020, to appear)
35. Yorsh, G., Musuvathi, M.: A combination method for generating interpolants. In: Nieuwenhuis, R. (ed.) CADE 2005. LNCS (LNAI), vol. 3632, pp. 353–368. Springer, Heidelberg (2005). https://doi.org/10.1007/11532231_26
36. Zhan, N., Wang, S., Zhao, H.: Formal Verification of Simulink/Stateflow Diagrams: A Deductive Approach. Springer, Cham (2017). https://doi.org/10.1007/978-3-319-47016-0
37. Zhao, H., Zhan, N., Kapur, D., Larsen, K.G.: A "hybrid" approach for synthesizing optimal controllers of hybrid systems: a case study of the oil pump industrial example. In: Giannakopoulou, D., Méry, D. (eds.) FM 2012. LNCS, vol. 7436, pp. 471–485. Springer, Heidelberg (2012). https://doi.org/10.1007/978-3-642-32759-9_38

Symbolic Verification of MPI Programs with Non-deterministic Synchronizations

Hengbiao Yu[1(✉)], Zhenbang Chen[1(✉)], Chun Huang[1], and Ji Wang[1,2]

[1] College of Computer, National University of Defense Technology,
Changsha, China
{hengbiaoyu,zbchen,chunhuang,wj}@nudt.edu.cn
[2] State Key Laboratory of High Performance Computing,
National University of Defense Technology, Changsha, China

Abstract. Message Passing Interface (MPI) is the current de-facto standard for developing applications in high-performance computing. MPI allows flexible implementations of message passing operations, which introduces non-deterministic synchronizations that challenge the correctness of MPI programs. We present in this paper a symbolic method for verifying the MPI programs with non-deterministic synchronizations. Insides the method, we propose a path-level modeling method that uses communicating sequential processes (CSP) to precisely encode the non-deterministic synchronizations of an execution path. Furthermore, for the execution paths without non-deterministic message receive operations, we propose an optimization method to reduce the complexity of the CSP models. We have implemented our technique on MPI-SV and evaluated it on 10 real-world MPI programs *w.r.t.* deadlock freedom. The experimental results demonstrate the effectiveness of our verification method.

1 Introduction

Message Passing Interface (MPI) [21] is the most widely used standard for developing applications in high-performance computing (HPC). MPI provides a rich set of *message passing* operations for developers. MPI programs are usually run in many processes spanned on network-connected machines. These distributed processes cooperate by message passings to accomplish a computation task. The development of MPI programs is challenging, and it is highly demanded to have methods and tools to ensure the correctness of MPI programs [8].

Existing approaches for verifying the correctness of MPI programs are mainly dynamic methods [6,24], which run the program under a specific input and verify the correctness of program paths. There are few static verification methods [2,18, 19], which abstract the MPI program and verify the correctness of the abstract model. There are also symbolic execution based methods [14,27], which achieve a balance between precision and scalability and provide a bounded verification support for MPI programs.

This work is supported by National Key R&D Program of China (No. 2018YFB0204301) and NSFC Program (No. 61902409, 61632015, 61690203 and 61532007).

J. Pang and L. Zhang (Eds.): SETTA 2020, LNCS 12153, pp. 160–176, 2020.
https://doi.org/10.1007/978-3-030-62822-2_10

For improving the performance further, the MPI standard [7] allows flexible implementations of MPI operations. Especially, the standard send operation can be implemented in *"rendezvous"* mode [1], where the send operation blocks the sending process until the message is received, or the *"eager"* mode [1], where the send operation's completion is independent of the corresponding receive operation and only requires that the sending message has been copied to the local system buffer. If the local system buffer is full, the send operation also blocks. Hence, the synchronizations in MPI programs depend on the MPI implementations, which we call *non-deterministic synchronizations*. Because of this, an MPI program failure (*e.g.*, deadlock) may appear only in some specific MPI implementations, which brings difficulties for developing MPI programs. However, the existing work of verifying MPI programs seldom considers the problem of non-deterministic synchronizations. As far as we know, the work in [1] is the only one, which provides a dynamic verification method that can find potential errors related to non-deterministic synchronizations. However, the method in [1] cannot find the errors that depend on the program input.

Figure 1 shows an MPI program running in two processes. Process P_0 first sends a message to process P_1. Then, if the input x is equal to 'a', P_0 will receive a messages from P_1. On the other hand, if x is 'a', process P_1 will first send a message to P_0. After that, process P_1 receives a message from process P_0. If the input x is 'a' and both the send operations are implemented in the "rendezvous" mode, a deadlock happens, *i.e.*, both P_0 and P_1 block at the send operation and wait for receive operations to receive the message. However, if send operations are implemented in the "eager" model with non-zero-sized local system buffers, there will be no deadlock, despite the input x. Hence, to verify the deadlock freedom of the MPI program, we need to cover both the input space and the non-deterministic synchronizations.

P_0	P_1
Send(1)	if ($x==$'a')
if ($x==$'a')	Send(0)
Recv(1)	Recv(0)

Fig. 1. A motivating example.

In this paper, we present a verification method that covers both the program input and the non-deterministic synchronizations. Our approach is based on the symbolic verification framework of MPI-SV [27]. Specifically, we propose a precise modeling method that utilizes communicating sequential processes (CSP) [17] to encode the non-deterministic synchronizations. The key idea is to use an internal choice to model the blocking or non-blocking of each send operation. Besides, we propose an optimization method for the MPI execution paths without non-deterministic receive operations, which improves the verification's efficiency.

We have implemented our method on MPI-SV [27], and evaluated it on 10 real-world MPI programs, totaling 46638 lines of code (LOC), *w.r.t.* the deadlock freedom property. Our tool successfully verified all the 26 tasks within 90 min, and found that 18 verification tasks have deadlocks due to the non-deterministic synchronizations and 8 tasks are deadlock free. We manually confirmed that all the detected deadlocks are real. These experimental results demonstrate the effectiveness of our approach.

There are following main contributions of this paper.

- A precise method for modeling the non-deterministic synchronizations of an execution path in terms of CSP.
- An optimization method that can reduce the complexity of CSP models for paths having no non-deterministic receive operations.
- A prototype tool and an extensive evaluation on real-world MPI+C programs.

Related Work. There already exist some approaches for verifying MPI programs. MPI-SPIN [18,19] utilizes model checking [5] to verify MPI programs *w.r.t.* LTL properties. However, MPI-SPIN needs manual efforts to build a model in Promela [9]. ParTypes [13] integrates type checking and deductive verification to verify MPI programs against a protocol. ParTypes's verification results hold for any number of processes but may have false positives. Besides, ParTypes only supports MPI programs without non-blocking or wildcard operations. Dynamic verification approaches, *e.g.*, ISP [24] and DAMPI [25], execute the same input multiple times to cover the schedules. MOPPER [6] and the tool in [10] encode the deadlock detection problem under concrete inputs in a SAT and SMT equation, respectively. Hermes [11] integrates dynamic verification and symbolic analysis to verify *multi-path* MPI programs. All these dynamic verification approaches do not support input coverage. MPI-SV [27] integrates symbolic execution and model checking to verify MPI programs *w.r.t.* a given property, but does not consider non-deterministic synchronizations.

The closest related work is the method in [1], where a two-step verification framework is proposed for MPI programs with non-deterministic synchronizations. They first build an abstract model by supposing all the non-deterministic synchronous operations using the "eager" mode. A post-processing method is then applied to the model to detect the potentially missed deadlocks introduced by the non-deterministic synchronous operations. However, they only consider communications under a specific input and may miss input-related deadlocks. In contrast, our approach covers program inputs, different schedules, and non-deterministic synchronizations.

The rest of this paper is organized as follows. Section 2 briefly introduces MPI programs. Section 3 presents the verification framework. Section 4 details our CSP modeling method. Section 5 gives the implementation and evaluation. We conclude in Sect. 6.

$$\begin{aligned}
\textsf{Proc} ::= \;&\textbf{var } l : \textbf{T} \mid l := \textsf{e} \mid \textsf{Comm} \mid \textsf{Proc} \; ; \; \textsf{Proc} \mid \\
&\textbf{if } \textsf{e } \textsf{Proc } \textbf{else } \textsf{Proc} \mid \textbf{while } \textsf{e } \textbf{do } \textsf{Proc} \\
\textsf{Comm} ::= \;&\texttt{Ssend(e)} \mid \texttt{Send(e)} \mid \texttt{Recv(e)} \mid \texttt{Recv(*)} \mid \texttt{Barrier} \mid \\
&\texttt{ISend(e,r)} \mid \texttt{IRecv(e,r)} \mid \texttt{IRecv(*,r)} \mid \texttt{Wait(r)} \mid \\
&\texttt{Bcast(e)} \mid \texttt{Gather(e)} \mid \texttt{Scatter(e)}
\end{aligned}$$

Fig. 2. Syntax of a core MPI language.

2   MPI Programs

In this section, we first define a core MPI language, including syntax and semantics. Then, we give some MPI related definitions used throughout the remainder of this paper.

2.1   Syntax

MPI is a library of message passing functions that can be used to create parallel applications in different languages, such as C, C++, and Fortran. This paper targets MPI+C programs. We define an MPI program $\mathcal{MP}$ as a *finite* set of MPI processes $\{\textsf{Proc}_i \mid 0 \leq i \leq n\}$, where there are $n + 1$ processes, and each $\textsf{Proc}_i$ is defined by the language in Fig. 2.

Figure 2 gives the syntax of a core MPI language considered in this paper, where $\mathbb{T}$ is a set of types, $\mathbb{N}$ is a set of names, and $\mathbb{E}$ denotes set of expressions. It is worth pointing out that we omit complex language features for brevity, *e.g.*, message related parameters of MPI operations, and pointer operations. Our tool does support real-world MPI+C programs.

The statement **var** $l : \textbf{T}$ defines variable l with type $\textbf{T}$ ($\textbf{T} \in \mathbb{T}$), and statement $l := \textsf{e}$ assigns the value of expression $\textsf{e}$ ($\textsf{e} \in \mathbb{E}$) to l. The statement $\textsf{Comm}$ defines an MPI operation, including both blocking and non-blocking message passing operations. An MPI process can be constructed by composing the basic statements using sequence, condition, and loop composition operators.

2.2   Informal Semantics

We present an informal semantics for MPI operations. In terms of the number of evolved MPI processes, we divide the MPI operations into two main groups, *i.e.*, two-sided operations and collective operations.

We first explain the semantics of two-sided operations. The parameter $\textsf{e}$ in two-sided MPI operations denotes the destination process's identifier, and the parameter $\textsf{r}$ denotes the handler of a non-blocking send or receive operation. $\texttt{Ssend(e)}$ is a blocking message send operation that blocks the process until its message has been received by the destination process e, while $\texttt{ISend(e,r)}$ is a non-blocking message send operation that returns immediately after being issued. $\texttt{Send(e)}$ also sends a message to process $\textsf{e}$, and blocks the process until its sending buffer can be reused. A message from process $\textsf{e}$ can be received using

Recv(e) and IRecv(e,r). Recv(e) will block the process until the message is well received, while IRecv(e, r) returns immediately after being issued. Note that Recv(*) and IRecv(*,r) are blocking and non-blocking wildcard receive operations, which can receive a message from any processes. wait(r) is used to ensure the completion of non-blocking operations, *i.e.*, it blocks the process until the non-blocking operation indicated by r is completed.

Collective operations include all the processes in the communicator. The parameter e represents the identifier of the root process. Bcast(e) means that process e broadcasts a message to the non-root processes, and the non-root processes are blocked until the messages are received. Gather(e) gathers data from all the processes to the root process e; hence, the root process is blocked until all the messages are received. Scatter(e) scatters the data from process e to all the processes, which will be blocked until the messages are received. Barrier will block the process until all the processes have called it.

2.3   Definitions

Given an MPI program $\mathcal{MP} = \{\mathsf{Proc}_i \mid 0 \le i \le n\}$, we define a global state S of $\mathcal{MP}$ as $(s_0, \ldots, s_n)$, where s_i is the local state of the ith process. The local state s_i is a 4-tuple $(\mathcal{M}, Stat, Seq_i, \mathcal{F})$, where $\mathcal{M}$ is a mapping from variables to values, $Stat$ is the next program statement to be executed, Seq_i records the issued MPI operations of Proc_i, $\mathcal{F}$ is the flag of process status belonging to {active, blocked, terminated}. An element $elem$ of s_i can be accessed by $s_i.elem$. For a global state S, we use $Seq(S) = \{Seq_i \mid 0 \le i \le n\}$ to denote the issued MPI operations of S.

The formal semantics of the language in Fig. 2 can be defined based on the definitions of global and local states. In principle, the semantics of an MPI program is a communicating finite state machine [3] with different buffer sizes determined by the MPI implementations.

3   Symbolic Verification Framework

This section explains the symbolic verification framework based on MPI-SV [27]. Algorithm 1 gives the framework. In principle, this framework combines symbolic execution and model checking in a synergetic manner. The framework employs symbolic execution to extract path-level models from the MPI program. Then, the path-level models are verified by model checking. The results of model checking are also used to prune paths in symbolic execution.

The inputs of the framework are an MPI program and a verification property. The framework's skeleton is a worklist-based symbolic executor [4]. In the beginning, the *worklist* only contains the initial state S_{init}. Then, the framework iteratively selects a state from *worklist* to advance the state for symbolic execution until all the paths are explored or timeout (omitted for brevity). Select at Line 4 can use different search heuristics for state exploration, such as depth-first

---

Algorithm 1: Symbolic Verification Framework

SV-Framework($\mathcal{MP}, \varphi$)

Data: $\mathcal{MP}$ is an MPI program $\{\text{Proc}_i \mid 0 \leq i \leq n\}$ and φ is a property

1 **begin**
2    $worklist \leftarrow \{S_{init}\}$
3   **while** $worklist \neq \emptyset$ **do**
4       $S_c \leftarrow$ Select($worklist$)
5       $s_i \leftarrow$ Scheduler(S_c)
6   Execute($S_c, s_i, worklist$)
7   **if** $\forall s_i \in S_c, s_i.\mathcal{F} =$ terminated **then**
8   **if** containWild(S_c) **then**
9             $\Gamma \leftarrow$ GenerateCSP(S_c)
10   **else**
11             $\Gamma \leftarrow$ GenerateCSP$^{\#}$(S_c)
12   **end**
13   ModelCheck(Γ, φ)
14   **if** $\Gamma \models \varphi$ **then**
15   Prune($worklist, S_c$)
16   **end**
17   **else if** $\Gamma \not\models \varphi$ **then**
18   reportViolation and **Exit**
19   **end**
20   **end**
21   **end**
22 **end**

---

search (DFS) and breadth-first search (BFS). For the state S_c, we select a process for symbolic execution. Scheduler at Line 5 selects the non-blocking process with the smallest rank. Then, Execute will symbolically execute the next statement in the selected process's state s_i, which may add new states to $worklist$. When each process terminates normally in the state S_c (Line 7), we build a CSP model Γ that encodes the equivalent states of S_c, *i.e.*, the states having the same path condition of S_c. Here, if there exists any wildcard receive along the path to S_c, we build the CSP model by GenerateCSP (*c.f.* Sect. 4.2); otherwise, we build an optimized model by GenerateCSP$^{\#}$ (*c.f.* Sect. 4.3). Then, we verify the CSP model Γ *w.r.t.* φ by model checking (Line 13). If Γ satisfies φ, we prune the equivalent states from $worklist$; otherwise, if the model checker gives a counter-example, we report the counter-example and exit.

Symbolic Execution. The symbolic execution step in the framework is the same as traditional symbolic execution [12] except for the message-passing operations. To get the possible matchings of wildcard receives, the framework executes the non-blocking processes as much as possible. The message operation matchings will be carried out when all the processes are blocked or terminated. The framework matches the message operations *w.r.t.* the happens-before requirements in the MPI standard [7]. When some message operations are matched, the framework will do the symbolic execution of these operations and continue to execute the processes that become active after matching. When a wildcard receive is matched with N send operations, the framework will fork the current state into N states to cover different cases.

P_0	P_1	P_2
Ssend(1)	Recv(*)	Ssend(1)
	Recv(2)	

Fig. 3. An illustrating example of MPI-SV.

Example. We use the example in Fig. 3 to show the workflow of symbolic verification. The symbolic executor first executes process P_0, and blocks at Ssend(1). After that the symbolic executor executes P_1 and P_2 in sequence and blocks at Recv(*) and Ssend(1), respectively. At this time, all the processes are blocked, symbolic verification handles the message matchings. Clearly, the wildcard receive Recv(*) has two matchings, i.e., P_0's Ssend(1) and P_2's Ssend(1). The symbolic executor forks two states for the two matchings. Suppose we first explore the state where Recv(*) matches P_0's Ssend(1), process P_1 continues to be executed, and blocks at Recv(2). Symbolic verification handles the message matchings again. After matching P_1's Recv(2) and P_2's Ssend(1), all the processes are terminated, and the issued MPI operation sequences are $Seq_0 = \langle \text{Ssend(1)} \rangle$, $Seq_1 = \langle \text{Recv(*)}, \text{Recv(2)} \rangle$, and $Seq_2 = \langle \text{Ssend(1)} \rangle$. Now, for all the three processes, we generate the CSP processes for each of them and then compose them in parallel to get the CSP model Γ (c.f. Sect. 4.2). The model checking of Γ w.r.t. deadlock freedom reports a counter-example, i.e., P_1's wildcard receive receives the message from P_2.

Discussion. Our framework integrates symbolic execution and model checking. Scheduler at Line 5 actually employs partial-order reduction (POR) [5] to reduce the full interleavings of different processes. Pure symbolic execution can only verify reachability properties [15]. However, leveraged by the synergy, the framework can verify a larger scope of properties, i.e., temporal properties, because the CSP model encodes the interleavings of the message operations in different processes.

4   CSP Modeling of Non-deterministic Synchronization

4.1   CSP Subset

We utilize a subset of CSP to model an execution path's equivalent communication behaviors, i.e., changing the matchings and interleavings of wildcard receive operations, and the implementations of the non-deterministic synchronizations.

Let Σ be a *finite* set of *events*, $\mathbb{C}$ be a set of *channels*, and $\mathbf{X}$ be a set of *variables*. Figure 4 gives the syntax of the CSP subset that we used, where P represents a CSP process, $a \in \Sigma$, $c \in \mathbb{C}$, $X \subseteq \Sigma$, $x \in \mathbf{X}$ and *cond* is a boolean expression.

$$P := a \mid P \, \mathbin{\fatsemi} \, P \mid P \sqcap P \mid P \square P \mid P \underset{X}{\parallel} P \mid c?x {\to} P \mid c!x {\to} P \mid [cond] {\to} P \mid \mathbf{skip}$$

Fig. 4. The syntax of the CSP subset.

A CSP process can be a single event a or an empty process **skip** that terminates immediately. There exist five operators to compose complex processes, *i.e.*, sequential composition ($\mathbin{\fatsemi}$), internal choice ($\sqcap$), external choice ($\square$), parallel composition with synchronization ($\parallel$) and guarded composition($\to$). Process $P \underset{X}{\mathbin{\fatsemi}} Q$ executes process P and Q in sequence. The choice of process P and Q executes P or Q, the selection of internal choice ($\sqcap$) is non-deterministic, while the selection of external choice ($\square$) is made by the environment, *i.e.*, which process is first enabled to execute. $P \underset{X}{\parallel} Q$ executes the interleaving of P and Q but requires P and Q to synchronize on the events in X. Let PS be a finite set of processes, $\underset{X}{\parallel} PS$ denotes the parallel composition of all the processes in PS. The guarded composition executes the guard and the guarded process in sequence. Channel operation $c?x$ and $c!x$ represent reading an element from channel c to variable x and writing the value of x to channel c, respectively. The guard $[cond]$ makes the guarded process unable to be executed until the boolean condition *cond* is true. *cond* can be the boolean condition of variables and channels, *e.g.*, $\mathsf{empty}(c)$ means that channel c is empty.

4.2   CSP Modeling

Algorithm 2 depicts the basic procedure of building a CSP model for a normally terminated path. The input is a normally terminated global state S for an MPI program running with $n + 1$ processes, and $Seq(S) = \{Seq_i \mid 0 \le i \le n\}$ contains the recorded message passing operation sequences of the processes, *i.e.*, Seq_i is the sequence of the MPI process Proc_i.

The algorithm generates a CSP process for each MPI process and composes the CSP processes in parallel to construct the whole CSP model. For each MPI process, we use the generation rules defined in Fig. 5 to derive its CSP process P_i'. The generation is to scan the operation sequence backward. For each operation, we generate its CSP model and compose the model with the previously generated model. The basic idea of modeling non-deterministic synchronizations is to use an internal choice between the "rendezvous" mode and the "eager" mode with an infinite buffer for modeling message send operations.

For the standard send operation `MPI_Send`, we allocate a zero-sized channel c_0 and a one-sized channel c_1, and use an internal choice of the channel writings

---

Algorithm 2: CSP Model Generation for a Terminated State

GenerateCSP(S)

Data: A terminated global state S, and $Seq(S)=\{Seq_i \mid 0 \le i \le n\}$

1 **begin**

2 $\quad PS \leftarrow \emptyset$

3 $\quad X \leftarrow \emptyset$

4 $\quad$ **for** $i \leftarrow 0 \ldots n$ **do**

5 $\quad\quad P_i \leftarrow \textbf{skip}$

6 $\quad\quad (Seq_i, P_i, X)_i \rightarrow^* (\langle\rangle, P_i', X')_i$ using the rules in Figure 5

7 $\quad\quad X \leftarrow X'$

8 $\quad\quad PS \leftarrow PS \cup \{P_i'\}$

9 $\quad$ **end**

10 $\quad$ **return** $\underset{\{X\}}{\|}\ PS$

11 **end**

$$\frac{S = S' \circ \langle op \rangle \wedge op = \mathsf{Send(j)} \wedge (c_0, c_1) = \mathsf{Chans}(op)}{(S, P, X)_i \rightarrow (S', (c_0!x \rightarrow \textbf{skip} \sqcap c_1!x \rightarrow \textbf{skip}) \, \mathbin{;} P, X)_i} \qquad \text{(Send)}$$

$$\frac{S = S' \circ \langle op \rangle \wedge op = \mathsf{Bcast(j)} \wedge i = j \wedge c_1 = \mathsf{Chan}(op)}{(S, P, X)_i \rightarrow (S', (c_1!x \rightarrow \textbf{skip} \sqcap \mathsf{Bcast}_k) \, \mathbin{;} P, X \cup \{\mathsf{Bcast}_k\})_i} \qquad \text{(Bcast-1)}$$

$$\frac{S = S' \circ \langle op \rangle \wedge op = \mathsf{Bcast(j)} \wedge i \ne j \wedge c_1 = \mathsf{Chan}(op)}{(S, P, X)_i \rightarrow (S', ([!\mathsf{cempty}(c_1)] \rightarrow \textbf{skip}\square\mathsf{Bcast}_k) \, \mathbin{;} P, X)_i} \qquad \text{(Bcast-2)}$$

$$\frac{S = S' \circ \langle op \rangle \wedge op = \mathsf{Gather(j)} \wedge i = j}{(S, P, X)_i \rightarrow (S' \circ \langle \mathsf{Send(j)}, \mathsf{Recv(0)}, ..., \mathsf{Recv(n)} \rangle, P, X)_i} \qquad \text{(Gather-1)}$$

$$\frac{S = S' \circ \langle op \rangle \wedge op = \mathsf{Gather(j)} \wedge i \ne j}{(S, P, X)_i \rightarrow (S' \circ \langle \mathsf{Send(j)} \rangle, P, X)_i} \qquad \text{(Gather-2)}$$

$$\frac{S = S' \circ \langle op \rangle \wedge op = \mathsf{Scatter(j)} \wedge i = j}{(S, P, X)_i \rightarrow (S' \circ \langle \mathsf{Send(0)}, ..., \mathsf{Send(n)}, \mathsf{Recv(j)} \rangle, P, X)_i} \qquad \text{(Scatter-1)}$$

$$\frac{S = S' \circ \langle op \rangle \wedge op = \mathsf{Scatter(j)} \wedge i \ne j}{(S, P, X)_i \rightarrow (S' \circ \langle \mathsf{Recv(j)} \rangle, P, X)_i} \qquad \text{(Scatter-2)}$$

Fig. 5. CSP Model Construction Rules. $S_0 \circ S_1$ represents the concatenation of two MPI operation sequences. In $(S, P, X)_i$, S is the current operation sequence, P is the currently generated CSP model, X is the set of the generated synchronization events, and i denotes the ith process Proc_i. $\mathsf{Chans}(op)$ returns a zero-sized channel and a one-sized channel. $\mathsf{Chan}(op)$ returns a one-sized channel. Besides, $\rightarrow^*$ represents applying the rules zero or multiple times.

to model it ($c.f.$, Rule Send). *Each send operation has its channels.* Hence, each send operation can finish immediately or wait for the message to be received. The internal choice models the non-determinism between the "rendezvous" mode and the "eager" mode with an infinite buffer.

For the collective broadcast operation MPI_Bcast, we model it as follows: for the root process (*c.f.*, Rule Bcast-1), we allocate a one-sized channel and use internal choice of a one-sized channel writing and a synchronization event (Bcast$_k$[1]) to model it; while for the non-root processes (*c.f.*, Rule Bcast-2), we use an external choice of a guarded process and the synchronization event process Bcast$_k$, where cempty is a boolean function to test whether a channel is empty or not. The external choice selects to execute the guarded process only if the root process has written the one-sized channel.

For other collective operations, *e.g.*, MPI_Gather and MPI_Scatter, we transform them into a sequence of MPI_Send and MPI_Recv operations, which preserves the semantics of these collective operations. For the remaining MPI operations, the modeling methods are the same as MPI-SV [27], which are omitted for brevity.

Example. Let's go back to the program in Fig. 1, even though there exist no wildcard operations, we build each terminated path a CSP model. For the false branch $x \neq$ 'a', process P_0 simply sends a message to P_1 using a standard send operation, and process P_1 receives a message from P_0. The issued MPI operation sequences of P_0 and P_1 are $Seq_0 = \langle \text{Send(1)} \rangle$ and $Seq_1 = \langle \text{Recv(0)} \rangle$, respectively. To model different implementations of the standard send operation, we use internal choice ($\sqcap$) to compose the "rendezvous" mode (corresponding to a zero-sized channel writing) and the "eager" mode that has infinite buffer (corresponding to a one-sized channel writing). Hence, we generate CSP_0 for process P_0, where c_0 is a zero-sized channel and c_1 is a one-sized channel.

$$CSP_0 := c_0!0 \rightarrow \textbf{skip} \sqcap c_1!1 \rightarrow \textbf{skip}$$

On the other hand, to model the receive operation, we use external choice ($\square$) to compose the two possible matched channel reading operations, *i.e.*, generating CSP_1 for process P_1.

$$CSP_1 := c_0?x \rightarrow \textbf{skip}\square c_1?x \rightarrow \textbf{skip}$$

We compose the two CSP models in parallel, *i.e.*, $CSP_0 \parallel CSP_1$, and verify that the model is deadlock free. The result is that the model satisfies the property.

Similarly, for the true branch $x ==$ 'a', the issued MPI operation sequences of P_0 and P_1 are $Seq_0 = \langle \text{Send(1)}, \text{Recv(1)} \rangle$ and $Seq_1 = \langle \text{Send(0)}, \text{Recv(0)} \rangle$, respectively. We generate CSP_0' for process P_0, and CSP_1' for process P_1, where c_0 and c_2 are zero-sized channels, c_1 and c_3 are one-sized channels.

$$CSP_0' := (c_0!0 \rightarrow \textbf{skip} \sqcap c_1!1 \rightarrow \textbf{skip}) \,\fatsemi\, (c_2?x \rightarrow \textbf{skip}\square c_3?x \rightarrow \textbf{skip})$$

$$CSP_1' := (c_2!2 \rightarrow \textbf{skip} \sqcap c_3!3 \rightarrow \textbf{skip}) \,\fatsemi\, (c_0?x \rightarrow \textbf{skip}\square c_1?x \rightarrow \textbf{skip})$$

When verifying the CSP model $CSP_0' \parallel CSP_1'$ *w.r.t.* deadlock freedom, the model checker gives a counter-example, where both the internal choices select to

---

[1] We allocate each group of MPI_Bcast operations a unique synchronization event Bcast$_k$.

write an element to the zero-sized channels, *i.e.*, c_0 and c_2. Hence, our approach detects the deadlock related to non-deterministic synchronizations.

Our CSP modeling method ensures that there will be no deadlock for the "eager" mode with an any-sized finite buffer if the generated model is deadlock-free. We prove this result in Theorem 1, where $\mathsf{CSP}_i(p)$ represents the CSP model built by Algorithm 2 for a normally terminated path p, and $\mathsf{CSP}_b(p)$ denotes the CSP model built by having a finite buffer in "eager" mode.

Theorem 1. *If* $\mathsf{CSP}_i(p)$ *is deadlock free,* $\mathsf{CSP}_b(p)$ *is deadlock free.*

Proof. The key idea of the proof is to use the refinement relation of CSP in stable-failures semantics [17]. The stable-failures semantic model of a process P is $(\mathcal{T}(P), \mathcal{F}(P))$, where $\mathcal{T}(P)$ contains the traces of P, and $\mathcal{F}(P)$ contains the elements formed as (s, X), which represents that P refuses to execute any event in X after executing the trace s.

The only different between $\mathsf{CSP}_i(p)$ and $\mathsf{CSP}_b(p)$ is the modeling of send operations. For $\mathsf{CSP}_i(p)$, any send operation can block or finish immediately, due to the infinite buffer. However, for $\mathsf{CSP}_b(p)$, a send operation's behavior depends on the size of the buffer when it selects "eager" mode. If the buffer is full, the send operation blocks; otherwise, it can finish immediately. Hence, for a send operation op, if $M_i(op)$ and $M_b(op)$ represent the models built by Algorithm 2 with infinite and finite buffers, respectively, we have $\mathcal{F}(M_i(op)) \supseteq \mathcal{F}(M_b(op))$ and $\mathcal{T}(M_i(op)) \supseteq \mathcal{T}(M_b(op))$. Because the modeling of all the remaining operations is same between $\mathsf{CSP}_i(p)$ and $\mathsf{CSP}_b(p)$, we can have $\mathcal{F}(\mathsf{CSP}_i(p))) \supseteq \mathcal{F}(\mathsf{CSP}_b(p))$ and $\mathcal{T}(\mathsf{CSP}_i(p))) \supseteq \mathcal{T}(\mathsf{CSP}_b(p))$.

Hence, we can prove that $\mathsf{CSP}_b(p)$ is a stable-failures refinement of $\mathsf{CSP}_i(p)$, which implies the theorem.

4.3   Optimization

For the execution paths without wildcard receives, we can optimize the CSP model construction by only considering the "rendezvous" mode. The intuition is that a model with more synchronizations tends to have a deadlock. The correctness of the optimization is ensured by Theorem 2, where $\mathsf{CSP}_r(p)$ represents the CSP model built by Algorithm 2 for a normally terminated path p considering only "rendezvous" mode.

Theorem 2. *Given an execution path p along which there are no wildcard receive operations,* $\mathsf{CSP}_r(p)$ *is deadlock free if and only if* $\mathsf{CSP}_i(p)$ *is deadlock free.*

Proof. The CSP modeling also complies with the happens-before requirements of the MPI standard [7]. Especially, the *non-overtaken rules* [24] are the ones that motivate the optimization. The rules require that:

- if there exist two send operations of a process that send messages to the same process and both can match a receive operation, the receive operation should receive the message of the first issued send operation;

– if a process has two receive operations that can match the same send operation, the send operation's message should be received by the first issued receive operation.

As a result, the message operation matchings are deterministic for the paths having no wildcard receive operations, despite the implementations of send operations.

With respect to the semantic definition [17] of internal choice, we can have that $CSP_r(p)$ is a stable-failure refinement of $CSP_i(p)$. Hence, if $CSP_i(p)$ is deadlock free, $CSP_r(p)$ is deadlock free. Next, we prove that the deadlock freedom of $CSP_r(p)$ implies that $CSP_i(p)$ is deadlock free by contradiction. Suppose $CSP_r(p)$ is deadlock free but there exists a deadlock in $CSP_i(p)$, and the deadlock happens after executing the trace s_d, i.e., $CSP_i(p)$ refuses to execute any event after executing s_d. Due to the non-overtaken rules and the assumption of no wildcard receives, the message matchings are deterministic. Hence, $CSP_r(p)$ can also executes s_d. Besides, the deadlock of $CSP_i(p)$ means that $CSP_r(p)$ cannot execute any event either. So, $CSP_r(p)$ also deadlocks, which contradicts with the assumption.

In summary, the theorem holds.

According to Theorem 2, when an execution path has no wildcard receive operations, we only need to treat the send operations as blocking operations for the verification of deadlock freedom. Such optimization can significantly reduce the complexity of CSP models because the state space of the original CSP model increases exponentially w.r.t. the number of send operations. We omit the optimization from the construction rules for brevity.

Example. We still take the program in Fig. 1 for example. For the terminated path p of the true branch $x ==$ 'a', the issued MPI operations of process P_0 and P_1 are $Seq_0 = \langle \text{Send(1)}, \text{Recv(1)} \rangle$ and $Seq_1 = \langle \text{Send(0)}, \text{Recv(0)} \rangle$, respectively. Since p has no wildcard receive operations, we use the optimization method to build the CSP model. We build the following two CSP processes, i.e., CSP_0 and CSP_1, where channel c_0 and c_1 are zero-sized channels.

$$CSP_0 := c_0!x \rightarrow c_1?x \rightarrow \textbf{skip}$$

$$CSP_1 := c_1!x \rightarrow c_0?x \rightarrow \textbf{skip}$$

When verifying the optimized model $CSP_0 \parallel CSP_1$ w.r.t. deadlock freedom, we can successfully detect the deadlock, because the standard send operations are implemented in "rendezvous" mode. Compared with the CSP model generated by the rules in Fig. 5, the optimized model is much simpler.

5   Experimental Evaluation

In this section, we first introduce the implementation of our approach. Then, we give the experimental setup. Finally, we present the experimental results.

5.1 Implementation

We have implemented our approach on MPI-SV [27], whose basic procedure is to compile an MPI+C program to LLVM bytecode using Clang, and then link it with a pre-compiled multi-threaded MPI library AzequiaMPI [16] to generate the input for verification. We implemented our path-level CSP modeling method as a module within the symbolic execution engine, which will be invoked if the generated path has wildcard receive operations or non-deterministic blocking operations. We adopt the state-of-the-art CSP model checker PAT [22] to verify the path-level CSP models *w.r.t.* deadlock freedom.

5.2 Setup

Table 1 lists the programs analyzed in our experiments. All the programs are real-world open source MPI programs. DTG is a testing program from a PhD dissertation [23]. Integrate_mw and Diffusion2d come from the FEVS benchmark suite [20]. Integrate_mw^2 calculates the integrals of trigonometric functions, and Diffusion2d is a parallel solver for two-dimensional diffusion equation. Gauss_elim is an MPI implementation for gaussian elimination used in [26]. We downloaded Pingpong, Mandelbrot, and Image_manip from github. Pingpong is a testing program for communication performance. Mandelbrot parallel draws the mandelbrot set for a bitmap. Image_manip is an MPI program for image manipulations, *e.g.*, shifting, rotating and scaling. The remaining three programs are large parallel applications. Depsolver is a parallel multi-material 3D electrostatic solver, Kfray is a ray tracing program that can create realistic images, and ClustalW is a popular tool for aligning multiple gene sequences.

We experiment on a laptop with 8G memory and 2.0 GHz cores. The operating system is Ubuntu 14.04. We set the time threshold as 90 min for each verification task. The conducted experiments are to answer the following two questions:

- Effectiveness: Can our tool effectively verify real-world MPI programs having non-deterministic synchronizations *w.r.t.* deadlock freedom?
- Optimization: Can the optimization for modeling the paths without wildcard receives reduce the cost of CSP model checking?

5.3 Experimental Results

Table 2 lists the verification results for the programs with different numbers of processes. To evaluate our approach, we verify each program under 6, 8, and 10 processes. The first column **Program** shows the program names. Column **#i** ($i \in \{6, 8, 10\}$) indicates the number of running processes. A verification task consists of a program and the number of running processes. Column **Deadlock** indicates whether a task is deadlock-free, where **no** denotes that our tool successfully

---

^{2}Integrat_mw is adopted from [6], in which a static schedule is employed.

Table 1. The programs in the experiments.

Program	LOC	Brief description
DTG	90	Dependence transition group
Integrate_mw	181	Integral computing
Diffusion2d	197	Simulation of diffusion equation
Gauss_elim	341	Gaussian elimination
Pingpong	220	Comm performance testing
Mandelbrot	268	Mandelbrot set drawing
Image_manip	360	Image manipulation
DepSolver	8988	Multimaterial electrostatic solver
Kfray	12728	KF-Ray parallel raytracer
ClustalW	23265	Multiple sequence alignment
Total	**46638**	**10 open source programs**

verified that the program is deadlock-free under the number of processes, and **yes** denotes that a deadlock exists. The column **Time(s)** gives the verification time. Table 3 lists the results for DTG and Pingpong that are developed under a fixed number of processes, where column **#Procs** gives the number of processes.

Table 2. Results for programs with variable number of processes.

Program	Deadlock			Time(s)		
	#6	#8	#10	#6	#8	#10
Integrate_mw	No	No	No	10.8	54.1	3783.4
Diffusion2d	Yes	Yes	Yes	20.3	12.9	13.1
Gauss_elim	Yes	Yes	Yes	16.1	21.1	28.6
Mandelbrot	Yes	Yes	Yes	11.7	12.6	14.1
Image_mani	Yes	Yes	Yes	11.6	13.3	15.4
Depsolver	Yes	Yes	Yes	127.9	204.8	322.8
Kfray	Yes	Yes	Yes	46.1	51.3	52.7
Clustalw	No	No	No	68.3	154.1	3651.2

Table 3. Results for programs with fixed number of processes.

Program	# Procs	Deadlock	Time(s)
DTG	5	No	7.8
Pingpong	2	No	343.8

To the best of our knowledge, there exist no verification tools that can cover both the inputs and the schedules of the MPI program with non-deterministic synchronizations. Hence, we evaluate our tool directly on real-world programs. Our tool successfully verified all the tasks within 90 min, $i.e.$, deadlock for 18 tasks, and no deadlock in 8 tasks. We manually confirmed that the detected deadlocks are real and are caused by the non-deterministic synchronizations. Even for the large tasks, $e.g.$, the last three programs running in 10 processes, Our tool can successfully verify them, demonstrating the scalability of our technique.

We evaluate the effectiveness of our optimization on the programs having no wildcard receive operations, $i.e.$, DTG[*3] and `Pingpong`. Table 4 gives the detailed results. The first column **PATH** is the label for the execution paths of symbolic execution, and the suffix of the program indicates the execution path's index. Column **Time(s)** gives the time consumption for verifying the corresponding CSP models and column **#States** gives the explored states in the CSP model. **CSP** and **CSP$^\#$** represent the default modeling method and the optimized modeling method, respectively. Column **Speedup** shows the speedups of optimization. In terms of time consumption for model checking the path-level CSP models, **CSP$^\#$** achieves an average 3x speedup. On the other hand, the number of states that need to be explored is reduced significantly by the optimization, $i.e.$, **CSP$^\#$** explores at least 2.4x fewer states than **CSP**. These results indicate that our optimization for the paths without wildcard receive operations can effectively reduce the verification complexity of path-level CSP models.

Table 4. Results for optimization.

PATH	Time(s)			#States		
	CSP	CSP$^\#$	Speedup	CSP	CSP$^\#$	Speedup
DTG$_1^*$	13.8	7.9	1.8	386	32	12.1
Pingpong$_1$	11.5	10.1	1.1	133	55	2.4
Pingpong$_2$	88.2	16.5	5.3	2413	967	2.5
Pingpong$_3$	63.2	14.7	4.3	1813	727	2.5
Pingpong$_4$	37.5	14.3	2.6	1213	487	2.5

6   Conclusion and Future Work

This paper has presented an approach for verifying MPI programs with non-deterministic synchronization features. We enhance the symbolic verification by proposing a precise method for modeling the non-deterministic synchronizations of an execution path in terms of CSP. To improve the scalability, for the execution paths without wildcard receive operations, we give an optimization to reduce the complexity of CSP models. We have implemented our approach as a

---

[3]DTG* is the version that replaces the wildcard receives by deterministic receives.

prototype tool and extensively evaluated it on real-world MPI+C programs. The experimental results demonstrate the effectiveness of our approach. Our future work mainly includes two directions: (1) reducing the complexity of CSP models for paths having wildcard receive operations; and (2) applying our tool to verify temporal safety properties related to non-deterministic synchronizations.

References

1. Böhm, S., Meca, O., Jančar, P.: State-space reduction of non-deterministically synchronizing systems applicable to deadlock detection in MPI. In: Fitzgerald, J., Heitmeyer, C., Gnesi, S., Philippou, A. (eds.) FM 2016. LNCS, vol. 9995, pp. 102–118. Springer, Cham (2016). https://doi.org/10.1007/978-3-319-48989-6_7
2. Botbol, V., Chailloux, E., Le Gall, T.: Static analysis of communicating processes using symbolic transducers. In: Bouajjani, A., Monniaux, D. (eds.) VMCAI 2017. LNCS, vol. 10145, pp. 73–90. Springer, Cham (2017). https://doi.org/10.1007/978-3-319-52234-0_5
3. Brand, D., Zafiropulo, P.: On communicating finite-state machines. J. ACM **30**, 323–342 (1983)
4. Cadar, C., Dunbar, D., Engler, D.: KLEE: unassisted and automatic generation of high-coverage tests for complex systems programs. In: OSDI, pp. 209–224 (2008)
5. Clarke, E.M., Grumberg, O., Peled, D.: Model Checking. MIT Press, Cambridge (1999)
6. Forejt, V., Kroening, D., Narayanaswamy, G., Sharma, S.: Precise predictive analysis for discovering communication deadlocks in MPI programs. In: Jones, C., Pihlajasaari, P., Sun, J. (eds.) FM 2014. LNCS, vol. 8442, pp. 263–278. Springer, Cham (2014). https://doi.org/10.1007/978-3-319-06410-9_19
7. MPI Forum: MPI: a message-passing interface standard version 3.0 (2012). http://mpi-forum.org
8. Gopalakrishnan, G., et al.: Report of the HPC correctness summit, 25–26 January 2017, Washington, DC (2017). https://science.energy.gov/~/media/ascr/pdf/programdocuments/docs/2017/HPC_Correctness_Report.pdf
9. Holzmann, G.J.: Promela manual pages (2012). http://spinroot.com/spin/Man/promela.html
10. Huang, Yu., Mercer, E.: Detecting MPI zero buffer incompatibility by SMT encoding. In: Havelund, K., Holzmann, G., Joshi, R. (eds.) NFM 2015. LNCS, vol. 9058, pp. 219–233. Springer, Cham (2015). https://doi.org/10.1007/978-3-319-17524-9_16
11. Khanna, D., Sharma, S., Rodríguez, C., Purandare, R.: Dynamic symbolic verification of MPI programs. In: Havelund, K., Peleska, J., Roscoe, B., de Vink, E. (eds.) FM 2018. LNCS, vol. 10951, pp. 466–484. Springer, Cham (2018). https://doi.org/10.1007/978-3-319-95582-7_28
12. King, J.: Symbolic execution and program testing. Commun. ACM **19**, 385–394 (1976)
13. López, H.A., et al.: Protocol-based verification of message-passing parallel programs. In: OOPSLA, pp. 280–298 (2015)
14. Luo, Z., Zheng, M., Siegel, S.F.: Verification of MPI programs using CIVL. In: EuroMPI, pp. 6:1–6:11 (2017)
15. Manna, Z., Pnueli, A.: The Temporal Logic of Reactive and Concurrent Systems - Specification. Springer, New York (1992). https://doi.org/10.1007/978-1-4612-0931-7

16. Rico-Gallego, J.-A., Díaz-Martín, J.-C.: Performance evaluation of thread-based MPI in shared memory. In: Cotronis, Y., Danalis, A., Nikolopoulos, D.S., Dongarra, J. (eds.) EuroMPI 2011. LNCS, vol. 6960, pp. 337–338. Springer, Heidelberg (2011). https://doi.org/10.1007/978-3-642-24449-0_42

17. Roscoe, B.: The Theory and Practice of Concurrency. Prentice-Hall, Upper Saddle River (2005)

18. Siegel, S.F.: Model checking nonblocking MPI programs. In: Cook, B., Podelski, A. (eds.) VMCAI 2007. LNCS, vol. 4349, pp. 44–58. Springer, Heidelberg (2007). https://doi.org/10.1007/978-3-540-69738-1_3

19. Siegel, S.F.: Verifying parallel programs with MPI-Spin. In: Cappello, F., Herault, T., Dongarra, J. (eds.) EuroPVM/MPI 2007. LNCS, vol. 4757, pp. 13–14. Springer, Heidelberg (2007). https://doi.org/10.1007/978-3-540-75416-9_8

20. Siegel, S.F., Zirkel, T.K.: FEVS: a functional equivalence verification suite for high-performance scientific computing. Math. Comput. Sci. **5**, 427–435 (2011)

21. Snir, M.: MPI-The Complete Reference: The MPI Core, vol. 1. MIT Press, Cambridge (1998)

22. Sun, J., Liu, Y., Dong, J.S., Pang, J.: PAT: towards flexible verification under fairness. In: Bouajjani, A., Maler, O. (eds.) CAV 2009. LNCS, vol. 5643, pp. 709–714. Springer, Heidelberg (2009). https://doi.org/10.1007/978-3-642-02658-4_59

23. Vakkalanka, S.: Efficient dynamic verification algorithms for MPI applications. Ph.D. thesis, The University of Utah (2010)

24. Vakkalanka, S., Gopalakrishnan, G., Kirby, R.M.: Dynamic verification of MPI programs with reductions in presence of split operations and relaxed orderings. In: Gupta, A., Malik, S. (eds.) CAV 2008. LNCS, vol. 5123, pp. 66–79. Springer, Heidelberg (2008). https://doi.org/10.1007/978-3-540-70545-1_9

25. Vo, A., Aananthakrishnan, S., Gopalakrishnan, G., De Supinski, B.R., Schulz, M., Bronevetsky, G.: A scalable and distributed dynamic formal verifier for MPI programs. In: SC, pp. 1–10 (2010)

26. Xue, R., et al.: MPIWiz: subgroup reproducible replay of MPI applications. ACM SIGPLAN Not. **44**, 251–260 (2009)

27. Yu, H., et al.: Symbolic verification of message passing interface programs. In: 42nd International Conference on Software Engineering, ICSE 2020, Seoul, South Korea, 27 June–19 July 2020, pp. 1248–1260 (2020)

Learning Safe Neural Network Controllers with Barrier Certificates

Hengjun Zhao[1], Xia Zeng[1($\boxtimes$)], Taolue Chen[2], Zhiming Liu[1],
and Jim Woodcock[1,3]

[1] School of Computer and Information Science, Southwest University,
Chongqing, China
{zhaohj2016,xzeng0712,zhimingliu88}@swu.edu.cn
[2] Department of Computer Science, University of Surrey, Guildford, UK
taolue.chen@surrey.ac.uk
[3] Department of Computer Science, University of York, York, UK
jim.woodcock@york.ac.uk

Abstract. We provide a novel approach to synthesize controllers for nonlinear continuous dynamical systems with control against safety properties. The controllers are based on neural networks (NNs). To certify the safety property we utilize barrier functions, which are also represented by NNs. We train controller-NN and barrier-NN simultaneously, achieving verification-in-the-loop synthesis. We provide a prototype tool nncontroller with a number of case studies. Preliminary experiment results confirm the feasibility and efficacy of our approach.

Keywords: Continuous dynamical systems · Controller synthesis · Neural networks · Safety verification · Barrier certificates

1 Introduction

Controller design and synthesis is the most fundamental problem in control theory. In recent years, especially with the boom of deep learning, there have been

H. Zhao is supported partially by the National Natural Science Foundation of China (No. 61702425, 61972385); X. Zeng is the corresponding author and supported partially by the National Natural Science Foundation of China (No. 61902325) and "Fundamental Research Funds for the Central Universities" (SWU117058); T. Chen is partially supported by NSFC grant (No. 61872340), Guangdong Science and Technology Department grant (No. 2018B010107004), and the Overseas Grant of the State Key Laboratory of Novel Software Technology (No. KFKT2018A16), the Natural Science Foundation of Guangdong Province of China (No. 2019A1515011689); Z. Liu is supported partially by the National Natural Science Foundation of China (No. 61672435, 61732019, 61811530327) and Capacity Development Grant of Southwest University (SWU116007); J. Woodcock is partially supported by the research grant from Southwest University.

© Springer Nature Switzerland AG 2020
J. Pang and L. Zhang (Eds.): SETTA 2020, LNCS 12153, pp. 177–185, 2020.
https://doi.org/10.1007/978-3-030-62822-2_11

considerable research activities in the use of neural networks (NNs) for control of nonlinear systems [8,15]. NNs feature versatile representational abilities of nonlinear maps and fast computation, making them an ideal candidate for sophisticated control tasks [16]. Typical examples include self-driving cars, drones, and smart cities. It is noteworthy that many of these applications are safety-critical systems, where safety refers to, in a basic form, that the system cannot reach a dangerous or unwanted state. For control systems in a multitude of Cyber-Physical-System domains, designing *safe* controllers which can guarantee safety behaviors of the controlled system is of paramount importance [1,2,4,5,9,10,12,19,20,23,24,26].

Typically, when a controller is given, formal verification is usually required to certify its safety. In our previous work [27], we have dealt with the verification of continuous dynamical systems by the aid of neural networks. In a nutshell, we follow a deductive verification methodology therein by synthesizing a barrier function, the existence of which suffices to show the safety of the controlled dynamical system. The crux was to use neural networks to represent the barrier functions. In this work, we follow a correctness-by-design methodology by considering synthesizing controllers which can guarantee that the controlled system is safe, which is considerably more challenging and perhaps more interesting. In a nutshell, we learn two neural networks simultaneously: one is to represent the controller (henceforth referred to as controller-NN), and the other is to represent the barrier function (henceforth referred to as barrier-NN). The synergy of the two neural networks, supported by an additional verification procedure to make sure the learned barrier-NN is indeed a barrier certificate, provides the desired safety guarantee for the application. The advantages of our approach are threefold: (1) the approach is data-driven, requiring considerably less control theory expertise; (2) the approach can support non-linear control systems and safety properties, owing to the representation power of neural networks; and (3) the approach can achieve verification-in-the-loop synthesis, owing to the co-synthesis of controllers and barrier functions, which can be seamlessly integrated to provide a correctness-by-design controller as well as its certification.

This short paper reports the general methodology, including the design of the NNs, the generation of training data, the training process, as well as the associated verification. We shall also report a prototype implementation and some preliminary experiment results. For space restriction, we will leave the discussion of related work (e.g., [3,7,25]), and further improvement of the performance of the learned controller (e.g., bounded and asymptotically stable controller), as well as more extensive experiments, to the full version [28].

2   Preliminaries

A *constrained continuous dynamical system* (CCDS) is represented by $\Gamma = (\mathbf{f}, X_D, X_I, X_U)$, where $\mathbf{f} : \Omega \to \mathbb{R}^n$ is the vector field, $X_D \subseteq \Omega$ is the system domain, $X_I \subseteq X_D$, and $X_U \subseteq X_D$. The system dynamics is governed by first-order ordinary differential equations $\dot{\mathbf{x}} = \mathbf{f}(\mathbf{x})$ for $\mathbf{f}(\mathbf{x}) = (f_1(\mathbf{x}), \cdots, f_n(\mathbf{x}))$, where $\dot{\mathbf{x}}$ denotes the derivative of $\mathbf{x}$ w.r.t. the time variable t. We assume that $\mathbf{f}$ satisfies the *local Lipschitz condition*, which ensures that given $\mathbf{x} = \mathbf{x}_0$, there exists a time $\mathcal{T} > 0$ and a unique trajectory $\mathbf{x}(t) : [0, \mathcal{T}) \rightarrow \mathbb{R}^n$ such that $\mathbf{x}(0) = \mathbf{x}_0$, which is denoted by $\mathbf{x}(t, \mathbf{x}_0)$. In this paper, we consider *controlled* CCDS

$$\begin{cases} \dot{\mathbf{x}} = \mathbf{f}(\mathbf{x}, \mathbf{u}) \\ \mathbf{u} = \mathbf{g}(\mathbf{x}) \end{cases} \tag{1}$$

where $\mathbf{u} \in U \subseteq \mathbb{R}^m$ are the feedback control inputs, and $\mathbf{f} : \mathbb{R}^{n+m} \rightarrow \mathbb{R}^n$ and $\mathbf{g} : \mathbb{R}^n \rightarrow \mathbb{R}^m$ are locally Lipschitz continuous.

The problem we considered in this paper is defined as follows.

Definition 1 (Safe Controller Synthesis). *Given a controlled CCDS $\Gamma = (\mathbf{f}, X_D, X_I, X_U)$ with $\mathbf{f}$ defined by (1), design a locally continuous feedback control law $\mathbf{g}$ such that the closed-loop system Γ with $\mathbf{f} = \mathbf{f}(\mathbf{x}, \mathbf{g}(\mathbf{x}))$ is safe, that is, system trajectory from X_I never reaches X_U as long as it remains in X_D.*

Barrier Certificate. Given a system Γ, a barrier certificate is a real-valued function $B(\mathbf{x})$ over the states of the system satisfying the condition that $B(\mathbf{x}) \leq 0$ for any reachable state $\mathbf{x}$ and $B(\mathbf{x}) > 0$ for any state in the unsafe set X_U. If such a function $B(\mathbf{x})$ exists, one can easily deduce that the system can *not* reach a state in the unsafe set from the initial set [17,18]. In this paper, we will certify the safety of a synthesized controller by generating barrier certificates.

There are several different formulations of barrier certificates without explicit reference to the solutions of the ODEs [6,14,17,22]. In this paper, we will adopt what are called *strict barrier certificate* [21] conditions.

Theorem 1 (Strict barrier certificate). *Given a system $\Gamma = (\mathbf{f}, X_D, X_I, X_U)$, if there exists a continuously differentiable function $B : X_D \rightarrow \mathbb{R}$ such that (1) $B(\mathbf{x}) \leq 0$ for $\forall \mathbf{x} \in X_I$, (2) $B(\mathbf{x}) > 0$ for $\forall \mathbf{x} \in X_U$, and (3) $\mathcal{L}_{\mathbf{f}} B(\mathbf{x}) < 0$ for all $\mathbf{x} \in X_D$ s.t. $B(\mathbf{x}) = 0$. Then the system Γ is safe, and such B is a barrier certificate. (Note that $\mathcal{L}_{\mathbf{f}} B$ is the Lie derivative of B w.r.t. $\mathbf{f}$ defined as $\mathcal{L}_{\mathbf{f}} B(\mathbf{x}) = \mathbf{f}(\mathbf{x}) \cdot \nabla B = \sum_{i=1}^{n}(f_i(\mathbf{x}) \cdot \frac{\partial B}{\partial x_i}(\mathbf{x})).)$*

3   Methodology

The framework of our safe controller learning approach is demonstrated in Fig. 1. Given a controlled CCDS $\Gamma = (\mathbf{f}, X_D, X_I, X_U)$, the basic idea of the proposed approach is to represent the controller function $\mathbf{g}$ as well as the safety certificate function B by two NNs, i.e. $\mathcal{N}_c$ and $\mathcal{N}_b$ respectively. Then we formulate the barrier certificate conditions w.r.t. $\mathcal{N}_b$ and the closed-loop dynamics $\mathbf{f}(\mathbf{x}, \mathcal{N}_c(\mathbf{x}))$ into a loss function, and then train the two NNs together on a generated training data set until the loss is decreased to 0. The resulting two NNs are the controller and barrier certificate candidates, the correctness of which is guaranteed by formal verification (SMT solver in this paper). The blue (solid), red (dashed), and green (dotted) arrows in Fig. 1 shows the information flow of forward propagation, backward propagation, and formal verification, respectively. Next, before giving more detailed steps of our approach, we first introduce a running example.

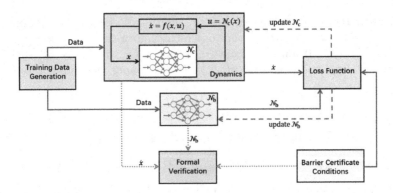

Fig. 1. The framework of safe neural network controller synthesis (Color figure online)

Example 1 (Dubins' car [7,25]). The control objective is to steer a car with constant velocity 1 to track a path, here the X-axis in the positive direction. The states of the car are the x, y position and the driving direction θ, which can be transformed to the distance error d_e and angle error θ_e between the current position and the target path (cf. the left part of Fig. 2). The controlled CCDS is:

$$\mathbf{f} : \begin{bmatrix} \dot{d}_e \\ \dot{\theta}_e \end{bmatrix} = \begin{bmatrix} \sin(\theta_e) \\ -u \end{bmatrix}, \quad \text{where } u \text{ is the scalar control input}$$

- X_D: $\{(d_e, \theta_e) \in \mathbb{R}^2 | -6 \le d_e \le 6, -7\pi/10 \le \theta_e \le 7\pi/10\}$;
- X_I: $\{(d_e, \theta_e) \in \mathbb{R}^2 | -1 \le d_e \le 1, -\pi/16 \le \theta_e \le \pi/16\}$;
- X_U: the complement of $\{(d_e, \theta_e) \in \mathbb{R}^2 | -5 \le d_e \le 5, -\pi/2 \le \theta_e \le \pi/2\}$.

The right of Fig. 2 shows simulated trajectories on the x-y plane from 50 random initial states in X_I using our learned NN controller u. The two red horizontal lines are the safety upper and lower bounds (± 5) for y (the same bounds as d_e).

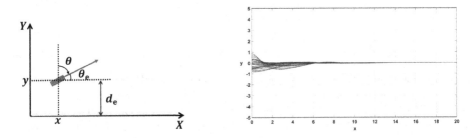

Fig. 2. Left: the car states; Right: simulated car trajectories with learned NN controller. (Color figure online)

3.1   The Structure of $\mathcal{N}_c$ and $\mathcal{N}_b$

We first fix the structure of $\mathcal{N}_c$ and $\mathcal{N}_b$ as follows, assuming that in Γ, $\mathbf{x}$ and $\mathbf{u}$ are of n and m dimension respectively, e.g. $n = 2, m = 1$ for Example 1.

- **Input layer** has n neurons for both $\mathcal{N}_c$ and $\mathcal{N}_b$;
- **Output layer** has m neurons for $\mathcal{N}_c$ and one single neuron for $\mathcal{N}_b$;
- **Hidden layer:** there is no restriction on the number of hidden layers or the number of neurons in each hidden layer; for Example 1, $\mathcal{N}_c$ has one hidden layer with 5 neurons, and $\mathcal{N}_b$ has one hidden layer with 10 neurons.
- **Activation function:** considering both the simplicity and the inherent requirement of local Lipschitz continuity [13] and differentiability, we adopt ReLU, i.e. $a(x) = \max(0, x)$ for $\mathcal{N}_c$, and *Bent-ReLU* [27], i.e., $a(x) = 0.5 \cdot x + \sqrt{0.25 \cdot x^2 + 0.0001}$ for $\mathcal{N}_b$ respectively for hidden layers; the activation of the output layer is the identity map for both $\mathcal{N}_c$ and $\mathcal{N}_b$.

3.2   Training Data Generation

In our training algorithm, training data are generated by sampling points from the domain, initial set, and unsafe region of the considered system. No simulation of the continuous dynamics is needed. The simplest sampling method is to grid the super-rectangles bounding X_D, X_I, X_U with a fixed mesh size, and then filter those points not satisfying the constraints of X_D, X_I, X_U. For example, we generate a mesh with $2^8 \times 2^8$ points from X_D for Example 1. The obtained three finite data sets are denoted by S_D, S_I, and S_U.

3.3   Loss Function Encoding

Given S_I, S_U, and S_D, the loss function can be expressed as

$$L(S_D, S_I, S_U) = \sum_{\mathbf{x} \in S_I} L_1(\mathbf{x}) + \sum_{\mathbf{x} \in S_U} L_2(\mathbf{x}) + \sum_{\mathbf{x} \in S_D} L_3(\mathbf{x}) \quad \text{with} \qquad (2)$$

$$
\begin{aligned}
L_1(\mathbf{x}) &= \text{ReLU}(\mathcal{N}_b(\mathbf{x}) + \varepsilon_1) && \text{for } \mathbf{x} \in S_I, \\
L_2(\mathbf{x}) &= \text{ReLU}(-\mathcal{N}_b(\mathbf{x}) + \varepsilon_2) && \text{for } \mathbf{x} \in S_U, \\
L_3(\mathbf{x}) &= \text{ReLU}(\mathcal{L}_\mathbf{f}\mathcal{N}_b(\mathbf{x}) + \varepsilon_3) && \text{for } \mathbf{x} \in \{\mathbf{x} \in S_D : |\mathcal{N}_b(\mathbf{x})| \le \varepsilon_4\}
\end{aligned}
\qquad (3)
$$

where the sub-loss functions L_1–L_3 encode the three conditions of Theorem 1. The basic idea is to give a positive (resp., zero) penalty to those sampled points that violate (resp., satisfy) barrier certificate conditions. $\varepsilon_1, \varepsilon_2, \varepsilon_3$ are three small non-negative tolerances, and ε_4 is a small positive constant approximating the zero-level set of $\mathcal{N}_b$. Note that in the expression $\mathcal{L}_\mathbf{f}\mathcal{N}_b$ above, $\mathbf{f}$ is $\mathbf{f}(\mathbf{x}, \mathcal{N}_c(\mathbf{x}))$.

3.4   The Training Process

We adopt a modified *stochastic gradient descent* (SGD) [11] optimization technique for training the two NNs. That is, we partition the training data set into mini-batches and shuffle the list of batches, rather than the whole training set, to gain some randomness effect. To start the training, we specify ε_1 to ε_4 in the loss function, as well as hyper-parameters such as learning rate, number of epochs, number of mini-batches, etc. The training algorithm terminates when the loss is decreased to 0 or exceeds the maximum number of restarts.

3.5   Formal Verification

The rigorousness of the NNs resulting from 0 training loss is not guaranteed since our approach is data-driven. Therefore we resort to formal verification to guarantee the correctness of our synthesized controllers. To preform the verification, we replace the $\mathbf{f}$ and B in the conditions of Theorem 1 by $\mathbf{f}(\mathbf{x}, \mathcal{N}_c(\mathbf{x}))$ and $\mathcal{N}_b$, and the negation of the resulting constraints are sent to the interval SMT solver iSAT3[1] for satisfiability checking. To reduce the degree of nonlinearity in the constraints, we compute piece-wise linear approximations of the Bent-ReLU function and its derivative.

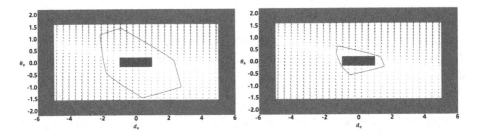

Fig. 3. Learned and verified NN controller and barrier certificate for Example 1. Left: $\varepsilon_1 = \varepsilon_2 = 0$, $\varepsilon_3 = \varepsilon_4 = 0.01$, the inner (green) and outer (red) shaded areas are the initial and unsafe regions, black arrows in the white area are the closed-loop vector fields $\mathbf{f}(\mathbf{x}, \mathcal{N}_c(\mathbf{x}))$, and the blue curve surrounding the inner shaded box is the zero-level set of $\mathcal{N}_b$; Right: $\varepsilon_1 = 0.02$, $\varepsilon_2 = 0.8$, $\varepsilon_3 = 0.01$, $\varepsilon_4 = 0.05$. (Color figure online)

Pre-training and Fine-Tuning. The success of synthesis and formal verification heavily relies on the choices of the four constants ε_1 to ε_4 in (2) and (3). In practice, we adopt a pre-training and fine-tuning combination strategy. That is, we start with small positive ε_4 and zero ε_1 to ε_3 to perform the training and verification, and gradually increase the values when formal verification fails. For Example 1, the first controller and barrier are synthesized with $\varepsilon_4 = 0.01$ and $\varepsilon_1 = \varepsilon_2 = \varepsilon_3 = 0$, and the fine-tuned controller and barrier are successfully verified when ε_3 was increased to 0.01 (cf. the left part of Fig. 3). Further fine-tuning gives a controller with larger safety margin (cf. the right part of Fig. 3).

4   Implementation and Experiment

We have implemented a prototype tool nncontroller[2] based on PyTorch[3]. We apply nncontroller to a number of case studies in the literature [7,25,29]. All experiments are performed on a laptop running Ubuntu 18.04 with Intel i7-8550u

---

[1] https://projects.informatik.uni-freiburg.de/projects/isat3/.
[2] Publicly available at: https://github.com/zhaohj2017/FAoC-tool.
[3] https://pytorch.org/.

CPU and 32 GB memory. The average time costs of pre-training for Example 1 over 5 different runs is 26.35 s. Formal verification of the fine-tuned controller for Example 1 (cf. the left part of Fig. 3) with iSAT3 costs 8.27 s. The other experiment results will be reported in the full version [28].

Acknowledgements. We thank anonymous reviewers for their valuable comments.

References

1. Ahmadi, M., Singletary, A., Burdick, J.W., Ames, A.D.: Safe policy synthesis in multi-agent POMDPs via discrete-time barrier functions. In: 2019 IEEE 58th Conference on Decision and Control (CDC), pp. 4797–4803. IEEE (2019)
2. Berkenkamp, F., Turchetta, M., Schoellig, A.P., Krause, A.: Safe model-based reinforcement learning with stability guarantees. In: Proceedings of the 31st International Conference on Neural Information Processing Systems, NIPS 2017, pp. 908–919. Curran Associates Inc., Red Hook (2017)
3. Chang, Y.C., Roohi, N., Gao, S.: Neural Lyapunov control. In: Advances in Neural Information Processing Systems, vol. 32, pp. 3245–3254. Curran Associates, Inc. (2019)
4. Cheng, R., Orosz, G., Murray, R.M., Burdick, J.W.: End-to-end safe reinforcement learning through barrier functions for safety-critical continuous control tasks. In: The Thirty-Third AAAI Conference on Artificial Intelligence, AAAI 2019, Honolulu, Hawaii, USA, 27 January–1 February 2019, pp. 3387–3395. AAAI Press (2019)
5. Choi, J., Castañeda, F., Tomlin, C.J., Sreenath, K.: Reinforcement learning for safety-critical control under model uncertainty, using control Lyapunov functions and control barrier functions (2020). https://arxiv.org/abs/2004.07584
6. Dai, L., Gan, T., Xia, B., Zhan, N.: Barrier certificates revisited. J. Symb. Comput. **80**, 62–86 (2017)
7. Deshmukh, J.V., Kapinski, J., Yamaguchi, T., Prokhorov, D.: Learning deep neural network controllers for dynamical systems with safety guarantees: invited paper. In: 2019 IEEE/ACM International Conference on Computer-Aided Design (ICCAD), pp. 1–7 (2019)
8. Duan, Y., Chen, X., Houthooft, R., Schulman, J., Abbeel, P.: Benchmarking deep reinforcement learning for continuous control. In: Proceedings of the 33rd International Conference on Machine Learning, ICML 2016, New York City, NY, USA, 19–24 June 2016. JMLR Workshop and Conference Proceedings, vol. 48, pp. 1329–1338. JMLR.org (2016)
9. Dutta, S., Jha, S., Sankaranarayanan, S., Tiwari, A.: Learning and verification of feedback control systems using feedforward neural networks. IFAC-PapersOnLine **51**(16), 151–156 (2018). 6th IFAC Conference on Analysis and Design of Hybrid Systems ADHS 2018
10. Fulton, N., Platzer, A.: Safe reinforcement learning via formal methods: toward safe control through proof and learning. In: Proceedings of the Thirty-Second AAAI Conference on Artificial Intelligence, (AAAI 2018), New Orleans, Louisiana, USA, 2–7 February 2018, pp. 6485–6492. AAAI Press (2018)

11. Goodfellow, I., Bengio, Y., Courville, A.: Deep Learning. The MIT Press, Cambridge (2016)

12. Ivanov, R., Carpenter, T.J., Weimer, J., Alur, R., Pappas, G.J., Lee, I.: Case study: verifying the safety of an autonomous racing car with a neural network controller. In: HSCC 2020: 23rd ACM International Conference on Hybrid Systems: Computation and Control, Sydney, New South Wales, Australia, 21–24 April 2020, pp. 28:1–28:7. ACM (2020)

13. Jordan, M., Dimakis, A.G.: Exactly computing the local Lipschitz constant of ReLU networks (2020). https://arxiv.org/abs/2003.01219

14. Kong, H., He, F., Song, X., Hung, W.N.N., Gu, M.: Exponential-condition-based barrier certificate generation for safety verification of hybrid systems. In: Sharygina, N., Veith, H. (eds.) CAV 2013. LNCS, vol. 8044, pp. 242–257. Springer, Heidelberg (2013). https://doi.org/10.1007/978-3-642-39799-8_17

15. Lillicrap, T.P., et al.: Continuous control with deep reinforcement learning. In: 4th International Conference on Learning Representations, ICLR 2016, San Juan, Puerto Rico, 2–4 May 2016, Conference Track Proceedings (2016)

16. Poznyak, A., Sanchez, E.N., Yu, W.: Differential Neural Networks for Robust Nonlinear Control. World Scientific, Singapore (2001)

17. Prajna, S., Jadbabaie, A., Pappas, G.J.: A framework for worst-case and stochastic safety verification using barrier certificates. IEEE Trans. Autom. Control $52(8)$, 1415–1429 (2007)

18. Ratschan, S.: Converse theorems for safety and barrier certificates. IEEE Trans. Autom. Control $63(8)$, 2628–2632 (2018)

19. Ray, A., Achiam, J., Amodei, D.: Benchmarking safe exploration in deep reinforcement learning. https://cdn.openai.com/safexp-short.pdf

20. Richards, S.M., Berkenkamp, F., Krause, A.: The Lyapunov neural network: adaptive stability certification for safe learning of dynamic systems. CoRR abs/1808.00924 (2018). http://arxiv.org/abs/1808.00924

21. Sloth, C., Pappas, G.J., Wisniewski, R.: Compositional safety analysis using barrier certificates. In: Proceedings of the Hybrid Systems: Computation and Control (HSCC), pp. 15–24. ACM (2012)

22. Sogokon, A., Ghorbal, K., Tan, Y.K., Platzer, A.: Vector barrier certificates and comparison systems. In: Havelund, K., Peleska, J., Roscoe, B., de Vink, E. (eds.) FM 2018. LNCS, vol. 10951, pp. 418–437. Springer, Cham (2018). https://doi.org/10.1007/978-3-319-95582-7_25

23. Taylor, A., Singletary, A., Yue, Y., Ames, A.: Learning for safety-critical control with control barrier functions (2019). https://arxiv.org/abs/1912.10099

24. Tran, H.-D., et al.: NNV: the neural network verification tool for deep neural networks and learning-enabled cyber-physical systems. In: Lahiri, S.K., Wang, C. (eds.) CAV 2020. LNCS, vol. 12224, pp. 3–17. Springer, Cham (2020). https://doi.org/10.1007/978-3-030-53288-8_1

25. Tuncali, C.E., Kapinski, J., Ito, H., Deshmukh, J.V.: INVITED: reasoning about safety of learning-enabled components in autonomous cyber-physical systems. In: 2018 55th ACM/ESDA/IEEE Design Automation Conference (DAC), pp. 1–6 (2018)

26. Yaghoubi, S., Fainekos, G., Sankaranarayanan, S.: Training neural network controllers using control barrier functions in the presence of disturbances (2020). https://arxiv.org/abs/2001.08088

27. Zhao, H., Zeng, X., Chen, T., Liu, Z.: Synthesizing barrier certificates using neural networks. In: HSCC 2020, pp. 25:1–25:11. ACM (2020)
28. Zhao, H., Zeng, X., Chen, T., Liu, Z., Woodcock, J.: Learning safe neural network controllers with barrier certificates (2020). https://arxiv.org/abs/2009.09826
29. Zhu, H., Xiong, Z., Magill, S., Jagannathan, S.: An inductive synthesis framework for verifiable reinforcement learning. In: Proceedings of the 40th ACM SIGPLAN Conference on Programming Language Design and Implementation, PLDI 2019, pp. 686–701. Association for Computing Machinery, New York (2019)

Software Defect-Proneness Prediction with Package Cohesion and Coupling Metrics Based on Complex Network Theory

Yangxi Zhou, Yan Zhu, and Liangyu Chen[✉]

Shanghai Key Laboratory of Trustworthy Computing, East China Normal University,
Shanghai 200062, China
lychen@sei.ecnu.edu.cn

Abstract. Driven by functionality requirements, software codes are increasingly inflated, and invocations between codes are frequent and random. This makes it difficult for programmers to be thoughtful when modifying code, increasing the risk of defects. In an object-oriented software system, packages take the role of a middle tier that aggregates classes and limits class access. However, as the software system evolves, the logic and correctness of packages are weakened. In this paper, we explore the relation between package metrics and object-oriented software defect-proneness. We use two metrics of package cohesion and coupling based on complex network theory to verify the impact of code structure on software quality. On six Java software systems, the experimental result shows that the cohesion and coupling metrics play a positive role in software defect prediction, and they can correctly and effectively evaluate package organization structure. Meanwhile, our study confirms that compliance with the design principle of high cohesion and low coupling can reduce the risk of software defect-proneness and improve software quality.

Keywords: Software package · Defect proneness · Cohesion and coupling metrics

1 Introduction

Software quality is a focus problem since software has involved everything in our lives. With the increase of software scale, software becomes more enormous, complicated and obscure. Then, software quality is weakened continuously, and the maintenance intensity and cost also go up ineluctably. Therefore, software quality must be evaluated quantitatively all the time. As everyone knows, software is an artifact developed carefully by programmers with professional skills, especially mastering software design principles. These design principles are important guidelines for software development to improve system maintainability, reliability, and efficiency.

© Springer Nature Switzerland AG 2020
J. Pang and L. Zhang (Eds.): SETTA 2020, LNCS 12153, pp. 186–201, 2020.
https://doi.org/10.1007/978-3-030-62822-2_12

Currently, software systems are mainly made by object-oriented (OO) programming language, such as C++, Java, C# and etc. Is well known that the common structure of OO software systems is two-tier: class and package. Class is the basic unit. And package, as an intermediate layer, can play the role of aggregating classes and regulate class access as well as can reduce system complexity and increase maintainability and understandability [1]. Note that the rationality of package organization affects software quality to a certain degree. Martin classified OO design principles into three categories: 1) class design principles; 2) package cohesion principles; 3) package coupling principles [14]. Among these principles, cohesion and coupling are two important measures for software modularity. However, it is difficult to get maximal cohesion and minimal coupling at all levels of software abstraction. Zhao verified that following the design principles of OO software packages is conducive to improving software quality and reducing defects [27]. Raji proposed a metric of the relation between package modules and stability [24], Albattah proposed a unified cohesion indicator based on class cohesion and package cohesion [3], but they did not verify the validity of their proposed metrics.

In this paper, we study the relation between package metrics and software quality from the perspective of defect-proneness and explore whether software package following the principle of high cohesion and low coupling can reduce software defect-proneness and improve software quality. First, we introduce nine software metrics, that is, seven existed metrics plus two newly proposed package cohesion-coupling metrics based on complex network theory. Secondly, experimental data is retrieved from several Java open-source software systems. We parse the source codes of six software systems, extract class dependencies, build corresponding software networks, and get the statistics of software metrics. We also collect open defect information from their official websites. Then, we construct a group of predictors, which reflects the relations of package cohesion and coupling metrics and software defects. The experiment results confirm that the package cohesion and coupling metrics are helpful for predicting package-level defects in Java software systems, and also verify that following the design principle of high cohesion and low coupling can reduce defects effectively.

The remainder of this paper is organized as follows. Section 2 introduces the related work of software metrics and defeat prediction. Section 3 describes the construction of software complex network and related network metrics. Section 4 states our prediction of software defect-proneness. Section 5 reports experimental results and analysis. Section 6 summarizes the whole paper.

2   Related Work

A software metric is a "thermometer". Good metrics can help people measure software quality and improve it quickly. In this paper, we focus on OO software systems. Currently, there are several metrics for OO software systems. The well-known CK metric suite is a set of class-level object-oriented metrics proposed by Chidamber and Kemer [5]. As to package-level measure, Martin proposed seven package-level metrics [15], including centripetal coupling, centrifugal coupling, abstraction, instability and etc. Misic et al. defined the cohesiveness measure of a package based on its external attributes, and concluded that relying solely on the internal relations of the package is insufficient to determine cohesion [17]. Abdeen et al. presented an automatic package coupling metric [2]. In our previous work, we proposed two effective package metrics based on complex network theory [16,28], to measure software structure correctly.

Some researchers have also done a lot on the relations between OO software metrics and defect-proneness. Chowdhury et al. used some metrics about coupling, cohesion and complexity of software to predict software vulnerabilities [6]. But they did not provide direct metrics of the cohesion and coupling for OO software packages. Gyimothy et al. analyzed the relations between code metrics and software defect-proneness, and confirmed a close relation between metrics and bug propensity [8]. Nagappan et al. also studied the use of metrics to predict buggy components in five Microsoft projects [19]. Their main finding is that there is no single metric can be used as a universal best predictor of errors. The technologies to predict potential defects for software systems are also hot in the field of software engineering [23]. Most of these prediction models currently used machine learning algorithms. Zimmermann et al. used logistic regression to build predictive models for multiple versions of Eclipse [29]. Koru et al. also used machine learning algorithms to construct a defect prediction model for NASA's public dataset [11]. Palomba et al. used Simple Logic (SL) technology to predict software defects related to code smell [20].

In recent years, the combination of complex network theory and software engineering has attracted much attention [18]. The software can be represented into a directed network according to multiple dependency relations between programs, such as object inheritance, function invocation and etc. Some researchers used the advantages of complex network to discover the cohesion and reconfiguration of OO software packages [22], but they did not involve the coupling of software. Shen et al. networked Java software systems, and found that the related networks contain many complex network properties, which confirmed the rationality of networking Java software systems [25]. Pan et al. used the theory of complex network to build Java software into a bipartite network, and proposed an algorithm to refactor the organization structure of packages [21].

3   Software Complex Network

3.1   CDG Construction

In this section, we introduce how to build software networks. Specially, we consider OO software systems made from Java. Java is a classical programming language, and widely used in many applications. Based on Java syntax, one can easily construct software networks. Generally speaking, all classes are labeled as vertices in a network, while the dependency relations between classes are edges linked between vertices. Then, packages, the organization delegates in Java, are deemed as communities in the network. The reasons for this are that, on one hand, the classes are defined in the package, which has a better granularity, and on the other hand, the amount of dependency relations between classes is larger. As a result, the complex network constructed is very similar to the actual network. Since the vertices are classes and the relations are dependencies, we also call this software network as Class Dependency Network (CDG).

Note that the dependencies between classes are directional, and there may be multiple edges between vertices. Therefore, CDG is a directed weighted graph. Define the CDG network graph $G = (V, E, C)$, where V is the set of vertices, $V = \{v_1, v_2 \ldots v_n\}$; E is a set of edges, and $e_{ij} = (v_i, v_j)(e_{ij} \in E)$ indicates that the number of edges from v_i to v_j; C is a collection of communities, $C = \{C_1, C_2 \ldots C_m\}$, and all packages are treated as communities in CDG networks. CDG has many types of dependency relations between classes. Detailedly, there is an edge $v_i \rightarrow v_j$ if and only if there exists at least one following dependency between the class codes of v_i and v_j:

- R_1–Inheritance and Implementation: v_i extends or implements v_j.
- R_2–Aggregation: v_j is the data type of member variable in v_i.
- R_3–Parameter: v_j is the data type of parameter/return value/thrown exception of a member function in v_i.
- R_4–Signature: v_j is the type of local member variable in v_i.
- R_5–Invocation: v_j is invoked insides the member function in v_i.

It is worthy noting that the above five dependencies include Kang's dependencies in [10] from the perspective of UML. Their classification is fine-granularity and fits for design evaluation. Then, in code implementation, these ten dependencies [10] can be transferred to ours from the perspective of code. Even, we consider some special associations, such as the type association of return value and thrown exception in the member function definition.

To solve the case of multiple edges between two vertices and the different effect of five dependencies, we design a multi-edge weighted merging model and calculate the total weight of the edges. First, the above five dependencies have different impact on package cohesion and coupling from the perspective of software engineering. To the best of our knowledge, there exists no quantitative standard about these dependencies. According to the classical theory in software engineering and some literatures [10], the dependency relation must be satisfied with the rule $w_1 > w_2 > w_3 > w_4 \geq w5$. In this paper, we design the weights of five dependencies as follows:

$$w_1 = 5, w_2 = 2, w_3 = 1.5, w_4 = 1, w_5 = 1.$$

Secondly, we consider the multiple edges between two vertices. Let N be the total number of vertices in CDG, the matrices $A^{(I)}$ ($I = 1, 2, 3, 4, 5$) represent the number of edges of five dependency relations, such as A_{ij}^1 represents the number of edges of vertex v_i pointing to v_j of the first relation. Since more edges between two vertices means more impact between two classes, the weighted model of CDG is expressed as a matrix M:

$$M = \sum_{I=1}^{5} w_I A^{(I)}. \tag{1}$$

We use a software system developed with Java programming language as an example, to show how to construct a CDG network. Corresponding to the source codes shown in Fig. 1, we can generate the CDG shown in Fig. 2. Different to the existing coarse-granularity software networks, our CDG describes the software structure more truly and clearly, since it is based on five fine-granularity dependencies $\{R_1, R_2, \ldots, R_5\}$.

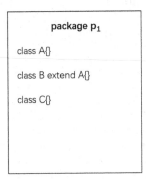

package p_1

class A{}

class B extend A{}

class C{}

package p_2

class D extend A{
  C obj1;
}
class E{
  public void f1(H obj) { }
}
class F{
  public void f2() { }
  public void f3() { }
}

package p_3

class H{
  public void f4() {
    F obj = new F();
    obj.f2();
    obj.f3();
  }
}

Fig. 1. An example of Java software

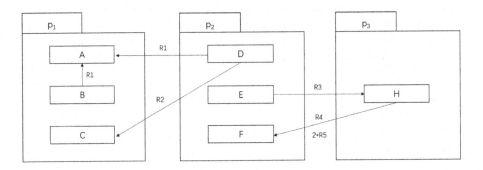

Fig. 2. An example of CDG

Table 1. The weight values of egdes

Edge	(B,A)	(D,A)	(D,C)	(E,H)	(H,F)
Weight values	5	5	2	1.5	3

In Fig. 1, there are three packages. Detailedly, the package p_1 has three classes: A, B, C; the package p_2 has also three classes: D, E, F, and the last package p_3 has one class: H. It is easily observed that there are seven dependencies between classes: B depends on A, D depends on both A and C, E depends on H and H (triple) depends on F. Based on the definitions of five dependencies $\{R_1, R_2, \ldots, R_5\}$, the CDG is generated and shown in Fig. 2. And, we calculate the weight values of all edges of CDG, shown in Table 1.

3.2   CDG Metrics

In this paper, we adopt some classic metrics proposed by Martin, and two package metrics about cohesion and coupling from our previous work, to measure the software design.

Martin's Metrics. Martin proposed seven representative metrics at package-level for software design evaluation [15]. They are shown in Table 2. Detailedly, Ce corresponds to independence. The smaller Ce is, the better the independence is. Ca corresponds to package responsibility. The larger Ca is, the higher the responsibility is. N corresponds to package scalability, and the larger N is, the better the scalability is. A corresponds to the abstraction. The larger A is, the better the abstraction is. I corresponds to package instability. The larger I, the package has the greater instability. D evaluates the balance between package abstraction and package instability. $Cycle$ is the number of cycles in which the package is directly involved.

Table 2. Martin's metrics.

Metrics	Definition
N	The number of classes (and interfaces) in a package
Ce	The number of other packages that the classes in a package depend upon
Ca	The number of other packages that depend upon classes within a package
A	The ratio of abstract classes (and interfaces) in a package to the total number of classes in the package
I	The ratio of Ce to total coupling $(Ce + Ca)$: $I = Ce/(Ce + Ca)$
D	The distance of a package from the main sequence: $D = |A + I - 1|$
$Cycle$	The number of package dependency cycles a package participates in

Cohesion and Coupling Metrics. Compared to Martin's metrics mainly on class level, the metrics of cohesion and coupling are measured on packages. Cohesion metric represents the degree of modularity within a package. In our previous work, we proposed a package cohesion metric ($COHM$) based on complex network theory [16]. According to the meaning of cohesion, it can be known that the larger value of $COHM$ indicates higher cohesion.

Inspired by Martin's efferent and afferent couplings (Ce, Ca) and $COHM$, in [28], we also proposed a package coupling metric $COUM$. This metric considers the relations between packages caused by all relations between classes, which can truly reflect the hierarchical relations between packages. Obviously, the smaller the $COUM$ value, the lower the degree of software coupling. For more information of $COHM$ and $COUM$, please refer to [16] and [28].

4   Software Defect-Proneness Prediction

In this section, we present defect-proneness prediction strategy. We also design some experiments to verify whether the package metrics of cohesion and coupling can effectively evaluate software quality from the perspective of defect-proneness.

4.1   Overview

For easy understanding, the whole process of experiments is shown in Fig. 3. After building the software networks, we can calculate Martin's metrics, $COHM$ and $COUM$. As shown in Fig. 3, we need do Redundancy detection for these nine metrics. It is very important to explore whether $COHM$ and $COUM$ are redundant to the existing Martin's metrics. If $COHM$ and $COUM$ are redundant, calculating these two metrics is meaningless. For defect-proneness prediction, correlation analysis between software metrics and software defects is necessary. The analysis explores the relation between metrics and software defect-proneness. Moreover, it can further explain whether these metrics are effective indicators for package-level defect-proneness prediction. More importantly, the performance of $COHM$ and $COUM$ in defect prediction is worth exploring. We need to verify whether it is reasonable to use these metrics to build a defect-proneness prediction independent variables for practical applications and whether the cohesion and coupling metrics are instructive in software design to avoid defects.

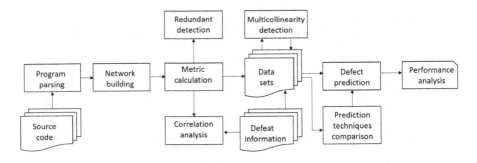

Fig. 3. Process of the experiments

4.2   Defect-Prediction Strategy

First, the choice of defect-prediction model technology is particularly important. Lessmann et al. [13] concluded that a simple modeling technique is sufficient to simulate the relation between static code characteristics and software defects. Therefore, in this paper, we use three commonly used simple prediction model technologies, namely, Support Vector Machine (*SVM*), Random Forest (*RF*), and Logistic Regression (*LR*). Then, we construct two groups of predictors: *MP*, which contains only Martin's metrics, and (*CMP*) which adds *COHM* and *COUM* with Martin's metrics. And, the software package defect information is the predictive dependent variable. Two sets of predictors and dependent variables constitute two prediction datasets respectively. And, Modeling technology is used to predict defect-proneness on two datasets and analyze performance.

There are several reasons of combining the package metrics with Martin's metrics to form the *CMP*. On one hand, Nagappan et al. found that there is no single metric that can be used as a universal best defect predictors to predict buggy components [19]. Thus, it is not enough to build prediction independent variables only using *COHM* and *COUM*. On the other hand, Martin's metrics all follow the software design principles. *COHM* and *COUM* are also defined according to the software design principles. Comparing to Martin's metrics, *COHM* and *COUM* are modular metrics, and they are different from Martin's metrics in meaning. So, they are added to make the prediction more comprehensive. Therefore, it is reasonable to combine *COHM* and *COUM* with Martin's metrics.

After datesets are executed to predict defects, the performance of the datesets need to be evaluated. Accuracy and F-measure are very useful evaluation indicators in the industry. In this paper, we use *Acc* and *F1* as the main evaluation indicators.

Table 3. Basic information of software.

Software	*PN*	*CN*	*KSLOC*	*DPN*	*DPP*
Axis 1.4	46	636	77	19	34%
Flume 1.4.0	41	329	32	24	34%
JDT core 3.6	45	1178	240	14	31%
Lucene 2.4	67	954	109	19	28%
Ant 1.5.1	54	670	84	18	33%
Hbase 2.0	130	3314	623	37	28%

PN: the number of packages;
CN: the number of classes;
KSLOC: the number non-empty and non-comment code lines (in thousands);
DPN: the number of defective packages;
DPP: the percentage of defective packages.

4.3   Experimental Object

This paper chooses six different open-source Java software systems as the experimental object, including Axis 1.4, Flume 1.4.0, JDT Core 3.6, Ant 1.5.1, Lucene 2.4, and Hbase 2.0. These software systems have different functionalities and have been widely applied in the industry. Moreover, the numbers of packages and classes are large enough for statistical analysis and good to obtain statistically meaningful conclusions. Table 3 describes the basic information about the six software systems.

4.4   Data Collection and Processing

The above six software systems are used as the experimental object. In every software, Martin's metrics, $COHM$, $COUM$ and package defect information of the packages are collected as items of the dataset. Specific steps are listed as follows:

Step 1: Software networks. First, perform static analysis on Java source files, and obtain the basic information of classes and the dependencies between classes. Then, according to the definition in Sect. 3.1, we build a directed weighted complex network for the software system.

Step 2: Metric calculation. Calculate the metrics from the corresponding class dependency graph (CDG).

Step 3: Redundancy metric detection. If $COHM$ and $COUM$ can be replaced by Martin's metrics, these two metrics are redundant. Therefore, we use multiple linear regression method to analyze the relations between $COHM/COUM$ and Martin's metrics. The determination coefficient R^2 in linear regression reflects the percentage of the dependent variable explained by the regression equation. $R^2 < 0.5$, indicates that the correlation is very weak or irrelevant [12]. $R^2 \in [0.5, 0.7]$, means correlation is a bit weak. When $R^2 = 1$, it means that the dependent variable can be represented by other variables, namely, it can be completely replaced. Therefore, we adopt R^2 to measure the redundancy of the cohesion and coupling metrics.

Step 4: Defect Information. There are many ways to obtain package defect information. The defect-proneness information of JDT core 3.6 and Ant 1.5.1 is obtained from the defect data disclosed on the official website of Eclipse[1] and Apache[2]. The defect information of the remaining four software systems can be found from JIRA[3]. Note that we only consider the $REAL$ defects, that is bugs, not functionality improvement. Table 3 summarizes the package defect-proneness information. For a package, if the class in the package has defect information, the value of the package defect is marked as 1; otherwise, it is 0. And, We add up the defect values of the package to form DPN in Table 3.

---

[1] https://bugs.eclipse.org/bugs.
[2] https://bz.apache.org/bugzilla.
[3] https://issues.apache.org/jira.

Step 5: Correlation analysis. Since the defect information in this paper is not a continuous value, we use Spearman's correlation coefficient to measure the correlation metrics and defect information, since this method is one of most useful correlation coefficients in statistics. Spearman's correlation coefficient, which is between -1 and $+1$, reflects the closeness of the relationship between two groups of variables.

Step 6: Multicollinearity detection. If the metric values obtained from the dataset are highly correlated, the prediction model is difficult to evaluate accurately. This highly correlated linearity between metric values is called multicollinearity. In order to make the predictions meaningful, the multicollinearity effect needs to be removed. Variance inflation factor (VIF) is a good measurement of multicollinearity [26]. It refers to the ratio of variance when there is multicollinearity between the variables, to the variance when there is no multicollinearity. The formula is $VIF = 1/(1 - R_i^2)$, where R_i is the negative correlation coefficient of the explanatory variable for regression analysis of the remaining explanatory variables. The larger VIF, the greater the possibility of collinearity between the variables is. In general, if $VIF < 10$, there is no collinearity problem [12]. Therefore, calculate VIF for all metrics; remove explanatory variables with VIF larger than 10 from the predictors; and recalculate VIF for the remaining metrics. Repeat the above operations until the values of VIF for all metrics are all less than 10.

5   Experimental Results and Analysis

In this section, we analyze the experimental results in detail and answer the following four questions:

- Q1: Are $COHM$ and $COUM$ redundant to Martin's metrics?
- Q2: What is the correlation between design metrics and software defect-proneness?
- Q3: Which of the three prediction techniques should be selected to predict software defect-proneness?
- Q4: Are $COHM$ and $COUM$ "GOOD" to improve the performance of defect-proneness prediction model?

5.1   Redundancy Detection

From Table 4, almost all R^2 values of $COHM$ and $COUM$ are less than the threshold value 0.5. For R^2 of $COHM$, the minimum is 0.071, while the maximum is 0.543. For R^2 of $COUM$, the minimum is 0.225, while the maximum is 0.579. Note that only one software system, Flume 1.4.0, has a value of R^2 of $COUM$ larger than 0.5, which is marked with ×. However, the values of 0.579, 0.543 and 0.502 are still less than 0.7, which means its effect is weak. In other words, $COHM$ and $COUM$ are almost irrelevant to Martin's metrics on six software systems and they cannot be replaced. So for the question Q1, the metrics of $COHM$ and $COUM$ are not redundant and irreplaceable.

Table 4. R^2 of *COHM* and *COUM*.

Software	*COHM*	*COUM*
Axis 1.4	0.201	0.345
Flume 1.4.0	0.502×	0.579×
JDT core 3.6	0.219	0.378
Lucene 2.4	0.543×	0.420
Ant 1.5.1	0.301	0.225
Hbase 2.0	0.071	0.263

Table 5. Spearman's correlation (the significance level of 0.05 marked with *, 0.01 marked with **).

	Ce	*Ca*	*I*	*N*	*A*	*D*	*Cycle*	*COHM*	*COUM*
Axis 1.4	0.094	0.357**	−0.266	−0.004	0.083	0.186	0	−0.165	0.115
Flume 1.4.0	0.347*	0.253	0.031	0.323*	0.085	−0.107	−0.202	−0.206	0.208
JDT core 3.6	0.134	0.218	−0.161	−0.041	0.258	−0.013	0	−0.166	0.311*
Lucene 2.4	0.085	−0.083	0.132	−0.308*	−0.335**	−0.216	−0.247*	−0.297*	0.355**
Ant 1.5.1	0.309*	0.169	−0.102	0.001	−0.127	0.137	0.125	−0.319*	0.306*
Hbase 2.0	0.156	0.241**	−0.203	0.056	−0.035	−0.084	0	−0.226**	0.169

5.2 Correlation Analysis

We execute Spearman's correlation tests on six software systems to explore the relation between all metrics and software defects. Table 5 lists the value of Spearman's correlation coefficient between each metric and the defects. The empty part of *Cycle* indicates 0.

From Table 5, most of Martin's metrics have positive correlations with software defects, that is, the larger the metric values, the more likely the software has defects. In most cases, I is negatively correlated. In other words, the smaller I, the more responsibility the package has, which may cause more defects. From this viewpoint, the correlation results are in line with the actual meaning of Martin's metrics. D is also negatively correlated, that is, the greater D, which means balance and be less likely to generate defects. Ce and Ca are significantly correlated in most cases, indicating that Ce and Ca may have greater effects on package defects. *COHM* has a negative correlation with software defects and *COUM* has a positive correlation, which is in line with the fact that software systems have good quality when they follow the design principle of high cohesion and low coupling. In most cases, *COHM* and *COUM* are significantly correlated, indicating that they may have a greater impact on package defects. In summary, for the question Q2, the metrics used in this paper are all valid independent variables and can be accepted by prediction models.

5.3   Defect-Proneness Prediction Performance

First of all, we carry out a multicollinearity check on the dataset with two groups of predictors *MP* and *CMP*. Table 6 shows the measurement results with *VIF* values. The first column indicates *MP* case, and the second column indicates *CMP* case. We just show the case *VIF* > 10 for Martin's metrics.

From these results, one can know that metric *D* appears multicollinearity on two software systems, while the *VIF* values of other six metrics are less than 10. This shows that *D* is strongly correlated with other metrics. When making predictions, the metrics which appear multicollinearity must be removed. And in *CMP*, all *VIF* values of *COHM* and *COUM* are less than 10. Therefore, *COHM* and *COUM* are used as effective independent variables in defect-proneness prediction.

Table 6. The values of *VIF*.

Software	*MP*	*CMP*		
	D	*D*	*COHM*	*COUM*
Axis	4	4	3	4
Ant	3	3	3	2
Flume	6	6	2	3
Hbase	125	55	2	2
JDT Core	2	2	2	2
Lucene	11	11	4	3

Table 7. Comparison of prediction technologies

Software	*F1*			*Acc*		
	LR	*RF*	*SVM*	*LR*	*RF*	*SVM*
Axis	0.54 ✓	0.52	0.52	0.65	0.67 ✓	0.63
Flume	0.67 ✓	0.53	0.65	0.73 ✓	0.62	0.73 ✓
JDT Core	0.57	0.47	0.58 ✓	0.68 ✓	0.63	0.68 ✓
Lucene	0.61 ✓	0.51	0.59	0.73 ✓	0.62	0.72
Ant	0.59 ✓	0.56	0.55	0.70 ✓	0.66	0.69
Hbase	0.62 ✓	0.55	0.59	0.75	0.70	0.76 ✓

Next, we compare the performance of the three model prediction technologies. Using Martin's metrics as independent variables for 50 times of 3-fold cross-validation defect-proneness prediction, the performance results of three model technologies are shown in Table 7. The "better" results are marked with ✓. From the comparison in Table 7, *LR* has the better results of *F1* in five software systems and better *Acc* in four software systems. In contrast, *F1* and *Acc* of *SVM* get better results in one software system and three software systems respectively. *RF* has the worst result whose *Acc* gets better on only one software system. Besides, *LR* has the highest value of *F1* and *Acc* on three software systems, while *RF* has one and *SVM* gets zero. In summary, compared with *RF* and *SVM*, *LR* has the best performance in predicting software package-level defect-proneness. In the review, Hall et al. [9] also pointed out that compared with other relatively modeling techniques, logistic regression performs excellently in defect-proneness prediction. Therefore, for the question Q3, the *LR* is selected to compare the prediction performance of *MP* and *CMP*.

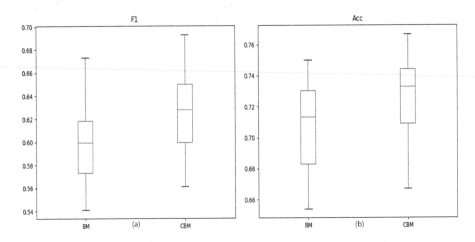

Fig. 4. Boxplot of the performance measure with the two groups of predictors

Table 8. Comparison of the performance of predictors

Software	MP		CMP		Improvement	
	F1	*Acc*	*F1*	*Acc*	*F1*	*Acc*
Axis	0.541	0.654	0.561 ✓	0.667 ✓	4%	2%
Flume	0.673	0.731	0.693 ✓	0.745 ✓	3%	2%
JDT core	0.568	0.678	0.590 ✓	0.704 ✓	4%	4%
Lucene	0.611	0.729	0.629 ✓	0.742 ✓	3%	2%
Ant	0.588	0.698	0.627 ✓	0.724 ✓	7%	4%
Hbase	0.621	0.750	0.657 ✓	0.767 ✓	6%	2%

Finally, multiple Logistic Regression is used to predict software defect-proneness with the *MP* and *CMP*. The average values of *F1* and *Acc* from the 50 times 3-fold cross-validation are used as an index for predicting performance. Figure 4 describes the overall performance of the two groups of predictors on six software systems. Figure 4(a) shows *F1* index distribution of two groups of predictors, and Fig. 4(b) shows *Acc* index distribution. For the predictors *CMP*, *F1* is distributed in [0.561, 0.693], and *Acc* is distributed in [0.667, 0.767]. Regardless of the value of *F1* or *Acc*, from the boxplot, the upper and lower bounds are both higher than *MP*'s. And the median, which represents the average level, also shows this situation. It is easily observed that *CMP* is more prominent than *MP*.

In order to further compare the performance of the two group of predictors, both *F1* and *Acc* values of two group of predictors are listed in Table 8. The data with better performance is marked with ✓. Compared with *MP*, both *F1* and *Acc* of *CMP* increase by 2% to 7%. *CMP* has better performance in all six software systems. Therefore, for the question Q4, the cohesion and coupling metrics are beneficial to improve the performance of software package defect-proneness prediction. It is also proven that the metrics *COHM* and *COUM* have guiding significance in OO software design.

In Sect. 4.2, we present two groups of predictors called *MP* and *CMP*. Now, we also compare the metrics *COHM* + *COUM* with a single metric *COHM* on prediction performance. The results are shown in Table 9. The data with better performance is marked with ✓. From the results, the prediction results considering *COUM* and *COHM* are better than those considering *COHM* alone. This illustrates that *COUM* we propose in this paper is an irreplaceable guide to software structure.

Table 9. The efficiency of *COUM*

Software	MP+COHM		CMP	
	F1(%)	Acc(%)	F1(%)	Acc(%)
Axis	55.2	66.1	56.1 ✓	66.7 ✓
Flume	68.1	73.3	69.3 ✓	74.5 ✓
JDT Core	57.4	68.8	59.0 ✓	70.4 ✓
Lucene	61.8	73.1	62.9 ✓	74.2 ✓
Ant	61.5	71.3	62.7 ✓	72.4 ✓
Hbase	63.9	76.1	65.7 ✓	76.7 ✓

6   Conclusion

This paper focuses on the relation between package organization structure and software design quality from the perspective of software defect-proneness. Taking advantage of complex network theory, we introduce two recent cohesion and coupling metrics which can better reflect the organizational structure of OO software systems. The experimental result has shown that the cohesion and coupling metrics can play a positive role that cannot be replaced by Martin's metrics in predicting defect-proneness, and can correctly and effectively evaluate the quality of software package structure. At the same time, it is confirmed that obeying the design principle of high cohesion and low coupling can reduce software defect-proneness and improve software quality.

References

1. Abdeen, H., Ducasse, S., Sahraoui, H.: Modularization metrics: Assessing package organization in legacy large object-oriented software. In: 2011 18th Working Conference on Reverse Engineering, pp. 394–398. IEEE (2011)
2. Abdeen, H., Ducasse, S., Sahraoui, H., Alloui, I.: Automatic package coupling and cycle minimization. In: 2009 16th Working Conference on Reverse Engineering, pp. 103–112. IEEE (2009)
3. Albattah, W., Melton, A.: Package cohesion classification. In: 2014 IEEE 5th International Conference on Software Engineering and Service Science, pp. 1–8. IEEE (2014)
4. Briand, L.C., Morasca, S., Basili, V.R.: Property-based software engineering measurement. IEEE Trans. Softw. Eng. 22(1), 68–86 (1996)
5. Chidamber, S.R., Kemerer, C.F.: A metrics suite for object oriented design. IEEE Trans. Softw. Eng. 20(6), 476–493 (1994)
6. Chowdhury, I., Zulkernine, M.: Using complexity, coupling, and cohesion metrics as early indicators of vulnerabilities. J. Syst. Architect. 57(3), 294–313 (2011)
7. Gupta, V., Chhabra, J.K.: Package coupling measurement in object-oriented software. J. Comput. Sci. Technol. 24(2), 273–283 (2009)
8. Gyimothy, T., Ferenc, R., Siket, I.: Empirical validation of object-oriented metrics on open source software for fault prediction. IEEE Trans. Softw. Eng. 31(10), 897–910 (2005)
9. Hall, T., Beecham, S., Bowes, D., Gray, D., Counsell, S.: A systematic literature review on fault prediction performance in software engineering. IEEE Trans. Softw. Eng. 38(6), 1276–1304 (2011)
10. Kang, D., Xu, B., Lu, J., Chu, W.C.: A complexity measure for ontology based on UML. In: Proceedings, 10th IEEE International Workshop on Future Trends of Distributed Computing Systems, 2004, FTDCS 2004, pp. 222–228. IEEE (2004)
11. Koru, A.G., Liu, H.: Building effective defect-prediction models in practice. IEEE Softw. 22(6), 23–29 (2005)
12. Kutner, M.H., Nachtsheim, C.J., Neter, J., Li, W., et al.: Applied Linear Statistical Models, vol. 5. McGraw-Hill, Irwin, Boston (2005)
13. Lessmann, S., Baesens, B., Mues, C., Pietsch, S.: Benchmarking classification models for software defect prediction: A proposed framework and novel findings. IEEE Trans. Softw. Eng. 34(4), 485–496 (2008)
14. Martin, R.C.: Design principles and design patterns. Object Mentor 1(34), 597 (2000)
15. Martin, R.C.: Agile Software Development: Principles, Patterns, and Practices. Prentice Hall, Upper Saddle River (2002)
16. Mi, Y., Zhou, Y., Chen, L.: A new metric for package cohesion measurement based on complex network. In: Cherifi, H., Gaito, S., Mendes, J.F., Moro, E., Rocha, L.M. (eds.) COMPLEX NETWORKS 2019. SCI, vol. 881, pp. 238–249. Springer, Cham (2020). https://doi.org/10.1007/978-3-030-36687-2_20

17. Misic, V.B.: Cohesion is structural, coherence is functional: Different views, different measures. In: Proceedings Seventh International Software Metrics Symposium, pp. 135–144. IEEE (2001)
18. Myers, C.R.: Software systems as complex networks: Structure, function, and evolvability of software collaboration graphs. Phys. Rev. E **68**(4), 046–116 (2003)
19. Nagappan, N., Ball, T., Zeller, A.: Mining metrics to predict component failures. In: Proceedings of the 28th International Conference on Software Engineering, pp. 452–461. ACM (2006)
20. Palomba, F., Zanoni, M., Fontana, F.A., De Lucia, A., Oliveto, R.: Toward a smell-aware bug prediction model. IEEE Trans. Softw. Eng. **45**(2), 194–218 (2017)
21. Pan, W.F., Jiang, B., Li, B.: Refactoring software packages via community detection in complex software networks. Int. J. Autom. Comput. **10**(2), 157–166 (2013)
22. Pan, W., Li, B., Jiang, B., Liu, K.: Recode: software package refactoring via community detection in bipartite software networks. Adv. Complex Syst. **17**(07n08), 1450006 (2014)
23. Radjenović, D., Heričko, M., Torkar, R., Živkovič, A.: Software fault prediction metrics: A systematic literature review. Inf. Softw. Technol. **55**(8), 1397–1418 (2013)
24. Raji, M., Montazeri, B.: On the relationship between modularity and stability in software packages (2018). arXiv preprint arXiv:1812.01061
25. Shen, P., Chen, L.: Complex network analysis in java application systems. J. East China Normal Univ. **1**, 38–51 (2017)
26. Weisberg, S.: Applied Linear Regression, vol. 528. Wiley, Hoboken (2005)
27. Zhao, Y., Yang, Y., Lu, H., Zhou, Y., Song, Q., Xu, B.: An empirical analysis of package-modularization metrics: Implications for software fault-proneness. Inf. Softw. Technol. **57**, 186–203 (2015)
28. Zhou, Y., Mi, Y., Zhu, Y., Chen, L.: Measurement and refactoring for package structure based on complex network. Appl. Netw. Sci. **5**(1), 1–20 (2020). https://doi.org/10.1007/s41109-020-00298-8
29. Zimmermann, T., Premraj, R., Zeller, A.: Predicting defects for eclipse. In: Third International Workshop on Predictor Models in Software Engineering (PROMISE'07: ICSE Workshops 2007), p. 9. IEEE (2007)

Author Index

Printed in the United States
By Bookmasters